UNIVERSITY OF WISCONSIN STUDIES
IN LANGUAGE AND LITERATURE
NUMBER 30

HENRY FIELDING'S THEORY
OF THE
COMIC PROSE EPIC

HENRY FIELDING'S THEORY
OF THE
COMIC PROSE EPIC

BY

ETHEL MARGARET THORNBURY

NEW YORK / RUSSELL & RUSSELL

1966

FIRST PUBLISHED IN 1931
REISSUED, 1966, BY RUSSELL & RUSSELL
A DIVISION OF ATHENEUM HOUSE, INC.
L.C. CATALOG CARD NO: 66—24766

PRINTED IN THE UNITED STATES OF AMERICA

TABLE OF CONTENTS

PREFACE

This study was originally written in partial fulfillment of the requirement for the doctor's degree at the University of Wisconsin. Since submitting it for that purpose, however, I have checked over all the quotations and notes, and in particular, checked the list of volumes in Fielding's library from photostatic reproductions of the pamphlet at the British Museum. What I have presented is, I therefore trust, as nearly accurate as a considerable number of proof-readings can make it.

Much of the material is already known, but it has not heretofore been gathered together and presented in this form. Nor has Fielding as critic ever received, I feel, quite the attention he deserves. At one time, I hoped to be able to omit a good deal of the account of epic theory before Fielding, but I found that, in order to make this position clear, I had to retain much of the general history of the subject. I could wish that the learning necessary to presenting all these facts sat as lightly in these pages as they do in Fielding's critical essays, but Fielding, writing for a different purpose, could afford a carelessness which is denied me.

I take this opportunity of acknowledging my indebtedness to many persons for the assistance they have given me. In particular, I am deeply indebted to various tutors and officials of Oxford University, especially to Miss C. M. Burrowes and Miss Cecile Hugon for many kindnesses; to my colleagues at the University of Wisconsin, especially to Professor Henry B. Lathrop, whose suggestions gave me help at every turn; and to the librarians of the Bodleian Library, the Taylorian Institute, and the British Museum, without whose courtesy, it would have been impossible to locate much of the material here presented.

CHAPTER I

FIELDING'S LIBRARY[1]

Fielding refers to his two novels, *Joseph Andrews* and *Tom Jones*, as "comic prose epics". The epic was highly venerated in his world and the term "comic epic" represented something very specific for him and for his contemporaries. In using the term, was he simply making a bid for fame by using a convenient label, or did he really mean that he considered these novels as epic in any sense? If the latter, then Fielding was something of a critic as well as novelist, for epic theory was one of the most important parts of criticism in the eighteenth century. The late Mr. Austin Dobson[2] performed a real service, not only to the biography of Fielding, but to the history of English criticism,[3] when he unearthed the little pamphlet containing the list of the books in Fielding's library from the depths of the British Museum and thus called attention to the probable reading of the "father of the English novel". A man's library is not necessarily identical with his reading, but the books a man owns do show the best of his interests. And if Fielding's library is, among other things, the library of a critic and student of letters, we can assume that the critical discussions and quotations from other authors scattered here and there in his writing are not the mere tossing about of current literary patter, but are instead probably serious statements of genuine beliefs and interests.

[1]See Appendix for the complete list of books in Fielding's library.

[2]Dobson, Austin, *Eighteenth Century Vignettes*, Vol. III, pp. 164-178. This essay was originally printed in *Bibliographica*, Vol. I, 1895, pp. 163-173.

[3]It seems strange that so little attention has been heretofore paid to Fielding's prefaces in histories of English criticism, or in anthologies. The prefaces to each book in *Joseph Andrews* and *Tom Jones* throw interesting light, not only on Fielding's own work, for which they are very important, but on the state of epic theory of his time.

7

Mr. Dobson called attention in his article on *Fielding's Library* to the striking fact that there were practically no novels in Fielding's possession. This seems a little strange at first, but perhaps one reason that we find so few novels was that he may have been less interested in the tales told by his contemporaries than he was in certain other books which would assist him in writing the comic prose epic, a "form not hitherto attempted in our language". He did not think of himself as the writer of the popular prose romances, nor even as the creator of a new form, but as the writer of a very old and respectable thing—the comic prose epic. There is in his library a copy of *The Female Quixote*[4] and another of *Pompey the Little*. There is a copy of Fielding's own prose narrative—hardly a novel—*Jonathan Wild*. But that is all. The list does not show a copy of *Joseph Andrews*, or of *Tom Jones;* there is nothing of Richardson, nothing of Marivaux, no *Gil Blas*, none of the heroic romances, although Fielding refers to *Clelia, Cleopatra, Astraea, Cassandra, The Grand Cyrus* in the *Preface* to *Joseph Andrews*. *Don Quixote* is there in Jervas'[5] translation, the edition of 1749. This translation was not made until 1742; Fielding must have read an earlier translation, possibly Motteux's, as he was already working on his *Don Quixote in England* when he was in Leyden, where he went in 1728. In fact, of the romance and the anti-romance, his library has, beside *Don Quixote*, only two ancient representatives of the species—Apuleius and Petronius.

Of course, one might account for the absence of novels by assuming that his own and perhaps those of the popular Richardson were kept back from the sale by relatives and friends, but his own pamphlet on *Some Causes of the Late Increase of Robbers* is included, as well as his dramatic works. There is no reason to suppose *Tom Jones* would be retained and

[4]This novel, by Mrs. Charlotte Lennox, was greatly esteemed by Fielding, who, writing in the *Covent Garden Journal* in 1752, compared it favorably with Cervantes' work. See Fielding's remarks on this which I quote in this study, p. 148.

[5]The author's name is spelled "Jarvis" in the catalogue, but the correct spelling, the one given in the translations, seems to be "Jervas".

Tom Thumb sold. And—for whatever this may be worth—the catalogue announces the sale of the *entire* library of Henry Fielding.

Though there are only one or two novels in his library, Fielding had a very complete collection of drama, ancient and modern. This would seem to indicate that, while he was *writing* plays, he *read* plays. If, then, he had no novels to read at the time when he was writing novels, one must conclude either that he took his plays more seriously than he took his novels or that he thought his novels were comic prose epics—built on a plan like the serious epic—and did not resemble the popular prose romances of the day. In any event, his dramatic library is strikingly complete. There are Aeschylus, Sophocles, Euripides, and Aristophanes; Plautus, Terence, and Seneca; Corneille, Racine, Moliére; Gherardi's *Le Théâtre Italien;* Shakespeare, Ben Jonson, Beaumont and Fletcher, Shirley, Otway, Dryden, Shadwell, Congreve, Wycherley, Vanbrugh, Farquhar, Southerne, Rowe, Lee, Steele, and his own works.

We may assume, I think, that he was a real student of the stage and knew a great deal about it. But the author of the burlesque *Tom Thumb* and its extravagant notes would already have shown this anyhow. The evidence of the library is simply corroborative.

Besides the dramatists, the library is equally complete in nondramatic literature. Among English writers, we find the complete works of Milton; the poems of Spenser, Suckling, Waller, Cowley, Denham, Butler, Prior, Dryden, Roscommon, Buckingham and Duke, Pope, Thomson, Young; the *Tatler,* the *Spectator,* the *Guardian*; the writings of Bacon, Fuller, Walton, Sir Thomas Browne, Boyle, Temple, Dennis, Addison; Hogarth's *Analysis of Beauty*; Harrington's *Oceana*. And, outside England, besides *Don Quixote* from Spain, there are Corneille, Racine, and Molière from France, Montaigne's essays, Fénélon's *Télémaque,* Pascal's *Pensées,* Boileau, Le Bossu, and other French critics. He did not own any of the Italian writers of the Renaissance—no Ariosto, no Tasso, none of the critics.[6] Fielding's library of Renaissance literature is French and English—and *Don Quixote*.

Of the eight persons whose inspiration he invokes at the beginning of Book XIII of *Tom Jones,* only two, that is, Marivaux and Rabelais, are not represented. It is not strange that Fielding did not own Marivaux; the really strange thing, to me, is that he should ever have included Marivaux in the company of Lucian, Cervantes, Swift, Molière, and Shakespeare, for there is very little in common between Marivaux,[7] who is of the hothouse, and Fielding. We know why Rabelais is not there. Fielding ultimately came to feel that Rabelais and Aristophanes used their ridicule to laugh at modesty and decency.[8] He owned Aristophanes, however, doubtless a relic of his earlier days. There are two editions, one in Greek and Latin, the 1710 Amsterdam edition, and a 1696 French translation of the *Plutus* and *The Clouds,* made by Madame Le Fèvre, later Madame Dacier. Of the other authors, the 1749 Jervas translation of *Don Quixote* in his library is not, as I have said, the one he could have read. Of Swift, he had the eight-volume 1742 Dublin edition, and Orrery's *Remarks on the Life and Writings of Swift.* He must, of course, have read Swift as his works came out, for Fielding early had an enthusiasm for that savage ironist. Of Shakespeare, he owned Warburton's 1748 edition, and another edition, undated, the number of volumes of which is not noted. His Molière was the eight-volume Paris edition of 1718.

And, finally, there is Lucian, probably his favorite, if one may judge by constant references to Lucian, by his plan for making an English translation, and by the number of editions he possessed. There is a two-volume 1697 Amsterdam edition in French, translated by Ablancourt; a four-volume 1619 Basle

---

[6]This is an interesting omission. Were the Italians too romantic? The influence of Italy had, of course, waned, and French influence had become ascendant in England of Fielding's day.

[7]Marivaux's *Le Paysan Parvenu* bears some likeness to *Joseph Andrews,* but the resemblance is superficial. And *La Vie de Marianne* is Richardsonian in everything except one *very* important aspect,—namely, that Marivaux is aware of his heroine's prudence, as she herself is also. But the novel has all of the subtle psychological analysis of Richardson.

[8]*Covent Garden Journal,* No. 10.

edition in Greek and Latin; Dryden's four-volume translation, edition of 1711; another French edition translated by Baudoin, the date of which is not given; another Greek and Latin (variorum) edition, printed in Amsterdam in 1687; still another Greek and Latin (variorum) edition, also of Amsterdam, dated 1743; another Greek and Latin (variorum) edition, edited by Benedict, dated 1619; a Latin edition of 1546 translated by Vascos; and a 1615 Paris edition, Greek and Latin, of Bourdelot. There are nine in all.

Besides Lucian, his collection of Greek and Latin works is astonishingly complete. He considered the classics a rich storehouse, a priceless heritage to the moderns. In the Preface to Book XII of *Tom Jones,* he says: "The antients may be considered as a rich common, where every person who hath the smallest tenement in Parnassus hath a free right to fatten his muse. Or, to place it in a clearer light, we moderns are to the antients what the poor are to the rich. By the poor here I mean that large and venerable body which, in English, we call the mob. Now, whoever hath had the honour to be admitted to any degree of intimacy with this mob, must well know that it is one of their established maxims to plunder and pillage their rich neighbors without any reluctance; and that this is held to be neither sin nor crime among them. And so constantly do they abide and act by this maxim, that, in every parish almost in the kingdom, there is a kind of confederacy ever carrying on against a certain person of opulence called the squire, whose property is considered free-booty by all his poor neighbors; who, as they conclude that there is no manner of guilt in such depredations, look upon it as a point of honour and moral obligation to conceal, and to preserve each other from punishment on all such occasions.

"In like manner are the antients, such as Homer, Virgil, Horace, Cicero, and the rest, to be esteemed among us writers, as so many wealthy squires, from whom we, the poor of Parnassus, claim an immemorial custom of taking whatever we can come at."

Fielding could roam freely in this ancient Parnassus, as may be seen if we consider the authors he owned. There are the poets, Pindar, Hesiod, Anacreon, Theocritus, Horace, Ovid, Lucretius, Lucilius, Martial, Juvenal, Catullus, Tibullus, Propertius, Persius, and, of course, Homer and Virgil, each in several editions, both in the original language and in translation. Not only the poets, but the critics, too; we find Aristotle's[9] *Poetics* and *Rhetoric,* Horace, Quintilian, Longinus. Finally, Homer, Virgil, Statius, Silius Italicus represent the epic. These are only a few of the best known names. His complete library contained most of the Greek and Latin writers known to his day.

If Fielding's library represents the authors in whom he was most interested,[10] we find that he studied the Greek and Latin epics and Greek and Latin critics chiefly. There are no writers either of the Renaissance epic—with the exception of Milton—nor of the Renaissance aesthetic theory, except Le Bossu, Boileau, and M. and Mme. Dacier, and such criticism as occurs in the works of Dryden, Dennis, Temple, Addison, Swift, Pope, and Hobbes, Locke, and Shaftsbury. There are a few of the best known Renaissance commentators—Scaliger's edition of Catullus, Tibullus, and Propertius, and of Lycophron; Heinsius' edition of Aristotle's *Politics,* and of Hesiod; Tollius' edition of Longinus; besides a very large number of the editions of the Greek and Latin classics in *Usum Dephini.*[11] Fielding did not own copies of the various French epic writers and epic theorists of the seventeenth century—with the exceptions already noted. But we find the works of Sarrasin. Here Fielding could have found dialogues between Chapelain and others, and the theories of the "Christian marvellous". With Boileau, Sarrasin, Le Bossu, Madame Dacier, especially her *Causes de la Corruption du Gout,* Fénélon, in the edition of 1742 which had

[9]There are a number of commentaries on Aristotle, including the Greek one of Alexander of Aphrodisias.

[10]We may assume that it does, if we examine the references to other authors in his writings where we find very few references to writers outside of the list in the library.

[11]Many of his editions of the Greek and Latin classics are Dutch, doubtless purchased during his residence at Leyden, or learned of there and purchased later.

Ramsay's preface on *Télémaque* as an epic, and Molière, Fielding could have had a pretty fair knowledge of the French epic of the seventeenth century and of French criticism of the epic. But Fielding was not man of letters and student of literature to the exclusion of everything else.[12] The number of histories, ancient and modern, which he owned is really amazing. If we think of Fielding as the man who most thoroughly describes the eighteenth century, it is because he knew and understood his century. The pictures which his early biographers, curiously hostile to the man, give of a dissolute, down-at-the-heels hanger-on of taverns have been pretty well disposed of by his more sympathetic and unprejudiced modern biographers, notably Mr. Austin Dobson and Mr. Wilbur Cross. But one could almost argue *a priori* that the Fielding of Arthur Murphy and Thackeray could never have known so much as he did, anyhow. Fielding apparently tried to understand the modern world by finding out the history of the past.

Time and again in his novels, Fielding insists that he is the *historian*. He did not mean, of course, that he was writing a history of his own times in the terms of battles or political struggles. But he obviously meant, among other things, that he was the historian of modern manners in contrast to the manners of former days. He owned the great Greek and Latin historians and biographers: Herodotus, Xenophon, Thucydides, Dionysius of Halicarnassus, Dion Cassius, Diodorus Siculus, Valerius Maximus, Plutarch, Livy, Tacitus, Sallust, Quintius Curtius, Polybius, Caesar's *Commentaries,* Arrian, Suetonius. These are a few of the striking names from the list of the ancient historians. And not only did he own these writers; he read them. He refers to them again and again, and discusses their writings with a keenly critical intelligence here and there, for example in Number Twelve of the *Covent Garden Journal.*

The list of modern European histories is equally wide and catholic, and perhaps even more important in showing us what Fielding was interested in. No one, not even the early bio-

---

[12] I omit any consideration of his very complete law library.

graphers, has denied that Fielding had had the conventional education of his day, and any English public school boy of the eighteenth century might have, left over from his Eton days, a good many of the Greek and Latin authors found in Fielding's library. The modern histories could not be school-boy texts. (Nor were all of the ancient histories, either, for that matter, as the editions were not those used in the schools.) Fielding was interested in the modern world and set himself to find out about it. Conceivably, a man might be able to write of the roads, the squires, the London drawing rooms, the taverns, in the realistic way in which Fielding does without being a scholar, or a student of any sort. Richardson seems to have evolved his characters and the predicaments which befall them out of a very slender stock of knowledge of any sort—always excepting the sensibilities of the tender female heart. But only a man of considerable learning could have written the prefaces in *Joseph Andrews* and *Tom Jones,* and various of the papers in the *Covent Garden Journal,* the *Jacobite's Journal,* and the *Miscellanies.* The list of modern histories is large, and the range of taste indicated is broad. One of the most interesting facts about this list of modern histories is the large number of books about the civil wars in England in the seventeenth century, books representing both sides of the quarrel—the *Eikon Basilike* and Milton's *Letters to Oliver Cromwell,* Clarendon's *History of the Rebellion* and a *Life of Oliver Cromwell* (the name of the author not given). There are histories of other countries— *Revolutions de Portugal,* by Vertot; *Histoire Critique de l'Etablissement des Bretons dans les Gaules;* Puffendorf's *Introduction to the History of Asia, Africa,* etc.; Osorio's *History of the Portuguese; Memoires de Sully; Le Siècle de Louis XIV.* The English histories naturally form the largest group. There are Geoffrey of Monmouth's *British History;* Holinshed's *Chronicles;* Polydore Virgil's *Historia Angliae;* Sidney's *Letters and Memorials of State in the Reigns of Queen Mary, Queen Elizabeth, King James;* Buchanan's *Detection of the Duinges of Marie Quene of Scottes;* Drake's *Secret Memoirs*

of Robert Dudley Earl of Leicester; the Earl of Strafford's
State Papers; Brady's *History of England;* Baker's *Chronicle
of the Kings of England;* Echard's *History of England;* Rapin's
History of England; Kennet's *Compleat History of England;*
Ralph's *History of England;* Speed's *History of Great Britain
under the Conquests of the Romans, Saxons, Danes, and Nor-
mans.*

The list is impressive. Fielding, the gay young playwright,
the lover of life whose income, according to the statement of
his cousin, Lady Mary Wortley Montagu, even had it been
tremendous, would still have failed to satisfy his desires,—this
man apparently read as avidly as he conversed and wrote and
talked and ate and drank. Fielding's papers in the *Covent
Garden Journal* are filled with references to historians. In the
first paper, he is commenting upon the prodigious number of
authors writing at his time. Should that, he asks, prevent him
from taking up his pen? And the answer is that it should not,
for the Rome of Juvenal abounded with writers likewise. In
his satire upon the Robinhoodians (Number 9 of the *Journal*),
in his attack upon Gossip in Number 14—to give just a few il-
lustrative examples—Fielding quotes freely from the Greek and
Latin historians to afford parallels to the conditions in his own
day. In his discussion of the punishments accorded adultery
in times past,[13] there are references to Speed, Echard, Rapin. In
Number 12, indeed, he takes up the relation of history to truth-
telling and has many amusing things to say. One quotation will
show his familiarity with the writings of great historians. The
entire essay is most entertaining—and quite in accord with some
of our modern predilections—for Fielding believes that history
should be picturesque rather than scientifically accurate. I suspect he liked Herodotus very well—in fact, he quotes him frequently. And it is interesting to note that Herodotus today is
enjoying a renaissance of reputation among historians.

"But if no Latitude should be given to Historians, I am
afraid not only Matthew Paris, the best of our antient Annalists,

[13]Number 68 of the *Covent Garden Journal.*

but the valuable Remains of Livy, Tacitus, Suetonius, Dion Cassius, and indeed almost every History must be condemned to the Flames . . . .

". . . For my own Part, though I have not quite so much Faith at present, as I once had in the Casualties related by Sir Richard Baker, in that wonderful Chronicle which was the great Favourite of my Youth; I do yet nevertheless acquit the Writer of any Design to impose on Posterity."

Besides history, Fielding seems to have been greatly interested in books of travel and in books dealing with the antiquities of various sections of England. The antiquarian spirit was strong in the eighteenth century, and Fielding, who loved the English country, especially the West Country, would naturally be interested in books about the antiquities in a given locality. There are books, too, on geography and travel from the ancients as well, such as Strabo and Pausanias. Thus, the author of a *Journal of a Voyage to Lisbon* knew his predecessors in the field of travel diaries. And, of course, his two great novels, *Joseph Andrews* and *Tom Jones,* are Odysseys of the road. Everything that the artist could learn about the road, about travel and travelling companions, about the aspect of a country side, about inns, was grist to his mill. Not but that Fielding knew all of his scenes at first hand. One can today follow Tom Jones' journey to London, although I fear that, in these degenerate—and decorous—days, one is hardly likely to have such adventures. The man who told of Tom's wanderings and of that delightful clerical Quixote and Odysseus, Parson Adams, knew how geographies and travel books were written.

But history and geography have to do with the spectacle of human life, with the pageant of civilization. A thoughtful man could scarcely live in the mid-eighteenth century and be untouched by metaphysical speculation. This was the age of Deism, of Methodism, of Quakerism, of the growth of the modern scientific spirit and technique. Mysticism and scepticism— both are to be found in the popular thought of the time. Fielding's philosophical and theological library was by no means contemptible. And we are sure that he read at least some of these works. For proof, there are, for instance, Parson Adams' debates with Parson Barnabas and the bookseller over Methodism and the Church of England doctrines in Book I, Chapter XVII of *Joseph Andrews*. M. Digeon[14] thinks that Fielding was in his youth a Deist, and later became a firm believer in the tenets of the Church of England. Certainly, it was an age of great intellectual ferment, when the beginnings of the first impact of traditional religious dogmas and the cold rationalism of science were felt among all groups of educated and thinking persons. Fielding was too much a child of his age to have escaped all this. His library shows that same catholicity and breadth of view in approaching these subjects as his historical library shows on matters of fact.

He has, for example, a work on the *Doctrines of the Mahometans,* with a *Life of Mahomet,* a *Life of St. Francis Xavier,* Bishop Burnet's *History of the Reformation,* Dr. South's *Sermons,* a book entitled *Deism Reveal'd,* Collins' *Grounds and Reasons of Religion,* Cruden's *Concordance to the Bible,* Hill's *Review of the Works of the Royal Society*—theology, church history, and science. Fielding has most of the standard works of philosophy, ancient and modern—Plato, Aristotle, Lucretius, Eusebius, Malebranche's *Recherche à la Verité,* Hobbes, Locke, Hume, Bolingbroke, Shaftesbury, and, curiously enough, Spinoza's *Posthumous works* (edition of 1677). Hobbes and Locke, the great rationalists, Hume, the sceptic, and Spinoza, the pantheist—all of them are represented. Spinoza seems a little out of place in such a library. At that time, his philosophy was either not known or held in bad repute because of its monism and anti-materialism. He is really a philosopher born out of his time, and belongs rather to the later Romantic thinking, the logical forefather of Kant and Hegel. I can find no reference to him in Fielding's works. Is he an author bought by Fielding in Leyden and never read? This, however, is merely an interesting subject for speculation.

[14]Digeon, Aurelien, *The Novels of Fielding*, pp. 210ff.

One may assume, after studying the list of books in Fielding's library and comparing the names there with references in his novels, plays, miscellanies, and various periodical essays that Fielding knew a great deal about many subjects and, in particular, about the epic and epic theories, as conceived by various Renaissance criticis, and by the critics and poets of antiquity. Not only Homer, Virgil, Statius, Silius Italicus, Aristotle, Horace, but also fugitive references such as that in Chapter CXVIII of the *Satyricon of Petronius*[15] may have been familiar to him. Among the modern writers, he possessed none of the Italian critics, and among the French he seems to have admired Le Bossu and Madame Dacier chiefly. But he could have become acquainted with such men as de Scudéry, Desmarets de Saint Sorlin, and Chapelain through the witty presentation of their ideas in the Socratic dialogues of M. de Sarrasin,[16] whose works Fielding owned. He owned none of the modern romances, poetic or prose. But he states that he had read some of the prose romances[17] and obviously knows a good deal about them. Many of the other writers, especially the Italian and French, who had attempted to create modern epics, had not been able to get away from the standards of the mediaeval romance. Fielding knew the ancient epics better than he knew the romances. When he came to study the principles of epic construction, his mind, not filled with the extravagances of the romances, could approach epic theory with a knowledge of that genre at its source and of the fundamental principles of epic construction. A full understanding of Fielding's achievement

[15]Petronius: *Satyricon*, Ch. CXVIII translated by J. M. Mitchell: "For not in a poem can we describe the deeds of men—the historians do this far better; nay, through dark ways and the services of the gods, through the tossing maelstrom of the imagination, must the free spirit be hurled, so that it may seem rather the prophecy of a soul inspired than the prosaic record of authenticated fact." This excerpt seems on the whole to justify the poetry of the romances rather than that of the *Iliad* or the *Odyssey*. Fielding nowhere in his prefaces quotes this à propos of his novels as histories. That idea, however, may owe something to Petronius and his commentators.

[16]M. de Sarrasin was a wit of the time of Louis XIV, whose writings, while not original as criticism, cleverly present, in the form of dialogues, the contrasting points of view of various critics among the Ancients and Moderns.

[17]Preface to *Joseph Andrews*.

really involves a knowledge of the whole artistic tradition of the epic.

In the following brief review of epic theory, I have confined myself, as nearly as possible, to those authors which Fielding, in all probability, knew well himself. Any others which I have discussed have been simply to show the sources of the theories.

CHAPTER II

The General Problem of the Modern Epic

In the Renaissance two very different civilizations, the Hellenic and the mediaeval Christian, meet. These two civilizations may have many points in common, but they have certain profound differences. A clash of ideas may be seen throughout the Renaissance, in the opposition of the ascetic suspicion of fleshly beauty to Greek joy in it, in the clash of the rather worldly Gods of Olympus and the awful Jehovah of Sinai. Nowhere is this clash more strongly felt than in the problem of the modern, Christian epic, which had to be built out of Christian materials upon the model of Homer and Virgil.

Virgil had been admired throughout the Middle Ages, but as the writer of moral lessons rather than writer of epic.[1] As the world of ancient Greece and Rome became a living imaginative force, interest in Virgil was gradually changed from a moral to a more purely artistic one and as Homer and Aristotle came to be known and reverenced as writer and critic of epic respectively, men desired to do for the modern world what Homer had done for his, and to write a great modern epic. Waiving for the moment the difference between Homer and Virgil, the poets and critics of the Renaissance were confronted with the necessity for determining what was essential to the epic and what was accidental. Most Renaissance critics agreed that human nature was the subject of all great art, and they felt that human nature is the same today, yesterday, and forever, a point of view most succinctly phrased for English readers in Pope's famous dictum:

[1]See Comparetti, D. *Virgil in the Middle Ages*, pp. 96-118.

20

"First follow Nature, and your judgment frame
By her just standard, which is still the same:
Unerring Nature, still divinely bright,
One clear, unchanged, and universal light,
Life, force, and beauty, must to all impart,
At once the source, and end, and test of Art."

But, though human nature may not change from age to age, social customs certainly do change, and it is even arguable that changes in social customs effect a change in human nature itself. Achilles would have seemed less heroic, possibly, in the court of Louis XIV than in the camp of Agamemnon, and surely Louis XIV would have found Agamemnon's position impossible. The intervention of the gods in Homer and Virgil does not lessen the hero's dignity, but the presence of the gods of Olympus or of Christian angels and devils in Renaissance epics frequently makes the heroes seem less important than they were intended to be.[2] Critics and poets of the Renaissance had, then, a very real problem before them of determining just what was meant by the conception of unchanging human nature.

One of the points which was most confusing to the critics was the general acceptance of Homer and Virgil as similar. Both wrote epics. Virgil had obviously used Homer as model.[3] Certain epic formulae in Virgil were derived from Homer. But there are striking differences as well.[4] Not until the late eighteenth century in England was the distinction between the

---

[2]Of course, Aeneas cuts a rather poor figure when he allows himself to be snatched from Dido's side at the bidding of the gods. But possibly this is true only to modern minds.

[3]Some of the ways in which Virgil followed Homer are: The wanderings of Aeneas in the first six books parallel those of Ulysses; the wars in the second part parallel the battles around Troy; the single combat between the heroes on opposing sides, Achilles and Hector, Aeneas and Turnus; the friendship of Nisus and Euryalus parallels that of Achilles and Patroclus; the Amazon queen, Penthesilea, killed by Achilles is like the warrior maid, Camilla, opposed to Aeneas, and killed by one of his men.

[4]Renaissance critics were quite aware of a difference in the spirit of the two poets— of the elegiac note in Virgil and his greater delicacy; of the zestful joy in combat in Homer, and the serene acceptance of life. One way in which realization of this difference found expression was in the effort made to decide which was superior. Muzio, Capriano, and Scaliger think Virgil greater because he observes the laws of decorum better. See Spingarn, *Literary Criticism of the Renaissance* p. 87 seq.

Le Bossu constantly points out that Virgil's poem is written in a softer mood than are the Homeric poems. He attributes this to the fact that Virgil wishes to inculcate the lessons of piety in writing the *Aeneid*.

Dryden also discusses their differences in his *Preface to the Fables*. See Dryden, *Essays*, Vol. II. p. 251 seq.

primitive and artificial epic emphasized. The Homeric epics are less of a *tour de force* than the *Aeneid*. The world of the *Iliad* and the *Odyssey* is a world *familiar* to Homeric audiences. The heroes are traditional heroes, whose deeds were known. The gods and their intervention on behalf of favorite warriors were commonplaces in narrative. The whole story in both epics was an artistic presentation of the business of life in a heroic age. Romantic love did not enter into this business of life. Andromache and Penelope are the heroines, respectively, of the *Iliad* and the *Odyssey*—not Helen, though she does pervade the scene of the *Iliad* as a kind of fate. It is not Homer, the writer of the heroic age, but the romantic Marlowe, who exclaims in ecstasy:

> "Was this the face that launched a thousand ships,
> And burned the topless towers of Ilium?
> Sweet Helen, make me immortal with a kiss!"

The choleric Achilles, although he sulked in his tent when he lost Briseis, would have been astonished that any man could think he would be made immortal with a kiss—even the kiss of Helen. Achilles was fighting to get the wife Helen back to her husband. A king does not care to have his wife carried off by an upstart young prince.

Virgil, living in a more sophisticated age, wrote his epic with a conscious desire to instruct not to be found in Homer. Homer's epics, though they are pictures of the heroic world of its heroes, are that rather by accident than by intention. The *Iliad* and the *Odyssey* tell primarily of the great deeds of Achilles and of the toilsome journey of Ulysses back to Ithaca. The tale of the deeds of great warriors inevitably forms a history of their times, but the history of the Trojan war was not the main subject, being sufficiently well-known anyhow to Homeric audiences so that there was no point in the poet's instructing his hearers precisely in this history. Virgil, in the age of Augustus, wrote to glorify the early traditions of his race when he wrote the *Aeneid*.

"I sing of arms and of the man, who first came from the shores of Troy, etc."

Thus runs the invocation to the *Aeneid,* in contrast to the more specific opening of the *Iliad*:

"Sing, goddess, of the wrath of Peleus' son, Achilles, etc."
There is, in the *Aeneid,* a self-conscious purpose entirely lacking in the Homeric poems. This does not imply that the *Iliad* and the *Odyssey* lack artistry, and conscious artistic finish. I refer simply to the difference in point of view about the *ends* which the Homeric poems and the *Aeneid* have in view. Virgil, in the *Aeneid,* wished to reveal the high origin of the race of Augustus, and to instruct his audience in the history of the Roman people.[5]

Another great difference between Homer and Virgil is in the introduction into the *Aeneid* of romantic love. The episode of Dido has no parallel in Homer.[6] The storm-tossed Ulysses is going home to his wife and to his subjects who are demoralized by his long absence from home. The storm-tossed Aeneas —though unknowingly, of course—is going to the arms of the susceptible Dido, arch-enemy of the Roman people. No great Homeric hero—not Achilles, nor Ulysses, nor Hector—was ever thought of by subsequent generations as one of the great lovers. But Aeneas and Dido take their place with Pyramus and Thisbe, Troilus and Cressida.

In spite of these differences, however, the Homeric poems and Virgil's have in common the same general religious background, so that their "machines" are much alike and equally relevant in their poems. And, as I have said, Virgil modeled many of his epic formulae directly upon Homer.

The Renaissance inherited not only this Greek and Latin tradition, but also a mediaeval tradition. Mediaeval narratives

[5] In this conscious desire to do for Rome what the *Iliad* did for Greece, Virgil really sets the conscious artistic purpose of the art epic. Tasso, Camoens, the French epic writers, all follow him. Even Milton does this, though he writes for a cosmos rather than for a nation, but it is a cosmos conceived in terms of his own religion.

[6] Even the story of Ulysses and Calypso is not done in terms of romantic love, though Ulysses' journey is delayed by Calypso as Aeneas' was by Dido. The feeling of Achilles for Briseis is wholly without romantic quality.

dealt with romantic love, with points of chivalrous behavior, and with strange enchantments and adventures. Such are the things to be found in the tales in the Arthurian cycle, or the Charlemagne stories. Aeneas, kept from his duty by Dido, is summoned by the gods to leave her and go on to Italy. But Tristan is the justification, the apotheosis of the lover. When the gods intervene in Homer, it is done in order to hasten the work of war. The gods simply take part in everyday life. But a knight of Arthur's court may expect, at almost any time, to ride into an enchanted forest where he will encounter bewildering magic of one sort or another. The supernatural is here an irrational force. As these secular tales become more and more popular, the influence of the Church made itself felt and chivalrous heroes became more and more monastic. In the early legends the knight to achieve the Grail is Parzival, who has sinned. In the later legends the hero of the Grail is the monastic and sinless Galahad. In the mediaeval ideal, art should have an other worldly purpose, certainly a moral purpose. Virgil in the Middle Ages was the repository of moral truths—as was Ovid. When the Renaissance felt the encounter of the pagan joy in earthly beauty with the ascetic repudiation of earthly beauty,[7] a really serious problem presented itself, the problem whether a work of art should be judged purely on aesthetic grounds, or on its definite and explicit moral purpose.

The didactic purpose in art is, of course, by no means a purely mediaeval interest. It is present in the Greek conception of the place of poetry in education, and, indeed, in a great many places. Aristotle, for instance, classifies poetry under the head of efficient metaphysics.[8] Horace, in his *Ars Poetica*, speaks of the purpose of poetry thus: "aut prodesse volunt aut dilectare poetae". The same point of view is evident in other writers—Longinus, Quintilian, Seneca. And finally, there is

[7]The contrast between the two ideals, *as moral ideals*, is revealed in the contrast between the pagan ideal, "Mens sana in corpore sano", and the Christian one, "to renounce the world, the *flesh*, and the devil."

[8]See Spingarn, op. cit. p. 24.

Plato's condemnation of Homer[9] as an imitation of an imitation of a divine idea, and also as telling scandalous tales of the gods. But even in this point where they seem similar, the Christian tradition was slightly different from the Greek tradition. In the Christian theology, there was an other-worldliness, in the Greek, a this-worldliness even in questions of morality. In its fundamentals, Christian theology removed its supernatural beings from the stage of this world more completely than did Greek theology. The marvellous in mediaeval literature had little to do with the mediaeval religious ideas; it was, in fact, largely opposed to the prevailing religious ideas. Almost all enchantments were the work of malignant beings rather than of beneficient ones, and almost all the magic was irrational. The Greek gods might be capricious, but they were intelligible. The aim of the Greek hero was to live a sane, reasonable, heroic life *in this world,* with the approval of the gods, and at times, their cooperation. The aim of the Christian hero was to live a humble, self-abnegating, chivalrous life in this vale of tears, with his high hopes fixed upon loyalty to his God, his liege lord, and his lady. His highest achievement would be achieving the Grail, an *other-wordly* ideal. The question of conduct was, therefore, less individualistic and practical for the Christian world than it had been for the Greek world. And, in this Christian world, where so many of men's best efforts were, theoretically at least, *ad majorem Dei gloriam,* works of art, as everything else, were conceived of more explicitly as didactic than they had been in the ancient world.

The justification of poetry, then, as a worthy human effort was one of the first problems which the Renaissance confronted when the clash of pagan antiquity and mediaeval Christianity occurred. After this, it was necessary for critics to analyze the different kinds of poetry and establish norms for each.

[9]*Republic,* Bk. II, fol. 377-78. But Plato's condemnation of the poet as being at two removes from reality is not mediaeval. The mediaeval moralist would not have elaborated a theory of beauty such as we find in the *Symposium,* where one goes from love of a beautiful body, through various stages, to love for the cosmos. The mediaeval idea based spiritual development on repudiation of love for a beautiful body.

Aristotle,[10] whose *Poetics* was taken as the great source of critical opinion by most of the critics of this period, had expressed his own belief that Tragedy is a higher form than Epic. He bases his opinion on the greater variety of artistic effects in drama, and on the greater condensation and closer unity of purpose in tragedy. Renaissance critics, however, did not always follow their master in preference. The spirit of the Renaissance was heroic and national. A world which had witnessed the exploits of Christopher Columbus, of Vasco da Gama, of Prince Henry the Navigator, which had just emerged from the long struggles with the Saracen and the wresting of their Christian civilization from the alien Mohammedan culture, could not fail to take a very special delight in the exploits of Achilles, whose defection almost brought ruin to the Greek cause, or in the wanderings of Odysseus, whose lonely sea voyages had so much in common with those wanderings of the actual Renaissance navigators. Furthermore, Virgil had been reverenced in the Middle Ages, and this reverence for the third great epic of classical antiquity held over into the period of the Renaissance.[11] On the other hand, drama at that time had fallen into disrepute as a vulgar, crude form. Most of the critics, therefore, expressing the interest of the times, gave the preëminent place to the epic.

Inasmuch as Aristotle's treatment of epic poetry was not very full, Renaissance critics occupied themselves with elaborating theories about the epic, frequently inferring epic formulae from what Aristotle has to say about tragedy, as for example, in the conception that epic action must be kept within a year, paralleling the unity of time of one day in tragedy. The *Iliad* and the *Odyssey,* and the *Aeneid* had celebrated the deeds of

[10]For a full discussion of epic theory in the Renaissance see Spingarn, *op. cit.,* especially pp. 107-125.

Most of the ideas developed by seventeenth century French and English critics are Italian in origin. In this chapter, I wish merely to state the problem and point out briefly how different men of genius solved it in part, and failed to solve it in part. The specific arguments will be developed in subsequent chapters about the French and English theorists of the seventeenth and early eighteenth centuries.

[11]No doubt, men's greater familiarity with Virgil than with Homer led to their emphasizing, and *seeing*, the conscious purpose of national glorification as the chief end of the epic.

great national heroes. Hence, Renaissance critics inferred that the epic *must be patriotic* in its conscious aims. Homeric epic undoubtedly is incidentally patriotic, but it may be questioned whether it is consciously. The epic must have—and this is derived from Aristotle—unity of action, not merely unity of hero. That is, it must develop a single important action. And finally, the poem must be expressed in a lofty style worthy the deeds and aims of the lofty action with which it deals. The definition of the epic most generally accepted would thus be somewhat like this: An epic poem is an imitation of one single, important, and unified action in the life of an important person or group of persons of worth to the state, written in language which is lofty and dignified.

But, once this definition was formulated, all sorts of problems remained. One of the first questions to be settled was an exact distinction between epic and romance. Part of the distinction between the ancient epic and such a poem as Ariosto's *Orlando Furioso* (1510) was contained in the definition—the epic must have unity of action, whereas the *Orlando Furioso* did not have this unity.[12] But this was not the whole difference. No such creature as the Hippogriff had appeared in Greek and Latin epic. What precisely is an "imitation" of which Aristotle speaks? What actually constituted Aristotle's "probable impossibility"? Hence arose the endless discussions over verisimilitude. Akin to this question was the question about the use of the marvellous. What exactly should be the function of "machines" in the epic? And, if the epic should have "machines", should there be a pagan marvellous, or a Christian marvellous? Should a Christian poet invoke the muse in writing his epic?

The answers to these questions seem more simple than they actually are. We of the present day answer many of the questions by pointing out that the *Iliad* and the *Odyssey* are primitive poems, and that the marvellous in them was not incredible

---

[12] I am omitting any discussion of Pulci's *Morgante Maggiore*, and of Boiardo's *Orlando Innamorato*, as antedating the real rise of the critical discussion.

to Homeric audiences. But this is by no means the whole answer. Is the sense of cosmic destiny which the presence of the Olympian deities gives to the Greek epics one of the *necessary* elements of the epic? Was Circe's enchantment in turning Ulysses' followers into swine a "probable impossibility"? If it was, how much might authors of the Christian epic make use of such magic?

One of the first aspects of the dispute over epic principles was the discussion of the claims of Ariosto to be called an epic poet. The *Orlando Furioso* was written before the critical war had got under way and was obviously inspired by the mediaeval romances more than by the Greek and Latin epics. Giraldi Cintio,[18] in his *Discorso intorno al Comporre dei Romanzi* (1549), defended the *Orlando Furioso*—and the romance generally—as worthy of serious consideration on two counts. First, as Aristotle did not know the romance, he could not have laid down rules for it. And second, the romance was more in keeping with the spirit of modern times than the ancient epic was, and hence, should be cultivated. This is one of the first statements of the quarrel of the Ancients and the Moderns which was to develop into open combat in France in the seventeenth century. In effect, it states this principle of the Moderns: the ancients had their literary forms; let the moderns develop theirs.

But the question was not to be settled thus. Something in the cool reasonableness of a tale *of this world* to be found in the *Iliad* and the *Odyssey*, and in the *Aeneid*—for all their apparent strangeness—appealed to the men of the Renaissance. The *Orlando Furioso* was not national in the way in which the *Iliad* was national. In Ariosto's poem, one gets many delightful things, but one gets very little sense of a great and important national struggle. The keen sense of achievement and of national power which was part of the Renaissance consciousness demanded expression.

<hr />

[18]For a full discussion of this struggle to define the romance, see Wolff, **Max Ledwig**, *Geschichte der Romantheorie*, especially pp. 11-25 for a discussion of **Giraldi Cintio.**

Torquato Tasso,[14] coming after much discussion of Aristotle, tried to write the modern epic in his *Jerusalem Delivered* (1581). Tasso scrupulously followed the epic formulae noted and practiced by Virgil. In this poem, we have an important action—the great struggle of Christendom against the Moslem. And the story of the struggle is managed in such a way that the action is single and unified. But, in limiting the actual narration of the poem to the capture of Jerusalem, Tasso had a rather thin subject for extended treatment. The Crusades were of great importance to the Christian world, but the actual capture of the city is, curiously enough, one of the least important events in the struggle. In order to extend his narrative to epic length, Tasso filled his poem with episodes, and these episodes frequently usurp first place in the story.[15] Finally, Tasso was deeply troubled by the bothersome business of "machines", without which no epic was supposed to be. The *Jerusalem Delivered* was written after the Counter Reformation, and, in the somewhat illiberal spirit of that time, a poet could not treat religious subjects with the levity with which Ariosto had treated the scene of Discord among the monks—nor with the slightly satiric irreverence with which the indecencies of Hephaistos, Ares, and Aphrodite are treated in the *Odyssey* in the tales told at the court of King Alcinous. Tasso introduced various kinds of magic to solve the problem of the marvellous, but his magic is not very convincing. His enchanters seem ineffectual, because they act, or fail to act, without giving reasons. The result is that Ariosto's extravagances seem somewhat more credible than Tasso's soberer efforts.

Thus, although Italy produced two great poems more or less in the epic manner, these were not quite successful as *epics*.[16]

[14]Tasso tried to solve the conflict between epic and romance in his *Discorsi dell' Arte Poetica* (1587). Here he states that a modern poem should have romantic material, but epic form. (See Spingarn, *op. cit.*, p. 119, and Wolff, op cit., p. 24). This is one solution, and one destined to be very popular. It is really a definition of the heroic poem—and the source of the theory of the prose heroic romance.

[15]To be sure, the same argument may be used against the *Aeneid* itself, where the episode of Dido certainly dominates the main story to the detriment of the latter. But the *Aeneid* had been somewhat mellowed by tradition, nor does it offend, on the whole, so badly as the *Jerusalem Delivered*.

[16]In a sense, neither of them pretended to be genuinely epic. Ariosto wrote before the problem had become all-important. His claims were put forward chiefly by his

The charm of these poems lies more in their extravagances, or
at least, their less realistic pictures, than in the sense they give
of the whole life of a period of human existence, which is the
sense back of the *Iliad* and the *Odyssey,* and to a lesser extent,
of the *Aeneid.* The primitive epic may contain genuinely
romantic qualities, for the simple reason that life contains such
qualities, and these great primitive epics are pictures of a civilization. But the *Iliad* and the *Odyssey* do not exist for their
romantic qualities, as the *Orlando Furioso,* and, to a lesser
extent, the *Jerusalem Delivered,* do. The problem which confronted Renaissance critics was that of discovering what material was genuinely romantic[17]—that is, a deliberate search for
the remote and strange—and what is realistic, however strange
it might appear.

Each country, as it felt the influence of the Renaissance,
tried to produce the great national epic which the spirit of the
times demanded. Portugal produced the *Lusiads,* (1572) of
Camoens. Spain produced no great epic which has taken rank
with those of Ariosto, Tasso, Camoens, Spenser, and Milton,
but still a number of attempts were made. Among others,
Lope de Vega somehow found time, in the midst of writing
his eighteen hundred or so plays, to write four epics—the
Dragontea (1598), a story of the last cruise of Sir Francis
Drake, *Angelica* (1602), a continuation of the *Orlando Furioso,*
the *Jerusalem Conquistada* (1609), in the manner of Tasso,
and *Corona Tragica* (1627), a religious epic about Mary Stuart
and Queen Elizabeth. The *Lusiads* deserves high praise. It had
really the best chance of any of the epics of the time—the
question of the author's genius apart—of being an *Odyssey* of
the Renaissance, for it had for its subject the great popular
interest of the period—the interest in exploration and voyages

admirers. And Tasso in his *Discorsi* says explicitly that he desired to unite romantic
material with epic form. This did not prevent Tasso's being criticized, however,
as a writer of epic. Nor was romantic material, ofter all, quite modern, so that the
Jerusalem Delivered was not the picture of *their* world which the Renaissance desired.

[17]I am using "romantic" here in a special sense, one of the senses which it may
have—that is, as having the qualities of the mediaeval romances. The word may
have so many meanings that it seems desirable to indicate the special limitations set
upon its meaning in this discussion.

to the East. Unfortunately, however, Camoens was troubled by the perplexing question of supernatural forces, and mingled Christian and Olympian deities in his poem in the most curious fashion. The Portuguese in India, whose deeds are watched over by a council of Olympian deities, who yet worship Jehovah, —surely this is as strange an assortment as one can hope to meet, especially when Bacchus, disguised as a priest, performs Christian rites! The *Lusiads,* then, satisfied a real thirst— the Renaissance thirst for exploration, which, if treated realistically, would have given us the picture of a great human epoch. But the poem fails to come off as epic because of the complete lack of realism in the handling of the machines.

Such, very briefly, is the history of the attempts made by various men of genius to write the epic of their own people. Meanwhile, as suggested above, the critics wrestled with the abstract principles. Much of the criticism seems pretty formal and illiberal today; yet I doubt if we do the critics justice. They were trying to solve a very perplexing problem, and an eternal problem. What have the great masters of the past to give us, and how far must we be bound by their discoveries? The beauty of the intricate, yet simple form of Homer is something which one who wishes to handle large groups of people and depict great events may very well wish to study. Yet, how intimately is the form an outgrowth of the material? It is the sense of an important struggle behind the actual events in the *Iliad* which gives it much of its power. How much does this sense depend upon the presence of the supernatural? How does Homer manage to make a "probable impossibility" out of the episode of Circe in the *Odyssey?* Tasso claimed, in his *Discorsi dell' Arte Poetica,* that in an epic poem the marvellous must be united with the verisimilar. How is the poet to achieve that? How did Homer and Virgil achieve it? Homer stops his direct narrative—as in the *Odyssey* where the action begins at the end of Ulysses' years of wandering,—to tell of things which have led up to this. Does this serve to give the action unity? He also stops this to tell seemingly irrelevant stories as the stories of the gods told at the court of King Alcinous. How, in spite of this—or because of this—does the action remain a unified whole?

From another point of view, what of the romance? Was the romance, as Cintio claimed, the real expression of the modern age? Here was another aspect of the problem, or a slightly different facet of the same problem. The world of the Medicis, or of Louis XIV, or of the Stuarts, was a very different world from that of Agamemnon. Had the Ancients indeed discovered all the forms of art? Perhaps some new form was more suited to the new world. Perhaps, as some claimed, the modern world was superior to the ancient world, just as Christianity was believed to be superior to paganism.

This quarrel of the Ancients and the Moderns[18] has its basis in a very real problem. At first, the re-discovery of the great authors of classical antiquity fired men's imagination. Yet when the creative fire died down—or when it had never been lighted—reverence for the ancients had sometimes a bad effect. And, even a man of genius may feel trammeled at times, as Corneille did after the famous battle over the unities when *The Cid* was produced. On the other hand, Racine, who observed the unities in his plays, probably gains much of his tragic effect from the austerity which the limitations of his form—a French version of classical tragedy—imposed.

Now, as I have said, though the sense of form and restraint in the great works of the past might afford a real inspiration to great men, it could become a dead weight to little men. If there was to be one form only for the epic, if every epic must have "machines," or some other set technical device, inferred as a rule from the practice of Homer, some very strange results would ensue. Sometimes there might result a kind of dull formalism; at other times, a kind of fantastic preciosity. The greatest Italian writers of epic managed to avoid this. But France, coming a little later to the attempt, suffered from just

[18]For a full discussion of the specific quarrel of the Ancients and Moderns, in France, see Rigault, H., *Histoire de la Querelle des Anciens et des Modernes.*

these things. Ronsard's *Franciade* is a purely "poetic" epic, almost wholly removed from the modern world, with its "machines" Olympian and its legends Virgilian, all couched in a language which had little reference to the language of everyday life. The influence of Malherbe, who insisted that the language of poetry *is* the language of everyday life, and of Descartes, with his rationalistic philosophy, brought about a reaction from this extreme, only to be followed by the ponderous and prosaic dullness of the writers of Christian epics—Desmarets de Saint-Sorlin, Georges de Scudéry, Chapelain, and a host of other writers of frigid epics. It was the desire of these men to write an epic which should be for modern France what the *Aeneid* had been for Rome, or what the *Iliad* had been for Greece. Inasmuch as their world was a Christian world, they repudiated the use of the pagan marvellous and used Christian deities. Some of them wrote Biblical epics,[19] but the greatest efforts were probably made to write a national epic, telling of some great French tradition. They followed the rules, as they knew them, faithfully, but they failed.

Yet, in the drama, where the rules were followed,—though by men of genius rather than by aspiring dilettantes or earnest pedants—we have the great age of French literature, with Corneille, Racine, Molière writing under a restraint which served to give depth to their work. Both about the drama and the epic, a critical war was always very near the surface, bursting out in such specific quarrels as the one over the unities in *The Cid,* or in the prolonged Quarrel of the Ancients and the Moderns at the end of the seventeenth century. The great men generally ranged themselves on the side of the ancients, for they had learned how to mold their own ideas into a work which gave expression to Christian material in a form learned from the study of the principles of the ancients.

Yet the critical problem remained. Even where the poets were successful—as Tasso undoubtedly was—in writing a

[19]Such, for example, as the *Jonas,* the *Josué,* the *Sanson,* the *David,* of Coras, written between 1662 and 1665; *l'Incarnation* (1624) of Masen; the *Moïse Sauvé* (1653) of Saint-Amant.

beautiful, Christian poem of heroic dimensions, how far was that poem national, realistic, and probable, in the manner of Homer? In England, Spenser, following one interpretation of Homer and Virgil popular in Reniassance criticism, made his *Faerie Queen*[20] allegorical. His poem is exquisite, but it is not an epic in the sense in which the men of the Renaissance generally conceived the epic. For one thing, it lacks unity of action. For another, its marvellous was undoubtedly largely the magic of the mediaeval romances. Spenser belongs to the early stage of the Renaissance when the clash of traditions of pagan antiquity and of mediaeval Christianity had not been subdued to the somewhat frigid harmony which later ensued. But Milton wrote almost a century later, when the principles had been fought over again and again, and rules more explicitly formulated than in the early days.

That Milton was able to achieve a successful solution of the problem and in *Paradise Lost* write the Christian epic was not especially helpful to his English followers, not only because it is always difficult to imitate a work of genius, but because, in a special sense, *Paradise Lost* could be done once and once only. That is, there could not be an indefinite number of poems in which the "machines" of epic theory become the protagonists, as they do in Milton. In the Homeric epic, the world presented to the reader was familiar, and the gods were at home in this world rather than in a divine abode of their own. But *Paradise Lost* takes us into chaos and Paradise, the remote and strange abodes of Jehovah and Lucifer. It is a picture, not of a civilization, but of a cosmos, and we know but one cosmos and even this only because Milton compels us to know it. And even were this not true, the spirit of the world changed at the close of the seventeenth century, and a spirit of scepticism came into being which would probably have made a repetition of Milton's achievement impossible even had a Milton existed.

Such is the history, very briefly sketched, of attempts to

[20]Spenser may have got his ideas in part from Thomas Wilson's *Arte of Rhetoricke*, published in 1553, where the author says that the allegorical is the important thing in composition, the story being just a framework for elaborating the fable.

write the epic up to the middle of the seventeenth century, when France begins to work upon the problem. In the field of narrative outside the epic, there were romances—both prose and poetic—and anti-romances. The romances have a long ancestry, dating back to the days of the late Greek civilization on the one hand, and to mediaeval Christendom on the other. But in the seventeenth century, they took on new life. The heroic romances of that time are compounded of many diverse elements—fictitious history; delicate, Dresden-China pastoralism; mediaeval magic; epic formulae; and the point of honor. Spain presided as godmother at this rebirth of the mediaeval romance in modern dress. During the time of the original flowering of romance for the rest of Europe—that is, during the twelfth, thirteenth, and fourteenth centuries—Spain had been either a Moorish country, or else occupied with getting rid of the Moors. The heroes of her thought at that time were actual Cids, and not beautiful, but perhaps dreamlike Parzivals or Launcelots. But romance, with its delicate sense of the point of honor, its delightfully incredible magic, its passionate and high-minded love, satisfied a longing which nothing else will satisfy; and somewhat late in life, to be sure, but with the passion of those who come late in life to the things of youth, Spain embraced the romance. Don Quixote's reading, which was Cervantes' own, reveals the power of the heroic romance, and though Don Quixote is the butt of all the jokes, he is the profoundest assertion of the dignity of a romantic faith that we have. And he is representative of Cervantes' world—the ideals of chivalry at war with Renaissance worldliness. The heroes of the serious heroic romances are a series of Don Quixotes, *taken seriously*. They are not merly improbable possibilities; they are improbable impossibilities, human Hippogriffs! The characters are remote from familiar life, but epic formulae are conscientiously adhered to. The action, however it may spread in reality, is put into the straight-jacket of the unity of time. The result is that these romances are terribly involved as narrative. The *Odyssey* begins when Odysseus is at the end of his wanderings, and we are made acquainted with what has gone before through the narration which he himself gives. The heroic romance scrupulously carries this device to extravagant lengths. A and B, let us say, are about to marry, when C and D appear. The nuptials are held up while C relates his adventures—through the course of a volume—and not only his adventures, but what E has told him of *his* adventures, and the various adventures may have taken the characters pretty much over the known world in the course of the tales. The result is very confusing—and terribly dull. Yet the witty Madame de Sevigné used to devour the things.

The anti-romance is deliberately vulgar and anti-heroic. Its characters are rogues, thieves, vagabonds,—anyone outside the pale of gentlemanly and courtly society. Their conception of the point of honor is Falstaffian. In the escapades of Gil Blas, and of the travelling players in *Le Roman Comique,* there is a very definite sense of recognizable human beings in an everyday world. But, even the vagabonds are romantic vagabonds, and the realism of the world of *Le Roman Comique* is picturesque. And, as narratives, these anti-romances lack a sense of form. The episodes are a series of disconnected adventures, joined together solely by the fact that they all happen to the same person or persons. The anti-romances are not pretentious, as are the heroic romances; and they are vivid pictures of certain aspects of their times. But they give no more a picture of the whole of an epoch, such as the writers of serious narrative desired, than would a collection of short stories, mostly of the fabliaux variety.

These heroic romances and the burlesques anti-romance offered readers the delights of prose fiction throughout the seventeenth century and for the first part of the eighteenth century, both in France and England, for what happened in France went to England shortly. The epic was the concern of serious writers. The heroic romance was pretentious, but it and the anti-romance were light reading—difficult as it may be to believe.

The critical problem of the nature of the epic remained, and a good deal, first and last, was written on the subject. The epic does something which no other kind of writing does, and men desire to see their world done with epic sweep. Curiously enough, it was not Blackmore, or even Milton, nor any of the writers of the poetic epic who wrote of English civilization after the Reformation and the Civil Wars with the epic sweep. Fielding, who had read what many dull and, it would appear, not too wise critics had to say about epic structure, gave us the picture of the whole of modern life in the life and adventures of a young man who is for his world as representative a figure as Achilles was for his—Tom Jones.

CHAPTER III

FRENCH EPICS AND EPIC THEORIES OF THE SEVENTEENTH CENTURY

Whatever else may be said about the seventeenth century French writers of narrative fiction of any sort, they were almost all prefatory. The authors of the uninspired epics of that day were very greatly addicted to airing their theories and to weighing their own merits in a voluminous foreword. We will pardon their poetic transgressions for the sake of their prefaces. In his extended discussion of the French epic of this period, M. Duchesne remarks: "La Grèce d'Achille avait attendu quatre cents ans ses deux Epopées; nos beaux esprits n'imposèrent pas à la France une si longue patience; Cinq ans (1653-57) produisent quatre Poëmes; le Saint Louis du Jésuite Lemoyne; Alaric, de Scudéry (1654); la Pucelle, de Chapelain (1656), et le Clovis, de Desmarets (1657): Les quartre auteurs s'announcèrent plus ou moins franchement comme émules de l'Epopée antique; mais etudions leurs aptitudes, leur passé, l'instant qui vit éclore leur entreprise, et nous préssentirons sans peine à quel genre ils allaient aboutir."[1] (M. Duchesne has previously made a careful distinction between the primitive epic and the art epic).

A consideration of the preface of Georges de Scudéry's *Alaric* will illustrate the degree of frankness with which he announced himself as emulating the ancient epic. It will be noted that he includes the various Italian critics among the list of his guides. The influence of Italy on French theory at this time was very great, following a period of revolt from the first Italian influence on the Pleiade.[2] Chapelain, in fact, was a

[1]Duchesne, Julien, *Histoire des Poemes Épiques Francois du XVIIe Siècle*, p. 77.
[2]See Spingarn, op. cit., pp. 232-253.

member of the Italian Accademia della Crusca, on whose model
the French Academy was founded. He was also, as was de
Scudéry, a member of the Hôtel de Rambouillet group, where,
under the aegis of the Italian Madame de Rambouillet, theories
of art and manners were discussed at length.

Georges de Scudéry begins thus:[3]

"Comme le Poëme Epique a beaucoup de raport, quant à
la constitution, avec ces ingenieuses Fables, que nous apellons
des Romans; il est presque superflu que j'en parle icy; puisque
j'en ay traitté assez amplement, dans l'avant-propos de mon
Illustre Bassa: & que d'ailleurs l'heureux succés de ce Grand
Vizir, & celuy du Grand Cyrus qui l'a suivy, ont assez fait voir,
ce me semble, que je n'ignore pas absolument ce genre d'escrire,
dont je me mesle quelquefois. Neantmoins comme il pourroit
estre qu'une partie de ceux qui liront ce Poëme, n'auroient pas
veu ces autres Ouvrages; j'ay creu que je ne ferois pas mal,
de mettre en ce lieu un Discours de l'Epopée: afin de faire voir
aux Lecteurs, que je n'ay pas entrepris d'eslever un si grand
Bastiment, sans sçavoir toutes les proportions, & tous les aligne-
ments que l'Art enseigne."

Thus, in the opening sentence of his *Preface,* he avows the
kinship between the epic and the romance. He knows how to
write an epic because he has written romances. (The romances
were certainly as much his sister Madeleine's work as his, and it
is probable that they were almost entirely hers). In the preface to *Ibrahim, ou l'Illustre Bassa* (1641), to which he refers
above, Georges, or Madeleine, had said:

"Comme nous ne pouuons estre sçavans, que de ce que les
autres nous enseignent; Et que c'est à celuy qui vient le dernier,
à suiure ceux qui le deuancent: I'ay creu que pour dresser le
plan de cet ouurage il faloit consulter les Grecs, qui ont esté nos
premiers maistres, suiure la route qu'ils ont tenuë; Et tacher en
les imitant, d'arriuer à la mesme fin, que ces grands hommes
s'estoient proposée. I'ay donc veu dans ces fameux Romans de

---

[3]Preface-*Alaric*. It will be observed that de Scudéry's ideas follow, in a somewhat confused way, the theories of Torquato Tasso about the heroic poem with romantic
material and an epic form.

l'Antiquité, qu'à l'imitation de poëme Epique, il y a une
action principale, où toutes les autres sont attachées; qui
regne par tout l'ouurage; & qui fait qu'elles n'y sont employées,
que pour la conduire à sa perfection.   Cette action dans l'Iliade
d'Homere est la ruine de Troye: dans son Odyssée, la retour
d'Ulysse à Itaque; dans Virgile, la mort de Turne ou pour
mieux dire la conqueste de l'Italie; plus pres de nous dans le
Tasse, la prise de Hierusalem, & pour passer du Poëme au
Roman, qui est mon principal obiet; dans l'Heliodore, le mariage
de Chariclée & de Theagenes.   Ce n'est pas que les Episodes en
l'un, & les diuerses histoires en l'autre, n'y soient plustost des
beautez que des deffaux."

Although it is not explicitly stated in the above excerpt, the
implication of the passage is that the epic and the romance
follow the same structural principles, and that they differ, if at
all, solely in that the epic is usually a poem and the romance
usually prose. This excerpt seems, in fact, to call the *Iliad,* the
Odyssey, and the *Aeneid,* romances.[4] At any rate, in the preface to *Alaric,* Georges de Scudéry feels that his creations in the
field of heroic romance have given him authority to speak on the
epic. He does not distinguish the primitive epic, the literary
epic, romance, and romantic epic. This is even better illustrated
by what he says in his next paragraph.

"J'ay donc consulté les Maistres là dessus: c'est à dire
Aristote & Horace: & aprés eux Macrobe, Scaliger, le Tasse,
Castelvetro, Picolomine, Vida, Vossius, Pacius, Ricobon,
Robortel, Paul Benni, Mámbrun, & plusieurs autres: et passant
de la Theorie à la Pratique, j'ay releu fort exactment l'Iliade
& l'Odyssée d'Homere; L'Eneide de Virgile; la Guerre civile de
Lucain; la Thebaide de Stace; les Rolands amoreux & furieux
de Boyardo & de l'Arisoste; l'imcomparable Hierusalem delivrée du fameux Torquato; & grand nombre d'autre Poëmes
Epiques en diverses langues: tels que sont les premiers Livres
de la Franciade de Ronsard, & de Saint Louis du Père le
Moine; & ce beau Poëme de la conqueste de Granada: le plus
bel Ouvrage que l'Italie nous ait donné depuis le Tasse."

<hr>

[4]In the phrase, "dans ces fameux Romans de l'Antiquité."

Homer, Virgil, Boiardo, and Tasso—they are all here. He either had not read, or did not accept, the critical conclusions of various Italian critics, differentiating epic and romance, who had followed Ariosto.[5] He notes that Castelvetro believes that the subject of the epic poem "doit estre absolument fabuleux."[6] But, de Scudéry goes on to say, "si cela estoit, l'Iliade seroit defecteuse, & l'Eneide ne vaudroit rien; puis que le Siege de Troye est veritable, & qu' Enée est venu en Italie, selon la plus commune croyance des Autheurs." This point is well taken. He then adds: "Ainsi je crois pour moy, contre l'advis de ce Commentateur d'Aristote, que le Sujet du Poëme Heroique, doit estre plutost veritable qu'inventée: parce que le Poëte Epique, devant sur toutes choses s'attacher au vray-semblable; il ne le seroit point, qu'une action illustre ne fust descrite dans aucun Historien." In these quotations, is stated, a problem, which de Scudéry does not attempt to settle; that is, if the subject of a heroic poem (which he identifies with the epic) should be true (historical) rather than invented (fictitious), because of the necessity for verisimilitude, can a poem like the *Orlando Furioso,* with its great element of the fantastic and grotesque, be said to have verisimilitude, the supreme quality of the epic? (He has just called the *Orlando* an epic.) Further more, how can the material be both historical and romantic, as Tasso and de Scudéry both claim it should be? Indeed, he apparently does not see the issue which he has raised, by implication rather than explicitly, of course.[7]

He then takes up the problem of "machines", phrasing it thus: "Or l'illustre Sujet du Poëme Epique, ne doit point estre pris maintenant, à mon advis, des Histoires du Paganisme: parce

[5]The arguments of Giraldi Cintio in favor of the romance, and Tasso's definition of the modern epic as a poem with romantic material and epic form had not been universally accepted. On the contrary, it was attacked by a large number of critics. See Spingarn, op. cit., pp. 122-124 for on account of the attacks on Tasso.

[6]The question whether the material of the epic should be historical, or fictitious engaged a good deal of critical attention. It all grew out of Aristotle's distinction between history as presenting *what is,* and poetry as presenting *what ought to be.* The majority of critics, including Tasso, said that the material should be historical. See Spingarn, op. cit., pp. 44-47.

[7]The problem of combining romantic, historical, verisimilar, and marvellous material in epic form was what finally led to the abandonment of Tasso's conception of the romantic epic.

(comme je viens de le dire, & comme le Tasse l'a dit devant
moy) que tous ces Dieux imaginaires, destruisent absolument
l'Epopée, en destruisant la vray-semblance, qui en est tout le
fondement. Il faut donc que l'Argument du Poëme Epique,
soit pris de l'Histoire Chrétienne, mais non pas de l'Histoire
Sainte: d'autant qu'on ne peut sans prophanation, en alterer
la verité, & que sans l'Invention, qui est la principal partie du
Poëte, il est presque impossible que l'Epopée puisse avoir toute
sn beauté . . . . & je suis fortement persuadé, que l'Histoire
Payenne ni l'Histoire Sainte, ne sont point propres presente-
ment à fournir un Sujet Epique: & que la Chretienne prophane
toute seule en nostre temps, nous peut donner ce merveilleux
& ce vray-semblable, qui en sont l'ame, pour ainsi dire. Car avec
elle, l'invention du Poëte introduit les Anges, les mauvaises
Demons, & les Magiciens: & sans choquer la vray-semblance,
par elle le Poëte divertit le Lecteur par des Prodiges: & em-
broüille & demesle le noeud de la Fable, par des voyes qu'on
ne sçauroit deviner. Par son moyen, une mesme action peut
estre merveilleuse & vray-semblable, le premier, par les choses
extraordinaires que fait la Magie: & le second, par la croyance
qu'elle trouve dans l'esprit de la plus part du monde."[8]

It is evident that he has not very clearly defined his problem.
He will not use pagan, by which he means Greek and Roman
mythology in his poem, nor Christian angels and devils. But
it seems to him justifiable, on the score of verisimilitude, to
use demons and magicians, surely not part of the credible world
as he knew it. This he had to do because of the necessity for
having some sort of marvellous element. His whole conception
seems, therefore, to be that of a writer of romances who would
divert his reader by prodigies while still preserving, if he can,
the air of verisimilitude. *Alaric* became, therefore, simply
another romance, without either the sober loveliness of *Jerusalem Delivered* or the gaiety of *Orlando Furioso* and whatever
charm it has—and it has little enough—is through its extrava-

---

[8]This follows Tasso precisely, as de Scudéry virtually admits—"comme le Tasse
l'a dit devant moy."

gances rather than through any imaginative realism.   There are,
M. Duchesne feels,[9] passages of genuine power in descriptions
of military affairs, but the effect of the whole is not unlike the
effect of *Le Grand Cyrus,* which also has passages about military affairs possessing a vigorous realism.

The purpose of the epic poem, Scudéry holds, with a great
many others, including many of the ancients, is to instruct. Here
is the statement from the *Preface* to *Alaric.*

"En effet, s'il est vray (comme il [Tasso] le dit en plusiers
endroits de ses Oeuvres) que l'Allegorie doit regner par tout
le Poëme Epique, quoy que tous les yeux ne l'y aperçoivent pas,
n'est-ce pas dire clairement, que le Poëte doit pour le moins
autant songer à l'utile qu'au delectable, & qu'il a pour principale fin, non pas de divertir, mais d'instruire?   Aussi ce
Grand homme estant revenu dans un meilleur sentiment, fit
imprimer à la fin de sa Hierusalem delivrée, un long Traité de
l'Allegorie :[10] par où il fait voir, qu'il n'y a pas une seule action
en tout son Poëme, qui ne soit instructive : & il conclud en
termes expres, que l'instruction doit estre l'objet du Poëte
Epique.

"C'est donc pour cela, que le Sens Allegorique regne par
tout dans ma *Rome Vaincuë* : entendant par Alaric, l'ame de
l'homme, par l'Enchantement où je le fais tomber, comme
Ulysse dans l'Isle de Calipso, la foiblesse des hommes, je dis
mesme des plus forts : qui sans le secours de la grace, tombent
dans les foiblesses, & dans des malheurs estranges : & qui par
ce puissant secours, s'en relevent & s'en desgagent apres : ainsi
que ce Prince sort d'un Palais enchanté, par l'assistance que le
Ciel luy donne.   Par le Magicien qui le persecute, les obstacles
que les Demons mettent toujours aux bons desseins, par la
belle Amalasonthe, la puissante tentation de la volupté, par ce
grand nombre d'ennemis qui le combattent, le Monde, qui est

[9]Duchesne, op. cit., p. 96.
  "Les discours militaires que remplissent le poeme portent un remarquable cachet
de vérité et de vigueur."
  [10]Here is the definition of the Epic as allegory,—a theory which had become
very important in criticism of the epic.

un des trois que l'ame Chrestienne a en teste, selon, le tesmoignage de l'Escriture & des Pères. . . . ."

This excerpt shows clearly enough Scudéry's conception
of the epic as an allegorical poem designed to teach morals,
heroic morals such as the heroic romances were supposed to
teach, through episodes where magicians not only appear but
dominate the scene; and the reference to Calypso in the above
passage shows that the most "romantic" section of the *Odyssey*
was the model for the whole of *Alaric*.

The influence of the heroic romances upon epic theory at
this time was considerable,[11] as has already been indicated in
the excerpt from the *Preface* to *Alaric*. The romances of Mlle.
de Scudéry, in particular, were realistic to the extent that the
characters in them were thinly disguised literary versions of
actual persons in Madeleine's own Saturday salons. The earlier
romances, *Astrée* of d'Urfé for instance, had been entirely
fictitious. Except that the scene of *Astrée* was a river familiar
to the author, the persons and the events, and the setting had
none of them actual originals, disguised or otherwise. According
to one school of criticism, however, the epic was to teach morals
through an account of the deeds of a well-known historical
figure. I have already pointed out how de Scudéry takes issue
with Castelvetro on the question of historical material as the
subject matter of the epic, de Scudéry maintaining that the
material of the epic should be "veritable." But it is necessary,
so the seventeenth century theorists think, to change history.[12]
(This idea is derived, besides its immediate Renaissance forebears, from Aristotle's distinction between history as what
happened—the particular—and tragedy as what may happen—
the typical). This is the way de Scudéry phrases it.

"Au reste, il est certain que le Poëte doit traiter les choses,
non comme elles ont esté, mais comme elles devoient estre: &

[11]Romance and Epic influenced each other as a result of efforts to harmonize
these two popular forms. See Duchesne, op. cit., pp. 81-84.

[12]See Duchesne, op. cit., pp. 62-66, for a discussion of the confusion regarding the
place of historical material in the epic. "Ainsi, pour garantir une apparente vérité aux
recits les plus imaginaires, il suffit de les mettre sur le compte de l'histoire: on la
recommonde non pour la respecter, mais pour l'alterer plus librement; elle n'est qu'un
prête-nom, un support sans valeur propre."

les changer & rechanger à son gré, sans considerer ny l'Histoire, ny la verité, qui ne sont ny sa Regle, ny sa fin." He bolsters up his argument by citing the practice of Virgil in the anachronism of having Aeneas and Dido contemporaries.

The chief difficulty which de Scudéry encountered in his undertaking, although he did not perceive it, was that his history was itself partly "invented." His historical sources are, as named in his *Preface,* Procopius, Orosius, Ritius. There was, besides, a considerable body of contemporary history, but this was confused, no effort being made, among other things, to distinguish the various Germanic tribes from each other nor to separate fact from fiction.[13] Christine of Sweden, to whom the poem was dedicated, was held to be a descendant of the Goths, in much the same way that Augustus was made by Virgil the heir of Aeneas, but the history of *Alaric* seems less true than that of the Aeneid, for de Scudéry's idea about the Germanic tribes was of the vaguest, whereas Virgil worked with a plausible and accepted tradition.

I have gone into the *Preface* of *Alaric* at some length because it illustrates clearly the sort of difficulty which the epic writers and theorists encountered. For de Scudéry, the epic is a poem on an illustrious (historical) subject, about an illustrious person (also historical), written with art to teach morals, upon the plan of the poems, not only of Homer and of Virgil, but also of Tasso, Ariosto, and other writers of the art epic and of romances. But he had to determine what seemed probable and what improbable. He made some attempt to grapple with this troublesome business of verisimilitude in his discussion of whether the matter of epic should or should not be historical, and, if historical, whether changes should not be made in the history. (Aristotle had, of course, pointed out that a history in verse was not an epic. But the question remained what kind of changes made history into epic). There is no suggestion that de Scudéry distinguishes between primitive and the art epic. And he obviously considers the epic and romance as

[13]See Duchesne, op. cit., pp. 85-86.

essentially the same form, whether the medium be verse or prose.

Desmarets de Saint-Sorlin, in his *Clovis,* whose subject was the Christianizing of France, encountered much the same problem in the choice of his subject matter. What was historically true and what was humanly probable were so imperfectly understood that verisimilitude became for him a sort of elusive dream, even had he had the genius to utilise his material with art. Chapelain, on the other hand, in *La Pucelle,* had a genuine subject, fit for epic treatment, a fact which is evidenced by the appeal the Maid of Orleans has had for subsequent generations of writers even unto Mr. Bernard Shaw. To be sure, Jeanne d'Arc was not appreciated by the seventeenth century,[14] whose ideals of correct feminine behavior were doubtless formed by those ladies of the Hôtel du Rambouïllet, or of Mlle. de Scudéry's Saturdays, subsequently to be satirised by Molière in *Les Précieuses Ridicules.* But, even so, during the course of the century, national pride—one of the great forces impelling authors toward the writing of epics—was fostering a growth of interest in France's most heroic historical figure. Had Chapelain had creative genius, he could have written an epic—or so one feels. Chapelain, a learned man, member of the Hôtel du Rambouïllet group, had considerable influence in shaping the destinies of French critical standards. But he is genuinely modest in offering his *La Pucelle* to the world. In the *Preface* to *La Pucelle,* he says:

"Je sçay que de toutes celles qui se peuuent faire dans l'Empire des Muses, celle-là [the heroic poem] est la plus hardie & la plus eleuée; & que pour y bien reüssir il faut estre si versé en toutes les Disciplines; auoir vn si grand usage du Monde; brusler d'vne si viue & si noble ardeur; regir sa Machine auec vn judgement si solide; enfin, y trauailler auec vn soin si assidu, & vn patience si courageuse, qu'encore que ces puissans Genies d'Homere & de Virgile, ayent porté ce genre de Poësie à vne tres-Sublime hauteur, l'on doute neantmoins qu'ils l'ayent conduit à sa derniere perfection; comme s'il estoit au dessus des forces humaines, et qu'il ne falust pas moins estre Heros, pour celebrer les grandes Actions, que pour les faire. Ce qui ne sçauroit estre vray, sans rendre coupable d'vne temerité fort presomptueuse vn homme tel que je suis, qui pretendroit donner, sans defauts, vn Ouvrage que ces Hommes incomparable n'aûroient pu donner qu'imparfait. On ne m'accusera, pour ce regard, ni d'estre temeraire, ni d'estre presomptueux. I'auoüe de n'auoir que bien peu des qualités requisés en vn Poëte heroique."

Chapelain tries in his *Preface* to reply in advance to those critics who will find it strange that, disregarding all precedent in Homer and Virgil, he has made his epic figure a woman. His argument is amusing, for he does not stress what seems the most obvious reply,—that the greatest "hero" of France was in point of fact a woman. But he falls afoul his own theory of the fable as that which should be rather than that which has been—the typical rather than the actual. And one must grant that there has been but one Jeanne d'Arc. She is exceptional to a degree which Achilles is not. Of course, to our minds, that makes her the more heroic, the more epic, but she had to wait until the twentieth century for her cannonization, and until long past Chapelain's day for the honor due her. That he saw her heroic stature shows that, though he might not be a Homer, he had the imagination to recognize epic material. He tries to bolster up his genuine insight by an appeal to logic and to fact. The result is, on the whole, unfortunate. Jeanne d'Arc is an epic figure. He cites historical instances, drawn from various sources, to show that women, besides being, as he affirms, capable of patriotic fervor and moral heroism, actually have been allowed to participate in the affairs of their nations. The countries of England, Scotland, Sweden, and Spain, for instance, permit women, as well as men, to rule. *La Pucelle,* therefore, is "vrai-semblable." By this, he apparently means that she is not unique, but typical. Besides, in the story of Joan, there is an added virtue—that is, the machines are also probable.[15]

"Enfin, ils m'en blasmeront d'autant moins, qu'ils verront que pour rendre cette Histoire plus susceptible de la forme Epique, le Ciel y concourt auec la Terre, de la sorte que l'Art le demande, dans les Sujets purement humains. Et qu'on ne pense pas m'objecter, comme vne chose considerable, que le concours du Ciel est vne Machine, qui choque la Vray-semblance, & qui, en la choquant, destruit l'Imitation. Car outre qu'on ne peut conceuoir de Heros, où il n'entre quelque chose de diuin, il faut, de plus, tomber d'accord que cette sorte de Machine, où la Diuinité interuient, lors-qu'elle passe pour vraye, deuient aussi-tost vray-semblable, aupres de ceux qui sont persuadés de pouuoir de cette Divinité. Et je n'en chercheray point la preuue hors des miracles les moins communs, que Dieu opere aucunes-fois, pour sa gloire, & qu'on ne sçauroit soupçonner d'auoir leur principe dans la Nature; lesquels n'ont besoin que d'estre creus vrays, pour estre creus vray-semblables; & où l'esprit acquiesce, sans repugnance, parce-qu'encore que la cause luy en soit inconnuë, la certitude de l'effet luy tient lieu de cause, pour n'en douter pas dauantage que s'il la connoissoit. Cette doctrine est tres-solide, suyuant mesme celle d'Aristote, qui dans les euenemens incroyables, quoy que produits par le seul hazard, & destituës du secours celeste, dit, & fort bien que plusieurs choses arriuent contre le vray-semblance, qui ne laissent pas d'estre vray-semblables, parce qu'il est vray-semblable qu'il arriue quelquesfois des choses, qui selon le cours ordinaire, ne deuroient point arriver. Que si l'on vouloit rejetter, comme contraire à l'Imitation & à la vray-semblance, tout ce qui se fait par l'inspiration, ou par l'assistance des Cieux; où en seroit Homere, & apres luy toute la Famille Poëtique, qui souuent, sans besoin, & souuent aussi, par necessité, ont introduit les Diuinités, dans les actions des hommes? Personne neantmoins ne leur a imputé cela, à defaut; au contraire, ils en ont esté

---

[15]The combining of the marvellous with the probable was the crux of epic theory. Chapelain is one of the first to find a subject where this combination can be achieved.

loüés & admirés, à cause du relief que de semblables Machines donnent à leurs Sujets; auxquels elles communiquent vne certaine majesté, qui leur fait maistriser les esprits, auec plus d'empire."

He goes on to add to this the argument that if pagan deities took an interest in human affairs, Christian deities may be supposed to do so as well. (He uses the plural "Machines Chrestiennes.") And a belief in some sort of divine assistance is part of the historical conception of the life of the Maid of Orleans. As Chapelain says: "Aussi n'ay-je employé la *Pucelle* pour Heroine, dans mon Poëme, que parce que c'estoit vne Personne vraye, & d'vne verité si connue, qu'elle ne le seroit pas dauantage, si les mereuilles de sa Vie auoient eu nos yeux pour tesmoins . . . . Ie ne l'y ay introduite comme animée de l'esprit de Dieu, que sur l'exemple de la vaillante Debora: . . . . Ie dis plus, bien que, dans le fait particulier de la Pucelle, j'eusse le tesmoignage de l'Histoire, l'euidence de sa Mission, & les effets de ses Miracles, pour fondement de cet employ, voulant conseruer neantmoins, dans ses actions, le plus de cette Vray-semblance que l'on desire, pour ne satisfaire pas moins Aristote que Platon; lors que je dressay mon Plan, & que je donnay la forme Poëtique à ce veritable Euenement, j'eus vn soin particulier de le conduire de telle sorte, que tout ce que j'y fay faire, par la puissance diuine, s'y puisse croire fait par la seule force humaine, eleuée au plus haut point, où la Nature est capable de monter."

He expressly states that he has not employed the "Machines de la Magie, à la maniere des vieux Romans," even abandoning the practice of Tasso, because they are contrary to the spirit of the age. "Il me suffira de dire que j'ay pris l'autre chemin [that is, away from the magic of romances] comme le plus seur, par des considerations que je dois bien auoir creuës fort solides, puis qu'elles m'ont fait renoncer à l'vn de ces ornemens, qui ont eu le plus de vogue en ce genre, parmy les Modernes; pour me renfermer dans ceux que souffre l'Art, & qui ne choquent, ni la Nature, ni la creance des Peuples."

Chapelain was, it seems to me, an original thinker, in spite of the fact that it was he who was largely responsible for forcing the three unities upon French drama, and has subsequently been laughed at for being a frigid pedant. In his *La Pucelle,* he failed, because he was no poet, to write an epic, but in his preface, he really grappled intelligently with the problem of verisimilitude in the modern epic. He chose a subject which was at once historical, heroic, probable, and marvellous. One is really sorry that his genius was not equal to the task before him, for the subject of La Pucelle is a subject for a really great epic, simple and moving and splendid. As it was, the work was not popular, and France's great epic figure has never been celebrated by a Frenchman in epic. Soon after Chapelain, the writing of epics at all was laughed at by the satirists. That in itself was no loss—on the contrary; but Chapelain had an idea which would have been worth another effort, by another man. He himself had got away from the idea of the romance and the epic being much the same thing. The subject matter of *La Pucelle* is not love, but national affairs. And the national affairs of *La Pucelle* were important, the figure of the maid herself dominant and powerful. Besides his own lack of genius, he was handicapped by the false impressions of his age regarding not only his heroine, but historical fact as well. But, as M. Duchesne says: "s'il arrive qu'il atténue les erreurs de son époque, si notamment il a restitué les traits principaux de son héroïne; si, animé d'une patriotique admiration pour La Pucelle, il s'élève jusqu'à des beautés que l'on ne pouvait attendre d'un faible génie, ne serons-nous pas heureux de rendre enfin justice à ce travailleur judicieux et clairvoyant?" When all is said and done, Chapelain had genius of a sort in discovering her at all.

After the outburst of the heroic poems of Scudéry, Desmarets, and Chapelain, a rapid change followed in French taste. In fact, these authors spoke to an age which already had much of the spirit of Molière in it. The work of Molière belongs more properly to a discussion of the drama than of the

epic, but inasmuch as his amused attacks upon pedantic prefaces in his own preface to *Les Précieuses Ridicules,* and his
identifying the rules of art with the rules of good sense made
in various places, notably in the *Critique de L'Ecole des Femmes,* applied equally to the heroic poem and to the drama, it is
not out of the way to discuss them here, especially in view of
the fact that Henry Fielding was a disciple of Molière.   In the
critical war which took place between the prophets of common
sense and the prophets of tradition, Chapelain did not play
the part of obstructionist, and although *La Pucelle* went through
six editions in a year and a half, the author was content to
speak of himself as a critic rather than as a poet.

Molière's equipment as a critic was the exact opposite of
that of Chapelain.   Whereas the latter was really learned, with
a discriminating taste which survived most of his tendencies
toward what was merely pedantic, Molière was a Bohemian.
For some years, he was a wandering player, and throughout
his life, he got his inspiration directly from watching people
around him.   His reading was not extensive—Plautus, Terence,
Lucretius, Rabelais and Montaigne chiefly.[16]

In the preface to *Les Précieuses Ridicules,* first presented
in 1659, Molière pokes fun at the habit his literary colleagues
had of writing prefaces, thus:

"Encore si l'on m'avait donné du temps, j'aurais pu mieux
songer à moi, et j'aurais pris toutes les precautions que MM.
les auteurs, à present mes confréres, ont coutumés de prendre
en semblables occasions.   Outre quelque grand seigneur que
j'aurais étés prendre malgré lui pour protecteur de mon ouvrage, et dont j'aurais tenté la liberalité par une epitre dedicatoire
bien fleurie, j'aurais tâché de faire une belle et docte préface;
et je ne manque point de livres qui m'auraient fourni tout ce
qu'on peut dire de savant sur la tragédie et la comédie,
l'étymologie de toutes deux, leur origine, leur definition, et le
reste."

[16]See Faguet, E., *En lisant Molière,* p. 7.

Molière, in his *Critique de l'Ecole des Femmes,* (1662), exalts good sense over ready-made rules. This is really the whole point of the sketch—pointing out the fact that the artist's equipment is his experience seen through the eyes of common sense, as is illustrated by such words as these of Dorante: "Il semble . . . que ces règles de l'art soient les plus grands mystères du monde; et cependant ce ne sont que quelques observations aisées, que le bon sens a faites sur ce qui peut ôter le plaisir que l'on prend à ces sortes de poëmes; et le même bon sens qui a fait autrefois ces observations les fait aisément tous les jours, sans le secours d'Horace et d'Aristote." Or this, of Uranie: "Pour moi, quand je vois une comédie, je regarde seulement si les choses me touchent; et, lorsque je m'y suis bien diverti, je ne vais point demander si j'ai eu tort, et si les règles d'Aristote me défendoient de rire."

Molière's whole conception of comedy doubtless had considerable influence on Fielding. Molière is one of the great group of comic authors whom Fielding thoroughly enjoyed and whose spirit he invoked in the invocation to Book XIII of *Tom Jones.* The spirit of Molière was for the seventeenth and eighteenth century France and England the Comic Spirit, as defined by Meredith later—a spirit of sanity and balance. Pretentiousness and dullness, the pseudo-heroic and the rigid conception of classical rules, were done for.

CHAPTER IV

FÉNÉLON, BOILEAU, LE BOSSU, AND MADAME DACIER

Desmarets, de Scudéry, and Chapelain were modernists.
They desired to write modern epics. More than this, they
wished to improve upon the old—a desire which rose out of
their belief in the superiority of Christian civilization over
pagan civilization, or perhaps, more precisely, a belief in the
superiority of Christian religion over pagan faith. For, they
argued, Homer made a great epic out of the materials of false
theology; ergo, a Christian epic may be much greater, in proportion as Christian theology is true, and the gods of Olympus
are false. A sound enough argument, of course, if the divine
beings of the epic had any hand in making the epic, and if
it were a truth universally admitted that one set of divine beings
was true and the other false. No one of the critics of Desmarets
and his fellows challenged the latter premise, but by implication at least, the idea of divine beings having anything to do
with the making of poetry was challenged by the whole group
of champions of the Ancients. In spite of their elaborate critical theorizing in the prefaces, the epics of Desmarets, de Scudéry, and Chapelain were simply laughed at by the wits. If
the modern epic had to have an element of the marvellous, it
had to have a marvellous which would be acceptable to moderns—and therefore, probably Christian. Desmarets' judgment
in this matter was perfectly sound. But none of these writers
could write—a fact which Boileau, Scarron, and their fellows
were not slow to point out, developing the while their own
theories of the place of machines in the modern epic.

The Quarrel of the Ancients and the Moderns, which developed into a fierce battle in the French Academy in the latter

53

half of the century, had its roots in a fundamental conflict, one which engages every artist—the old struggle between convention and revolt in poetry. The prefaces to the feeble epics of the great age of Corneille, Racine, and Molière at least tried to state the issues, although the poems themselves did not contribute anything toward a solution. Ronsard, in the sixteenth century, had used pagan mythology in his *Franciade*. The seventeenth century writers used the magic of mediaeval Christian romance. No one of them wrote an *Aeneid*. And the authors became, by their dull pretensions, fit subjects for the ridicule of clever men.

Boileau,[1] with his eye for human absurdity, could not resist an attack. He followed Molière as champion of common sense and succeeded to a great extent in establishing his principles as the critical norm for his own generation. Yet his work is essentially reactionary in its conclusions and facile rather than profound in its grasp of the problem of verisimilitude and the use of the marvellous in the epic. Boileau was not a learned man, but a very clever one. Although he set forth the rules of a rigid neoclassicism, he seems to have done so without much sense of the real spirit of the ancients. [He did not read Greek]. He conceives the epic as a thing purely decorative. The gods and goddesses of the *Iliad* have for him precisely the reality of the painted Cupids on the ceilings of Versailles—whatever artistic value they have is symbolic, and they exist as part of a conventional pattern. Here is what he says of "machines" in Canto III of L'Art Poëtique (1674).

> "D'un air plus grand encor la poésie épique,
> Dans le vaste récit d'une longue action,
> Se soutient par la fable, et vit de fiction.
> Là pour nous enchanter tout est mis en usage;
> Tout prend un corps, une âme, un esprit, un visage.
> Chaque vertu devient une divinité:
> Minerve est la prudence, et Venus la beauté;

---

[1]Boileau derived his ideas from Vida's *Ars Poetica* (1527) and both are the offspring of Horace's *Ars Poetica*. Horace discussed chiefly style and minor points of construction rather than a philosophy of composition which is emphasized in Aristotle. Hence, Boileau and Vida are concerned with style and technical difficulties.

Ainsi dans cet amas de nobles fictions,
Le poëte s'égaye en mille inventions,
Orne, élève, embellit, agrandit toute choses,
Et trouve sous sa main des fleurs toujours écloses"

Thus, for him, the epic is the recital of an extended action, based on an invented fable, by implication a fable to teach manners. The whole is an "amas de nobles fictions". When Aeneas is borne by tempests to the shores of Africa—

"Ce n'est qu'une aventure ordinaire et commune,
Qu'un coup peu surprenant des traits de la fortune.
Mais que Junon, constante en son aversion,
Pour suivre sur les flots les restes d'Ilion" . . . .

This is a tale of ordinary adventure, and Juno is added simply to prettify the poetry. It is vain for modern poets to try to use the "machines" of Christian theology.[2]

"C'est donc bien vainement que nos auteurs déçus,
Banissant de leurs vers ces ornemens reçus,
Pensent faire agir Dieu, ses saints et ses prophètes,
Comme ces dieux éclos du cerveau des poëtes."

Divine beings are thus explicitly called "ornaments", and pagan deities are more fitted to decorative effects than are Christian ones. But although pagan deities should be used in a Christian poem, they should not occupy too much of the scene.

"Ce n'est pas que j'approuve, en un sujet chrétien,
Un auteur follement idolâtre et païen;
Mais, dans une profane et riante peinture ,
De n'oser de la fable employer la figure,
De chasser les Tritons de l'empire des eaux,
D'ôter à Pan sa flûte, aux Parques leurs ciseaux,
D'empêcher que Caron, dans la fatale barque,
Ainsi que le berger ne passe le monarque,
C'est d'un scruple vain s'alarmer sottement,
Et vouloir lecteurs plaire sans agrément."

2. Vida, to whom Boileau owes most of his ideas, actually thought the glory of translation not less that of creation. See *Ars Poetica*, Bk. II, 246-248.
"Haud minor est adeo virtus, si te audit Apollo,
Inventa Argivum in patriam convertere vocem,
Quam si tute aliquid intactum inveneris ante".
It would follow from such a principle that the poet need not seek his material from the credible world around him.

Since the whole thing, then, is largely *décor,* Boileau takes up such minor points as the names of the protagonists. He condemns Desmarets for the choice of a harsh name for his Christian hero, when he might have chosen Ulysses, Agamemnon, or some other mellifluous Greek or Latin name.

> Là tous les noms heureux semblent nés pour les vers,
> Ulysse, Agamemnon, Oreste, Idoménée,
> Hélène, Ménélas, Paris, Hector, Énée.
> O le plaisant project d'un poëte ignorant,
> Qui de tant de heros va choisir Childebrand!"

In general, we can say that Boileau contributed almost nothing to epic theory. His ideas about poetry in general are the precepts of common sense—be plain, make a good beginning, study the manners of the court. In his *Dialogue des Héros des Romans* (1664), he laughed at the pretentious heroes of the heroic romances, and showed how far they were from the ancient heroes whose names they bore. But everything he said was rather fitted to instruct courtiers in a highly sophisticated court on good taste than to analyze the nature of epic poetry.

His contemporary, Le Bossu, whose *Traité du Poëme Epique* appeared in 1675, the year following the publication of *L'Art Poëtique,* held practically the same ideas as Boileau about the fable, the fiction, machines, etc., but his work by its more complete treatment, offers a more complete justification for these views, and yet at the same time, has been more often ridiculed by later generations than has Boileau's *L'Art Poëtique.* The *Traité du Poëme Epique* was very popular in its day. Boileau himself praised it. It was translated into English, and was quoted with favor by a number of English critics, among others by Dryden, who refers to Le Bossu in several places, but notably in the *Preface to Troilus and Cressida,*[3] where he refers to "Bossu, the best of modern critics". Henry Fielding, too, esteemed him highly. In the prefatory chapter of Book

[3]Dryden, *Essays,* edited by Ker, W. P., vol. I, p. 211.

XI of *Tom Jones,* for instance, in speaking of good and bad critics, he says:

"I will therefore endeavor, in the remaining part of this chapter, to explain the marks of this character, and to show what criticism I here intend to obviate: for I can never be understood, unless by the very persons here meant, to insinuate that there are no proper judges of writing, or to endeavor to exclude from the commonwealth of literature any of those noble critics to whose labors the learned world are so greatly indebted. Such were Aristotle, Horace, and Longinus among the ancients, Dacier and Bossu among the French, and some perhaps among us; who have certainly been duly authorized to execute at least a judicial authority *in foro literario*".

One has only to call to mind the almost reverential esteem in which Aristotle and Horace were held by all the men of Fielding's age, and by his literary forebears who had given him the tradition, to realize how highly Fielding ranks Le Bossu in placing him in a list with Aristotle and Horace.

It is hard not to laugh at the solemn canon of Ste. Geneviéve, setting about with canonical fervor to prove that Homer wrote the *Iliad* to teach the moral that division in the ranks of an army is harmful, or that the moral of the Odyssey is that it is bad for a country to remain long without its ruler. He searches for the moral as assiduously as ever the Duchess does in *Alice in Wonderland* and produces it with as triumphant a flourish. Today, a belief in the didactic in art is out of favor. But, for all that, Le Bossu gives a complete statement of one point of view about the epic, and analyzes the epics of Homer and Virgil, carefully, with a view to finding out what actually they were.[4] Nor was he so hide-bound that he could not recognize the presence of elements which he did not altogether expect to find there—such as the "romanesque" elements in the *Odyssey*, for example.[5] He avoided one dif-

---

[4] Le Bossu's treatise is both theoretical and concrete. He develops a theory of allegory, for example, but he compares concretely the work of Homer with Virgil, and of both with Statius. In this, he is directly in the spirit of neo-classicism of the time. See Spingarn, *op. cit.*, pp. 132-133.

[5] Le Bossu, *Traité du Poeme Epique*, tom. II, p. 166.

ficulty by making no attempt to apply his rules to the epic of his own day, nor indeed, to any other epics than those of Greece and Rome.

It is hard to be wholly just to the work of Le Bossu today. At first we feel disposed merely to laugh at le Père Bossu and say that the ecclesiastical office of the author changed the usual "Cherchez la femme" into a "Cherchez la morale." Even the critic who today emphasizes the ethical element in a work of art would say Le Bossu is too narrowly didactic. But one has to recognize that he stands in the line of a direct tradition from the past, and that throughout the Renaissance every critic had much the same view. He presents his ideas clearly and logically. He analyzes technical elements. And his prestige among contemporaries was enormous.

His treatise is divided into six books,—Book One, *De la nature du Poëme Epique, & de la Fable;* Book Two, *De la Matière du Poëme Epique, ou de l'Action;* Book Three, *De la Forme du Poëme Epique, ou de la Narration;* Book Four, *Des Moeurs;* Book Five, *Des Machines;* and Book Six, *Des Sentimens et de l'Expression.*

He starts out with a comparison of art with science in terms which place him immediately among the prophets of reason and of common sense. He says: "Les Arts ont cela de commun avec les Sciences, qu'ils sont comme elles fondez sur la raison, et que l'on doit s'y laisser conduire par les lumieres que la nature nous a données. Mais," he goes on to say, "les Sciences ne laissent point à ceux qui les trouvent ou qui les cultivent, la liberté de prendre d'autres guides que ces lumieres naturelles; Et les Arts au-contraire, dépendent en beaucoup de choses, du choix et du génie de ceux qui les ont inventez les prémiers, ou qui y ont travaillé avec l'approbation la plus générale de tout le monde".[6]

From a study of the ancients one can come at the principles, not only of writing the epic, but also of criticism of the epic, Homer and Virgil having given us the former, Aristotle and

[6]Le Bossu, *Traite du Poeme Epique,* tom. I, p. 1.

Horace the latter. From these four writers, he deduces his definition: "L'Epopeé est un discours inventé avec art, pour former les moeurs par des instructions déguisées sous les allégories d'une action importante, qui est racontée en Vers d'une maniere vrai-semblable, divertissante, et merveilleuse".[7] This is in the usual manner of definitions of the epic—a discourse related in verse and invented with art to form manners. Le Bossu goes on to distinguish between the epic and other forms of poetry, following Aristotle in the distinction he makes between the epic and versified history, or biography.

The epic may be in prose, although, if in prose, it is not an epic *poem*. "Mais si l'on écrivoit une Epopée en Prose, seroit-ce un Poëme Epique? Je ne le croi pas, parcequ'un Poëme est un discours in Vers. Cela néantmoins n'empécheroit pas qu'elle ne fût une Epopée; de méme qu'une Tragédie en Prose n'est pas un Poëme Tragique, & est toujours une Tragédie. Ceux qui ont douté si la Comédie Latine etoit un Poëme, ou si elle n'en étoit pas un; n'ont point douté qu'elle ne fût une Comédie."[8] In other words, the epic may be written either in prose or in verse and still be an epic,—a view by no means original with Le Bossu.[9] While he does not discuss prose as a possible medium, Aristotle himself had pointed out that imitation and structure constitute the essential qualities of the epic, and not verse. That is, a history in verse is history, not epic. And many of the commentators on Aristotle from Robortelli on accepted the principle. All critics and authors of epics, however, deemed the epic poem a more worthy enterprise than the prose epic. Le Bossu, after this one remark on the epic in prose, limits his discussion to the question of the epic poem.

An example of the almost universal acceptance of this idea that there might be both prose and poetic epics may be found in Huet's *Lettre à Segrais sur l'Origine des Romans* (1670). He says: "Je ne parle donc icy des Romans en Verse, & moins

[7]*Ibid.*, tom. I, p. 14.
[8]Le Bossu, *Traité du Poeme Epique*, tom. I. p. 29.
[9]For a full discussion of this, see Spingarn, *op. cit.*, p. 31, pp. 35-36.

encore des Poëmes Epiques, qui outre qu'ils sont en Vers, ont encore des differences essencielles qui les distinquent des Romans: quoy qu'ils ayent d'ailleurs un tres-grand rapport, & que suivant la maxime d'Aristote, qui enseigne que le Poëte est plus Poëte par les fictions qu'il invente, que par les Vers qu'il compose, on puisse mettre les faiseurs de Romans au nombre des Poëtes."[10]

The key to the whole of the epic, according to Le Bossu, "le prémier fondement du Poëme, comme le principe qui donne la vie & le mouvement à tous ses membres, & qui en fait joüer tous les ressorts", is the fable.[11] The fable is an abstract summary of the moral, and may be compared, says Le Bossu, to the fables of Aesop. Thus, the fable of the *Iliad* is that division among leaders brings disaster to an enterprise. Having found his fable, Homer found a story which would illustrate it—the story of the wrath of Achilles. The epic begins with the beginning of that wrath and concludes with the final triumph which reconciliation among the leaders effects. Thus, Achilles exists not for himself—that is, as a national hero whose deeds are absorbing—but as the means of fulfilling a didactic purpose. Hence in reading Homer, the reader must bear in mind the following ideas. "La différence la plus considérable que mon sujet me présente, entre l'eloquence des Anciens & celle des derniers Siecles, est que nôtre maniere de parler est simple, propre, & sans détour: & que celle des Anciens étoit pleine de mysteres & d'allegories. La vérité étoit ordinairement déguisée sous ´ces inventions ingenieuses, qui pour leur excellence portent le nom de Fables, c'est à dire de paroles."[12]

Since the ancients thus spoke in parables rather than directly, it follows, for Le Bossu, that the "machines" are allegorical. Thus:

". . . nous avons vû que toutes ces Personnes Divines sont allégoriques.

[10]Huet, *Lettre à Segrais sur l'Origine des Romans*, p. 6.
[11]Le Bossu, *op. cit.*, tom. I, p. 31.
[12]*Ibid.*, tom. I, p. 5.

"Nous en avons trouvé de trois sortes. Les unes sont Théologiques, & ont été inventées pour expliquer la Nature de Dieu: les autres sont Physiques; & elles représentent les choses Naturelles: les dernieres sont Morales, & elles sont les figures des Vertus & des Vices."[13]

That is, of course, the point of view of Boileau, and Boileau defended Le Bossu when Charles Perrault ridiculed the *Traité du Poëme Epique* in his *Paralleles des Anciens et des Modernes* (1688-1699). The value of Le Bossu's work, the thing that probably gave it the tremendous vogue it had, lies in his analysis of details. In spite of the fact that he sees in the *Iliad,* the *Odyssey,* and the *Aeneid* elaborate parables whose mysteries must be uncovered in order for us to appreciate the poems, he really does have a grasp of their structure. Although he mentions the invocation and other relatively non-essential features of the epic with reverence, he concentrates his attention upon the technical problems of management of plot, the complication and denouement, characterization, problems of verisimilitude, etc. De Scudéry, Desmarets, and Chapelain could not learn from him how to write their "Christian" epic, for Le Bossu does not conceive of an epic in relation to the author's world, but an author who had his material in hand might learn from Le Bossu how to handle it—or, at any rate, might learn why Statius is less effective than Homer as a manipulator of plot, and hence, less impressive in his total effect. Nor, viewed in one light, is the conception of the central allegory altogether absurd. Something does hold the *Iliad,* or the *Odyssey* together—something which is not the unity of having a single hero, or of treating of a whole historical event like the siege of Troy. The events which are selected in the *Iliad* are selected upon the basis of some pattern, an ideal pattern. It may not have been to teach the limited fable which Le Bossu draws from the *Iliad* that the poem was written, but there is a central idea, and that idea includes, among other things, truths about human conduct. Nor does Le Bossu preach the doctrine that

[13]Le Bossu, *op. cit.* tom. II, p. 144.

the hero of the epic has to be perfect himself in order to teach manners. Achilles, Le Bossu points out, wrought fully as much damage by his choler as he achieved glory by his prowess. This is certainly a step away from a very popular conception of Le Bossu's time that one could teach one's moral in the epic only by having a hero who was the pattern of all the virtues. Thus, Le Bossu says:[14]

"Il faut donc ici faire la même distinction entre un Héros en Morale, & un Héros en Poësie, que nous avons faite, entre le Bonté Morale, & la Bonté Poëtique: & dire que comme Achilles & Mézence ont autant de part à la bonté Poëtique qu'Ulysses & Enée: de même ces deux hommes cruels et injustes sont des Héros Poëtiques aussi reguliers que ces deux princes si justes, si sages & si bons."

The whole basis of the epic was, for Boileau, an "amas de nobles fictions", a collection of marvels, the sense of which was allegorical. And so it was for Le Bossu, but the latter succeeds, through his analysis of practice, in presenting a reasonable study of narrative technique.

In his theory of imitation, Le Bossu certainly used the word as meaning a copying of the great models from ancient times. But his theory, as illustrated by the above excerpt, implies that imitation should remain true to human nature, *as observed*. This point leads to consideration of his treatment of the marvellous and the verisimilar. He says, "Nous pouvons donc conclure qu'une Machine dans le Poëme Epique, n'est point une invention pour se tirer d'une difficulté embarassante, affectée, & propre à quelques endroits du Poëme: mais que c'est la présence d'une Divinité, quelque action surnaturelle & extraordinaire, que le Poëte insère dans presque tous les incidens de son Ouvrage, pour le rendre plus majestueux & plus admirable, & pour instruire ses Lecteurs à la piété & à la vertu."[15]   The marvellous exists to heighten the allegory and should not therefore be confused with the credible.   It is not

---

[14]Le Bossu, *op. cit.*, tom. II, p. 37.
[15]Le Bossu, *op. cit.*, tom. II, p. 177.

used to get heroes out of difficulties, but rather to reveal the divine in human affairs. Thus, in reference to the veri-similar and to the marvellous, he has an explanation of how the verisimilar and the marvellous may be mingled in the same poem without rendering the poem incredible.[16]

After the *Traité du Poëme Epique* came out in 1675, it sub-sequently went through many editions in French and was trans-lated into English. It was not universally praised, however. The author's reverence for the Greek and Latin epics, and his silence upon the question of modern epics fell upon a few rebellious ears. Love for antiquity might imply contempt for the modern, and France in the seventeenth century was con-scious of her greatness. The same war between the ancients and moderns had taken place in Italy when the revival of learn-ing brought keenly before men's minds the glory of the past, and raised the question whether this glory could ever be sur-passed, or even equalled. All the advocates either of the "merveilleux chrétien" or of the "amas de nobles fictions" had compelled a comparison between the glories of pagan Greece and those of Christian France. In 1687, Charles Perrault read before the French Academy his poem, *Le Siècle de Louis le Grand,* beginning:[17]

> "La belle antiquité fut toujours vénerable,
> Mais je ne crus jamais qu'elles fut adorable,
> Je vois les Anciens sans plier le genou:
> Ils sont grands, il est vrai, mais hommes comme nous."

The poem then proceeded to compare the age of Augustus with that of Louis XIV, and to point out the progress made in the arts and sciences and in knowledge since the age of Aug-ustus. It was the Manifesto of the Moderns. The poem brought all previous critical differences to a focus, and writers ranged themselves on one side or the other—the creative artists,

---

[16]For Le Bossu, as for Boileau, the gods of ancient epic are poetic and allegorical. The historian, says Le Bossu, would say that Aeneas decided he must leave Dido to go to Italy, but Virgil—to show the presence of the supernatural—has him receive a message from the gods, given by Mercury.

[17]For a complete treatment of the whole quarrel, both the earlier and later phase, in France, see Rigault, *op. cit.,* Parts I and III.

for the most part, on the side of the ancients, the philosophers, like Bayle and Fontenelle, on the side of the moderns. The very men who are the chief glory of the age of Louis XIV—Racine, Corneille, Boileau—all eagerly acknowledged their debt to classical antiquity. After about thirteen years of arguing about it, Boileau was prevailed upon to write a letter to Perrault in which, while he still maintains the greatness of the ancients, he nevertheless admits that the age of Louis XIV was superior in certain arts and sciences, and even in certain forms of literature.

This letter was written in 1700, but in the preceding year, Madame Dacier had published her prose translation of the *Iliad* and the *Odyssey*. Madame Dacier was another real lover of the great authors of classical antiquity, and she prefaced her translation of Homer with a eulogy of the poet and a brief treatise on the rules for the writing of epics. This preface, which is founded on Père Bossu's *Traité,* was not couched in a tone to give aid and comfort to the champions of the Moderns. Among other things, she says: "La pluspart des gens sont gastez aujourd'huy par la lecture de quantité de livres vains & frivoles, & ne peuvent souffrir ce qui n'est pas dans le mesme goust. L'amour, aprés avoir corrómpu les moeurs, a corrómpu les ouvrages. C'est l'âme de tous nos escrits. Les· païens ont bien mieux jugé que nous de cette passion; ils ont parfaitement connu que ne venant que de foiblesse, elle ne pouvoit jamais avoir rien de grand, ni contribuer au grand". Inasmuch as love was a very popular subject, then as now, among authors of romances, this description of the nature and origin of the grand passion was not especially flattering to the champions of the modern spirit.

She confesses that she had felt despair about the difficulty of communicating the glory of Homer to her readers, but she had taken courage upon reflecting that two events had conspired to dissipate the fogs of ignorance then prevailing. "Tous ces sujets de crainte m'avoient extrémement decouragée; mais enfin j'ay fait reflexion que l'ignorance, où l'on a esté si longtemps sur la nature du Poëme Epique, a pu estre entirement dissipée par deux ouvrages excellents, qui ont paru sur cette matiere. L'un est le *Traité du Poëme Epique* du R. P. le Bossu, chanoine regulier de sainte Geneviéve, où ce sçavant Religieux explique admirablement l'art des poëmes d'Homère & de Virgile par les règles d'Aristote; & l'autre, la Poëtique mesme d'Aristote traduite en François, & enrichie de commentaires qui font parfaitement sentir la certitude & la vérité de ces régles par l'experience mesme & par la raison".

Madame Dacier's translation of Homer was the work of an intelligent and sincere lover of Homer, and enjoyed a merited esteem for many years. (Fielding, as will be observed, had a copy of this translation in his library,—one of the five editions of Homer he owned, and the only translation except that of Pope.) Her translation of Homer threw still another competent person into the ranks of the champions of the ancients. But in 1713, a certain Houdart de la Motte, a man who did not know a word of Greek, after using her translation to make a rhymed version of the *Iliad,* re-opened the old quarrel of the Ancients and the Moderns by disparaging Homer in his preface, and, upon Madame Dacier's replying in *Causes de la Corruption du Gout,* where she repeats and develops her ideas in the Preface to her Homer, he further pursued the attack in asserting, in his *Reflexions sur la Critique* that *Clovis,* with its Christian hero, was greater than the pagan *Iliad.* The battle was on once more, but before it could gain greater intensity, Fénélon, in his *Lettre à l'Academie Française,* made peace by conceding something to both sides, much as Boileau had done earlier in his *Lettre à M. Perrault.*

In the meantime, Fénélon had brought out his *Télémaque* (1699). Published in the same year with Madame Dacier's translation of Homer, it is a curious and interesting example of the ideas of the champions of the Ancients, when applied. Its scene is supposed to be the island of Ithaca. The tale employs Greek deities and Greek names. Superficially, it belongs to the world of Odysseus and Ithaca. The work is actually, in part, a contemporary satire, in part, an educational tract. And the whole is pervaded by a seventeenth century Christian tone. The deities of the piece, although they bear Greek names, are allegorical. They are, in reality, the personifications of Christian moral virtues, and the whole book is essentially a presentation of the ideals of Fénélon's own time. Thus Fénélon settles the problem of the marvellous by making the marvellous symbolic. The hidden parable is sufficiently obvious so that one is aware of the meaning of the marvellous. In fact, the narrative is interrupted by such explanations as: "C'est que les Dieux Supérieurs cachent aux inférieurs tout ce qu'il leur plaît".[18] In Book XVIII Télémaque visits Hades, where most of the mysteries of religion are explained in terms of true and false belief.[19] Although no mention is made of Christian beliefs as such, the philosophy of the whole treatment is really an exposition of Christian doctrine as understood by Fénélon. Thus, the book makes one solution of the marvellous by making the marvellous a philosophical parable, comparable to various religious and philosophical symbols—as it is phrased, for example, in the words of the Catechism, "the outward and visible signs of an inward and spiritual grace".

In the 1714 edition of *Télémaque*, a preface was added by a certain A. M. Ramsay. This preface was entitled *Discours de la Poësie Epique, et de l'Excellence du Poëme de Télémaque*. The title of this preface is, in itself, interesting, inasmuch as the author specifically names the prose *Télémaque* a poem. The ideas in this preface are derived from Le Bossu's *Traité*. The purpose of the epic is to instruct. The definition of the epic follows Le Bossu's almost exactly. "Une Fable racontée par un Poëte pour exciter l'admiration, & inspirer l'amour de la Vertu, en nous representant l'Action d'un Héros favorisé du Ciel, qui execute un grand dessein en triomphant de tous les

---

[18]Fenelon, *Telemaque*, p. 2.

[19]This solution of the problem of the marvellous is, in theory, like that of Spenser. In reality, his allegory had something of the strange and romantic about it, whereas Fenelon's was rationalistic. Neither solution, of course, was in the spirit of the ancient handling of the marvellous.

obstacles qui s'y opposent".[20]   The author then proceeds to point out the ways in which *Télémaque* fulfills all the requirements of the epic.

Of all the attempts at epic in seventeenth century France, *Télémaque* was the most successful. And, in spite of the fact that Fénélon was on the side of the Ancients, the success of his work is due to the fact that it was essentially of his own age, that is, modern. Externally, pagan and narrative, in reality it was Christian and satiric, or, at any rate, didactic. (It is hard to determine just how far Fénélon meant his picture of the ideal commonwealth to be a criticism of the existing social order.) With its views on education and upon freedom for development, it accorded well with the growing critical spirit of the age, and foreshadowed somewhat the coming Romantic ideas. In this famous quarrel of the ancients and the moderns, then, neither side won, or both sides won, as you like. *Télémaque* is both ancient and modern, written according to a set of rules which should have hampered creation, but did not. It is too *sweet* for epic; yet it has a kind of epic view of the civilization of Fénélon's own times.

The curious thing—or another curious thing—about this quarrel of the Ancients and Moderns is that the real moderns were the champions of the ancients. That is, the champions of the moderns, while protesting that their own times were superior to the ancients in various ways, nevertheless based their arguments for superiority largely upon the superiority of the moderns in *following the rules*. If Christianity is the true religion, they argue, the writer of the Christian epic can observe the rules about the marvellous more easily than can the ancients, who had a false religion. Nor were all the epic heroes of the past "honnetes hommes", they said. Achilles was surely not a hero, in that he allowed his private wrath to upset the affairs of the side on which he fought. Modern heroes, embodying all the known virtues, were therefore superior.

[20]This discussion in the *Preface* to *Telemaque* elaborates the allegorical theory of the marvellous proportionally much more fully than Le Bossu does in his *Traité*.

Today we should reply, first, that Achilles' wrath was not precisely a vice in the Homeric days when personal prowess was the prime virtue of heroes, and a man of Achilles' virtue might be expected to have a "heroic" sense of what he would and would not endure, and, second, that he is a whole, self-sufficient, credible human being. The champions of the Ancients in seventeenth century France replied, however, that Homer could teach his moral in this particular instance by showing the evil effects of Achilles' wrath whereas he could not have done so had Achilles been more pliable, like the pious Aeneas. This was Le Bossu's argument. Nor was it absurd. Whether we grant that the *Iliad* was written to teach a lesson or not, it is certainly true that the story would not move us emotionally had Achilles possessed all the virtues of a seventeenth century hero. Le Bossu says, for instance:

"Ou pour mieux dire, ce Poëte ne donneroit aucunement à son Héroes, les qualitez de ces deux autres Héros. Il y a bien de la difference entre un visage en général, & le visage d' Enée : entre un front, un nez, une bouche, & des yeux en général ; & le front, les yeux, le nez, & la bouche d'Achilles. Il y a de-même, bien de la différence entre la Valeur en général, & la Valeur d'Achilles ; & entre la Piété en général, & la Piété d'Enée."[21]

Boileau's influence upon criticism was probably less beneficial than that of other champions of the Ancients. Yet we must remember that it was not Boileau, but Chapelain, the apostle of the Christian epic, and champion of the Moderns, who did most to fix the rule of the three unities upon French classical drama. It was Boileau's graceful and satiric superficiality, not his respect for rules, which made his influence on the whole bad. He treated art as a game. Homer was, for him, an "amas de nobles fictions", not a serious account of heroic deeds. The spirit of Boileau is enshrined in the palace of Versailles—a decorative, but too splendid palace, designed for ornament and display, rather than for use. The fact that

[21]Le Bossu, op. cit. tom. II, p. 103.

Louis XIV's gravies were inedible masses of cold grease by the time they had been handed from the kitchens to the royal table would probably have seemed to Boileau of little account as a criticism of the architecture of the most beautifully decorated palace in Europe.

CHAPTER V

Epic Theory in England, Dryden to Fielding

The conception of the epic in its origin as a disembodied fable, and subsequently clothed in a story seems almost fantastic when we think of the excellent narrative power of the *Iliad*. It was the desire of the French from the time of Ronsard on to have a great national epic. Yet, in spite of the books written, the *traités* on the *poëme épique,* France produced no epic comparable to any of the great epics of the past. One might infer that the theory and theorizing got in the way. But when we turn to England, we encounter a fact which gives us material for speculation. *Paradise Lost* was conceived in terms of the critical theory of Milton's time. Milton had a disembodied fable in mind long before he had hit upon his subject. As is well known, he was long undecided whether he should write upon the subject of Arthur or something else. And when he does select his subject, it is with the fable clearly in mind.

> "Of Man's first disobedience, and the fruit
> Of that forbidden tree, whose mortal taste
> Brought death into our world, and all our woe,"

This invocation may be contrasted with Virgil's

> "I sing of arms and the man, who came first from the shores of Troy to Italy's shores," etc.

or the invocation to the *Iliad*—

> "Sing, goddess, of the wrath of Peleus' son, Achilles, who brought woes innumerable to the Achaians," etc.

Milton is certainly speaking in terms of general cosmic purpose here as compared with the specific deeds which are the subject of the *Iliad* or of the *Aeneid*. In this connection, it is interesting to compare Milton's opening lines with those of some of the other Renaissance epics. Tasso begins his *Jerusalem Delivered* thus:

> "Canto l'arme pietose e'l Capitano
> Che'l gran sepolcro liberò di Cristo," etc.

This invocation is obviously modelled upon that of Virgil. The one sings of arms and the man who first came from the shores of Troy; the other, of the holy arms of the leader who freed the Holy Sepulchre. The invocation of the *Lusiads* and of Chapelain's *La Pucelle* are in the same mode.

> "Ie chante la Pucelle, & la sainte Vaillance,
> Qui dans le point fatal, où perissoit la France,
> Ranimant de son Roy la mourante vertu,
> Releua son Estat, sous l'Anglois, abatu."

Thus Chapelain begins, with perhaps somewhat more emphasis upon his central figure than has Virgil. But the *Lusiads* opens in true Virgilian form.

> "The feats of Arms, and famed heroick Host,
> from occidental Lusitanian strand,
> who o'er the waters ne'er by seamen crost,
> fared beyond the Taprobane-land," etc.[1]

In none of these is there the Miltonic emphasis upon the abstract fable.

The invocation to *Orlando Furioso* shows us something of the poem's kinship with the mediaeval romances.

> "Le donne, i cavallier, l'arme, gli amori,
> Le cortesie, l'audaci impresi io canto
> Che furo al tempo che passaro i Mori
> D'Africa il mare, e in Francia nocquer tanto," etc.

The material of this—ladies, gentlemen, arms, and lovers—is out of the mediaeval romance. But the interest in the abstract—in courtesy and brave enterprises—has more connection

---

[1] Translation of Richard Burton.

with the theory of the disembodied fable as it came to receive greater emphasis in Renaissance criticism than it has with the concrete material which is the subject of Homer, Virgil, Tasso, and Chapelain. The conception of the abstract fable as it was gradually worked out seems to be a harmonization of mediaeval interest in allegory and of what Aristotle has to say about the purpose of poetry being to paint what ought to be rather than what is.

By the time Milton came to write his epic, criticism of the epic had elaborated the theory of the fable, Whereas Tasso had admitted that the fable was ultimately the essential form of the poem, "Ultimamente la favola è la forma essenziale del poema, come nissun dubita: or, se piú saranno le favole distinte fra loro, l'una de le quali da l'altra non dependa, piú saranno conseguentemente i poeme,"[2] later critics, like Le Bossu, had started their treatises on the epic by making the allegorical fable the germ of the poem. Milton's epic was written in accord with this later theory—around the "fable" of justifying the ways of God to man.

After the Restoration, the Stuarts brought back to England French ideas, manners, and literary theories. In particular, discussions over the Christian marvellous *versus* the pagan marvellous and the Quarrel of the Ancients and the Moderns, were speedily reflected in England. The English of the seventeenth century were, however, in a wholly different position from the French of the same period. During the period when France, in the sixteenth century, had been torn by civil war and demoralized by the lack of a central government, England had enjoyed the greatest period of peace and tranquility she had known. For this reason, and for many others, largely imponderable, England had had her Elizabethan age. So, whereas in the seventeenth century the French were in the throes of bringing their golden age to birth, the English of Dryden's time could look back upon a "classical" past of their own. In some ways, the disputes of Chapelain and Boileau and their fellows

[2]Tasso, *Discorsi dell'Arte Poetica*, p. 35.

are comparable to those of Gabriel Harvey and Spenser rather than to the critical writings of Dryden and his contemporaries. With this difference in historical background, the course of the dispute over the ancients and moderns was bound to be different in England from what it was in France. Then, too, the English have always modified whatever they have borrowed.

When the new French ideas arrived, then, after the Restoration, there already existed a body of criticism, and of literature upon which the principles could be tested, or, as sometimes happened, which could be tested in the light of the principles. Hence, the conflict over the rules and the quarrel of the Ancients and Moderns took a slightly different form. Discussion was not restricted to Greek and Latin authors. Dryden, for instance, recognized that the great Elizabethans were truly great. The tribute to Shakespeare paid by Neander (Dryden) in the *Essay of Dramatic Poesy*[3] is well known: "He was the man who of all modern, and perhaps ancient poets, had the largest and most comprehensive soul".

If this attitude was modern, there was no champion of the ancients to challenge it, although there were, of course, persons like Rymer who lacked Dryden's critical acumen and were disturbed by the high-handed Elizabethan way of dealing with the rules.[4] In general, there was not the intense interest in fundimental critical problems among the English as there had been among the French. No writer of first importance, for instance, concerned himself immediately with the claims of the pagan marvellous against those of the Christian marvellous. The whole question of the relative greatness of ancient and modern learning has two important facets,—first, whether the moderns are superior to the ancients in learning, and second, whether, in any event, the moderns may be independent of the ancient ways of doing things. In France, the Quarrel of the Ancients and the Moderns had ended with a compromise on the first

---

[3]Dryden, *Essays*, W. P. Ker, ed., vol. I, p. 79.

[4].For a discussion of neo-classical opinions in England of this period, see Wood, Paul Spencer, *The Opposition to Neo-Classicism in England between 1660 and 1700*, Pub. Mod. Lang. Assoc., Vol. XLIII, No. 1, March, 1928, pp. 182-197.

question. It was conceded there that the moderns were superior in science, but that, in literature, progress might not exist. Mankind can perfect his scientific technique, but art, being a matter of genius, does not necessarily improve from age to age.

On the whole, although Temple, Dryden, Wotton, and others took part in the English quarrel of the Ancients and the Moderns, their interest in this first side of the question was but half hearted, perhaps for the reason which I have already pointed out, namely, that there was already a respectable English tradition.[5] But the second question of independence of the rules of the ancients received fuller attention. Of course, the problem of the rules is a natural outgrowth of the first question. If, as Boileau asserted, the modern poet must accept the mythology of the ancients as a poetic "amas de nobles fictions," indispensable to his work because of the superiority of the ancients over moderns, then the question of the rules "discovered, not devised" by the ancients becomes of paramount importance. Even if one were not a champion of the Ancients like Boileau, the rules might be interesting in themselves to persons interested in criticism. Hence the numerous French treatises on epic—and other—poetry were immensely popular in England, especially in view of the fact that there had been no English treatise of the same sort since Puttenham.[6]

The compromise which had ended the French quarrel was not wholly accepted in England. The new scientific spirit which found its expression in the Royal Society was not sympathetic to the belief that literature is not suitable for scientific investigation and is not subject to the laws of progress. The psychological investigations of Hobbes and Locke necessarily had aesthetic implications. One of the questions raised in regard to the rules was: If these rules are valuable, how do we know that they are? Grant for the moment that Homer discovered the rules for the epic and that Aristotle formulated

[5]M. Rigault's discussion of the English side of the Quarrel of the Ancients and Moderns seems to me to be interpreted somewhat too much in terms of the French side of the quarrel.

[6]England had *no* single treatise on the epic as a separate genre.

them, how do we *know* they are the rules? Obviously, each individual must re-judge the rules, or at least evaluate the authority. This attitude is reflected in Pope's *Essay on Criticism* when he tells us of Virgil that "Nature and Homer were, *he found,* the same." The French critics had by no means overlooked this point, but when a critic has made his evaluation and embodied the results in a treatise, he may sometimes seem to be saying: "Here are the rules; follow them," while actually he is merely giving his own study of what he believes to be the practice of the masters.

All these points are, after all, matters of emphasis. Temple and Wotton debated the question of superiority of Ancients and Moderns in genius. Le Bossu certainly implies throughout his *Traité* that the rules are good because Nature and Homer are the same. Only there is a difference in spirit between the French and the English quarrel which one is tempted to try to define. With all the preoccupation among the French critics over the matter of the rules of the epic for modern writers, there was, by most of the writers, the recognition that there was an imponderable element in creative composition— the "je ne sais quoi" of the Précieuses, of Corneille, and of Pascal.[7] As I have said before, it is only in the hands of little men that genius seems to be made into a matter of knowing and following the rules.

When the Quarrel of the Ancients and Moderns opened in France, Saint-Evremond, then in exile in England—his exile began in 1661—took up the quarrel in London. He was associated with Dryden and his group at Will's, and many an argument went on there over the whole matter, Saint-Evremond acting partly as moderator, partly as instigator. Sir William Temple, not a learned man, championed the cause of the An-

---

[7] See Pascal, Pensées, Art. VI. "Qui voudra connaître à plein la vanité de l'homme n'a qu'à considérer les causes et les effets de l'amour. La cause en est 'un je ne sais quoi'; et les effets en sont effroyables."
And Corneille, Rodogune, vers 359-362.
    "Il est des noeuds secrets, il est des sympathies,
    Dont par le doux rapport les âmes assorties
    S'attachent l'une à l'autre et se plaissent piquer."
Mr. Spingarn discusses this briefly in his introduction to *Critical Essays of the Seventeenth Century*, vol. I. p. c.

cients. William Wotton, a very learned man, who, it seems, knew Greek and Latin and I should hesitate to say what else besides—Hebrew, Italian, Spanish, French, Arabic—and had long known them—William Wotton took up the cause of the Moderns. Sir William had faith in the justice of his cause, but William Wotton had knowledge and common sense. So, in the matter of champions, the Moderns would have won, except that Swift at the death of Temple, took up the cause of his benefactor and wrote *The Battle of the Books* (1704, written 1698). Even this book is certainly as much on the side of the Moderns as of the Ancients, being essentially a satire against stupidity and in favor of common sense, and hence as modern as ancient. Nor does it really have the learning and sanity of Wotton's book. But Swift was Swift, and today we think of *The Battle of the Books* as the last word of the quarrel, which was really never very violent.

This quarrel of the Ancients and the Moderns concerned itself little with epic theory, except incidentally. To find out what was being done on the troublesome matter of the epic, we have to go back to Sir William Davenant's *Preface* to his *Gondibert* (1650). This gentleman knew de Scudéry, Chapelain, and Desmarets personally, having associated with them when he was in exile. On the whole, he shared many of their prepossessions, although with a difference. He takes as his models Homer and Virgil chiefly, but comments upon Lucan and Statius, and admits Tasso and Spencer as epic poets. He does not admit Ariosto nor Du Bartas, chiefly because he does not wish to be forced to admit Dante, Marino and others.[8] He is troubled by the question of Christian marvels in Tasso. In all of these points, Davenant reveals to us something of what he had been listening to in his Paris conversations.[9] Here is what he has to say on Tasso:

"But Tasso, though he came late into the world, must have

---

[8]Spingarn, *Critical Essays of the Seventeenth Century*, vol. II, p. 5.

[9]The champions of the Christian epic generally take Tasso for their model, and the presence of romantic material in the *Jerusalem Delivered* is frequently troubling to the later writers who look upon Tasso as their guide.

his share in that Criticall warr which never ceases amongst the Learned; and he seems most unfortunate, because his errors which are derived from the Ancients, when examin'd, grow in a great degree excusable in them, and by being his, admit no pardon. Such as are his Councell assembled in Heaven, his Witches Expeditions through the Air, and enchanted Woods inhabited with Ghosts. For though the elder Poets, which were then the sacred Priests, fed the world with supernaturall Tales, and so compounded the Religion of Pleasure and Mysterie, two Ingredients which never fail'd to work upon the People, whilst for the eternity of their Chiefs, more refin'd by education, they surely intended no such vain provision: Yet a Christian Poet, whose Religion little needs the aids of Invention hath less occasion to imitate such Fables as meanly illustrate a probable Heaven by the fashion and dignity of Courts, and make a resemblance of Hell out of the Dreams of frightened Women, by which they continue and increase the melancholy mistakes of the People."[10]

He wrestles with the problem of the Christian epic, as had his friends de Scudéry, Desmarets, and Chapelain. His criticism of the use of pagan marvels is virtually the same as theirs, and his arguments in favor of the superiority of the Christian religion are the familiar ones. But he does two new things. He decides that he will discard the marvellous altogether and he does not use national material for his poem. Both of these are innovations in epic practice and theory. His purpose is definitely to teach principles of conduct, and he agrees with Plato in thinking that Homer degraded the gods by having them mix in human affairs.[11] In the passage about Tasso just quoted, Davenant shows why he does not approve of the use of the marvellous by a Christian poet—namely, that it is not needful in the Christian belief. The use of material from remote times and another country will, he thinks, make his moral so much the clearer. Distance gives one perspective— and also permits liberties with facts!—and hence enables the

[10]Spingarn, op. cit. m vol. II, p. 5.
[11]Spingarn, op. cit., vol. II, p. 51.

poet to teach his lesson without fear of arousing envy. In this connection, he has something to say on the subject of comedy.[12] "This leads us to observe the craftiness of the Comicks, who are only willing when they describe humor (& humor is the drunkeness of a Nation which no sleep can cure) to lay the Scaene in their own Country, as knowing we are, like the Son of Noah, so little distasted to behold each other's shame, that we delight to see even that of a Father; yet when they would set forth greatness and excellent vertue, which is the Theme of Tragedy, publiquely to the people, they wisely, to avoid the quarrels of neighbourly envy, remove the Scene from home." The serious epic he thus identifies with tragedy in its purpose, a comparison often made and derived from Aristotle ("for his mock-heroic Margites stands in the same relation to Comedy as the Iliad and Odyssey to Tragedy".)[13] Davenant's idea that material for comedy should be contemporary and domestic is not found in Aristotle, but is inferred.

The *Preface* to *Gondibert* was addressed to Davenant's friend, the philosopher Hobbes, who replied in *An Answer* to *Sir William Davenant's Preface before Gondibert* (1650).[14] The most important aspect of his criticism is, I suppose, the division he makes of the kinds of poetry—Heroique, Scommatique, and Pastoral, corresponding to the divisions of social life of which each treats, namely, Court, City, and Country.[15] Each of these divisions is furthur divided according to the form of treatment—that is, dramatic or narrative,—so that we have tragedy and epic as the forms of the heroic; comedy and satire for the scommatique; and pastoral and pastoral comedy for the pastoral. This is simply a further elaboration of the Aristotelian divisions, although, of course, Aristotle does not make

[12]Ibid., Vol. II, p. 12.

[13]Aristotle, *Poetics*, edited by Lane Cooper, p. 12.

[14]Text found in Spingarn, op. cit., vol. II, pp. 54-76.

[15]This division of poetry had been worked out for the drama by an Italian architect, Sebastiano Serlio, who published a treatise in seven books called *Architettura*, published in 1545. He writes with the banquetting hall of a prince in mind, but his work had considerable influence on the art of stage-decoration. His work was translated into English in 1611, and was used by the Master of Revels in constructing scenes.

For a full discussion of this, see Campbell, Lilly Bess, *Scenes and Machines on the English Stage during the Renaissance*, pp. 29-42.

the social division, nor does he treat of the pastoral. Hobbes spends most of his essay in comment upon problems of style, but he has something to say about not using the marvelous and he comments upon the fact that *Gondibert* is, unlike all other epics, not national. Speaking of Davenant's failure to invoke the Muse, Hobbes says: "In that you make no small account of the example of almost all the approved Poets, ancient and modern, who thought fit in the beginning, and sometimes also in the progress of their Poems, to invoke a Muse or some other Deity that should dictate to them or assist them in their writings, they that take not the laws of Art from any reason of their own but from the fashion of precedent times will perhaps accuse your singularity. For my part, I neither subscribe to their accusation, nor yet condemn that Heathen custom otherwise then as accessory to their false Religion. For their Poets were their Divines, had the name of Prophets; Exercised amongst the People a kinde of spiritual Authority, would be thought to speak by a divine spirit, have their works which they writ in Verse (the divine stile) pass for the Word of God, and not of man, and to be hearkened to with reverence . . . . .

". . . Against such I defend you (without assenting to those that condemn either Homer or Virgil) by dissenting onely from those that think the Beauty of a Poem consisteth in the exorbitancy of the fiction. For as truth is the bound of Historical, so the Resemblance of truth is the utmost limit of Poeticall Liberty. In old time amongst the Heathen such strange fictions and Metamorphoses were not so remote from the Articles ot their Faith as they are now from ours, and therefore were not so unpleasant. Beyond the actual works of nature a Poet may now go; but beyond the conceived possibility of nature, never."[16]

These two excerpts show that Hobbes realized that some of the things found in the ancient epic grew out of the facts of an earlier civilization. But he does not infer from this the necessary superiority of the moderns over the ancients. His

[16]Spingarn, op. cit., vol. II, pp. 58-62.

attitude towards his subject was that of a man who made no
professions to being a poet himself and who was of a cool,
analytical turn of mind.

Of all the men of the Restoration engaged in the art of
letters, none was greater than Dryden. Posterity has laid many
faults at his door—that he was a turncoat in his religious principles, that he helped to foist a limited conception of poetry
upon English taste, that he dragged indecencies into his plays
by the hair of their head, and so on. Some of the charges
have some truth in them; others, like so many of posterity's
careless traditions, have very little truth, or none at all. And
of them all, the one with the least truth is the theory that he
did a very great deal to shackle the free soul of English poetry
with foreign rules. He was interested in the laws of his art—
not external laws, but principles upon which poetry is created.
He naturally was interested in those laws as interpreted by the
learned men of his own and former ages. He accepted some
of them and did not accept others, or accepted certain ones at
some times and not at others. The ones which he accepted are
not always those any one of us would accept. But, when one
has said this, one has said practically all that can be said about
Dryden and the rules. Perhaps it is scarcely necessary to repeat this, after the illuminating comments made by Professor
W. P. Ker in his edition of Dryden's *Essays*. But one must
bear it constantly in mind in reading Dryden's criticism, for
Dryden is interested, deeply interested, in the rules, as a
creative artist usually is interested in the technical principles
of his art.

Dryden did not have a system of criticism. He knew a
great deal about the accepted critical theories of other men,
and indeed believed them to a greater or less extent. But he
usually judged the author by the effect that author had upon
John Dryden rather than by any testing in the light of rules.
(Applying a system of criticism is, of course, ultimately more
or less personal). Thus, Dryden could believe in rhyme at one

period and in blank verse at another.[17]   He admired the heroic
poem greatly, as did most men of his time.   He translated the
Aeneid and wrote about epic poetry in his preface to his translation.   He loved Homer even more, however, than he did
Virgil.   Homer was, he said, more congenial to his own tempera-
ment.[18]   Le Bossu he esteemed highly, saying, indeed, that
"Spencer wanted only to have read Bossu."[19]   He apparently
enjoyed the interminable heroic romances which so delighted
his age, if one can judge from his use of them as sources for
his heroic plays and his defense of the heroic play.   Granted
that he may have written the heroic play because of a popular
demand, still Dryden was a child of his age, and a great many
persons enjoyed the heroic romances, even so unsentimental a
person as Madame de Sévigné confessing that they move her
greatly.

Dryden has something to say about the Ancients and
Moderns in his *Essay of Dramatic Poesy,* but it is little other
than we should expect—he likes both and he steers a common-
sense course through the problem.   This essay appeared in
1668, long before Perrault read his challenge to the French
Academy, but not before the argument had started in literary
circles in Paris.   In 1677, Dryden discussed *Heroic Poetry and
Poetic Licence* in a preface to his *State of Innocence and Fall
of Man.*   Here he has something to say about the old problem
of verisimilitude and the use of the marvellous, and also on the
question of poetic language.   He is too much of a poet, too
sensitive to the real beauties of poetry not to feel the constraint
of some of the purely rationalistic theories of his day.   In
poetry, he says, "you are not obliged, as in history, to a literal
belief of what the poet says, but you are pleased with the image,
without being cozened by the fiction."[20]   This is a breath of

[17]In his earlier heroic plays, he used rhyme, but in *All for Love,* blank verse, saying
in his preface to the latter: "In my style, I have professed to imitate the divine
Shakespeare; which that I might perform more freely, I have disencumbered myself
from rhyme.   Not that I condemn my former way, but that this is more proper to my
present purpose."   Ker's edition of *Dryden's Essays,* vol. I, p. 200.
[18]Ibid., *Preface to the Fables,* vol. II, p. 251, seq.
[19]Ibid., *Dedication of the Aeneis,* vol. II, p. 220.
[20]Dryden, op. cit., Vol. I, p. 185.

real common sense as against the dull and super-cautious common sense of some of the champions of correctness. Thus, he goes on to say:

"Imaging is, in itself, the very height and life of Poetry. It is, as Longinus describes it, a discourse, which, by a kind of enthusiasm, or extraordinary emotion of the soul, makes it seem to us that we behold those things which the poet paints, so as to be pleased with them, and to admire them.

"If poetry be imitation, that part of it must needs be best which describes most lively our actions and passions; our virtues and our vices; our follies and our humours: for neither is Comedy without its part of imaging; and they who do it best are certainly the most excellent in their kind. This is too plainly proved to be denied. But how are poetical fictions, how are hippocentaurs and chimeras, or how are angels and immaterial substances to be imaged; which, some of them, are things quite out of nature; others, such whereof we can have no notion? . . . The answer is easy to the first part of it: the fiction of some beings which are not in nature (second notions, as the logicians call them) has been founded on the conjunction of two natures, which have a real separate being."[21]

He pays his respects to Boileau and Rapin, "amongst the French, the greatest of this age," of whom the latter "is alone sufficient, were all other critics lost, to teach anew the rules of writing."[22] But his own defense of the marvellous is far ahead of Boileau's "amas de nobles fictions."

In his Preface to *Troilus and Cressida* (1679) he quotes Le Bossu for the first time. (Le Bossu's *Traité* came out in Paris in 1675). In this preface, Dryden accepts explicitly Le Bossu's initial premise—that the first rule for the heroic poem is to make the moral of the poem. Dryden elaborates this point somewhat, pointing out its aesthetic, or at any rate technical, value, however, rather than stressing the didactic side. The moral, he says, gives the center to the action.

---

[21]One interesting aspect of this quotation is Dryden's discussion of the theory of imitation. His attitude here and elsewhere is very liberal. Imitation means not copying, but "imitating" the ideal.

[22]Dryden, *op. cit.*, vol. I, p. 181.

"The first rule which Bossu prescribes to the writer of an Heroic Poem, and which holds too by the same reason in all Dramatic Poetry, is to make the moral of the work; that is, to lay down to yourself what that precept of morality shall be, which you would insinuate into the people; as namely, Homer's (which I have copied in my *Conquest of Granada*), was, that union preserves a commonwealth, and discord destroys it . . . . 'Tis the moral that directs the whole action of the play to one centre; and that action or fable is the example built upon the moral, which confirms the truth of it to our experience: when the fable is designed, then, and not before, the persons are to be introduced, with their manners, characters, and passions."[23]

The spirit of this essay is, on the whole, less liberal than that of the earlier *Essay of Dramatic Poesy,* but even while accepting the theories of Le Bossu and his school, Dryden had his eye upon poetry as an art rather than as a handmaiden of morality. And though he seems to side with the champions of the Ancients here and elsewhere, he never forgets the great modern English poets, as for example, in a passage from his *Dedication of Examen Poeticarum,* (1683), where he says: "Indeed, there is a vast difference betwixt arguing like Perrault, in behalf of the French poets, against Homer and Virgil, and betwixt giving the English poets their undoubted due, of excelling Aeschylus, Euripides, and Sophocles."[24]

In his *Dedication of the Aeneid* (1697), he has little new to say. Much of what he does say is borrowed from his French predecessor, Segrais. He repeats the commonplaces of the writers of treatises on the epic poem. "A heroic poem, truly such, is undoubtedly the greatest work which the soul of man is capable to perform. The design of it is to form the mind to heroic virtue by example; 'tis conveyed in verse, that it may delight, while it instructs. The action of it is always one, entire, and great . . . Even the least portions of them

---

[23]Ibid., vol. I, p. 213.
[24]Dryden, *op. cit.,* vol. II, p. 6.

must be of the epic kind: all things must be grave, majestical, and sublime; nothing of a foreign nature, like the trifling novels, which Ariosto, and others, have inserted in their poems: by which the reader is misled into another sort of pleasure, opposite to that which is designed in an epic poem."[25]

Dryden really added nothing to epic theory. He planned an epic on King Arthur, or on the Black Prince, as he tells us in his *Preface to Juvenal,* wherein he was to use Guardian Angels as "machines", but he did nothing with it. His chief contribution to English criticism of this period was simply that he knew good poetry and liked it, that he was interested in rules and theories only in so far as they helped to make good poetry or determine what it was in poetry that made it exciting. He gave English criticism something of a craftman's point of view toward the whole business, so that much of what he says has a reality which other criticism with the same views lacks. He borrows freely in his plays, as his critic, Gerald Langbaine, points out in *An Account of the English Dramatic Poets,* (1691).[26] But he had a really original mind, and in criticism, never accepted for a long time any opinion which violated his own standards of taste and reason, into which qualities he had keener insight than some of his contemporaries.

The influence of the French quarrel of the Ancients and the Moderns was to stimulate critical writing in England. Much of it, as I have said before, is concerned less with the theoretical definitions of the verisimilar or the marvellous than it is with such things as diction and versification, or the problem of whether the Elizabethans were justified in their violation of the rules. A worthy doctor of medicine of the City, by the name of Richard (later Sir Richard) Blackmore wrote, between the years 1695 and 1723, in his spare moments, a number of epics, *Prince Arthur, King Arthur, Alfred,* and *Eliza,* being some of them. All of these epics except *Eliza* (1705) had the usual voluminous preface, the ideas of which are derived largely

[25]Dryden, *op. cit.,* vol. II, pp. 154-155.
[26]Spingarn, *Critical Essays,* vol. III, pp. 110-147.

from Le Bossu—thus, "An Epic Poem is a feign'd or devis'd Story of an Illustrious Action, related in Verse, in an Allegorical, Probable, Delightful, and Admirable Manner, to cultivate the mind with instructions of Virtue. 'Tis a feign'd or devis'd Discourse, that is, a Fable."[27] Unlike Le Bossu, however, he wrestles with the problem of the Christian epic. "The Pagan Poets had in this [the problem of the marvellous] a great advantage; their Theology was such as would easily mix itself with their Poems, from whence they received their greatest Beauties. Homer, indeed, to raise his Subjects by his frequent Machines, seems to have debas'd his Religion. Virgil's Conduct, in my Opinion, is more careful and chast. But some of our modern Criticks have believ'd 'tis scarce possible for a Christian Poet to make use of this advantage of introducing Superiour, Invisible Powers into the Action, and therefore seem to despair of seeing an Heroick Poem written now that shall reach to the Dignity of those of the Pagans. They think the Christian Religion is not so well accommodated to this matter as the Pagan was: and that if any Attempt be made this way, Religion will suffer more than the Poem will gain by it. My opinion has always differ'd from these Gentlemen's; I believe a Christian Poet has as great advantages as the Pagan had, and that our Theology may enter into an Epick Poem, and raise the Subject without being it self debas'd."[28]

In his *Preface to Alfred,* (1723), Blackmore challenges Boileau explicitly, "These are the Reasons, which Mr. Boileau has alleged to prove that the Christian Revelation is unfit to enter into an Epick Poem: And when I consider them, I cannot but conclude, that either that Gentleman, being happily turned for Satyr, and having but little contemplated the Nature and Design of this Species of Writing, had acquired but a superficial Knowledge of the Nature and Properties of an Epick Composure; or that he lay under some obstinate Pre-possession in Favour of the Pagan Religion, as only capable of en-

---

[27]Spingarn, op. cit., Blackmore, *Preface to Prince Arthur*, vol. III, p. 235.
[28]Spingarn, op. cit., vol. III, p. 239.

livening and adorning an heroick Writing: And I shall here give a distinct and full Answer to his three Reasons, and show how weak and inconclusive they are."[29]

Sir Richard could not write a poem, but his ideas about how to do it are no worse than those of many of the persons who could. His attempt, however, to revive the dead struggle over the Christian epic was not successful, and his is the last effort made. He identifies himself with the group of Moderns in France who based their claim to superiority of the modern on the superiority of their religion.

John Dennis wrote a scathing criticism of *Prince Arthur* in 1696, attacking not so much Blackmore's ideas as his performance, but pointing out certain critical principles regarding the Christian epic which should be considered. In general, Dennis has been remembered by posterity because of Pope's attacks upon him in the *Dunciad*, his own absurd revisions of Shakespeare's plays, and because of Fielding's burlesque of his critical method in *Tom Thumb*. Dennis can easily be ridiculed, but, at the same time, he was not without intelligence. He admired Milton extravagantly. In the quarrel over the Ancients and the Moderns, he conceived of the element of religious passion in the ancients as constituting their chief claim to superiority. This idea is not far from Matthew Arnold's "high seriousness." And it is a truth, if not the whole and only truth. Dennis, in fact, had some excellent ideas, but little balance of judgment. His theory that humour (in the Jonsonian sense) not wit was the source of comedy has in it an element of truth. Charming as is the scintillating dialogue of Congreve's plays, for example, the humor (I use the word in the Jonsonian sense) of Molière is greater—that is, has more of Meredith's "Comic Spirit"—than the wit of Congreve's lines. But, again, Dennis' statement, while a truth, is but half a truth. No one would wish to give up *The Way of the World* simply in order to stick to one *kind* of comedy. The fact is that Dennis had

---

[29]Blackmore, *Preface to Alfred*, p. V.

little of the historical sense,[30] and was bound down by rather rigid definitions of kinds of literature.

Addison's defense of Milton's epic practice in various numbers of the *Spectator*, beginning with 267, is well-known. He has been laughed at, among others by Professor Saintsbury in his *History of English Criticism,* for testing Milton by the rules of Aristotle. Yet the process does not seem altogether far-fetched, when it is done with the reasonableness with which Addison does it. For one thing, Milton himself wrote with this theory of the epic in mind. Addison starts out, as do all his contemporaries, with the assumption that his readers are familiar with Aristotle, Horace, and Longinus, and with some of their commentators, and also with Homer and Virgil. In the light of the principles practiced by Homer and Virgil, and formulated by Aristotle and Horace, has Milton written a great epic? Dryden, while admiring Milton, was not inclined to call *Paradise Lost* a heroic poem.[31] His argument is given in the *Original and Progress of Satire,* and is as follows: "As for Mr. Milton, whom we all admire with so much justice, his subject is not that of an Heroic Poem, properly so called. His design is the losing of our happiness; his event is not prosperous, like that of all other epic works; his heavenly machines are many, and his human persons are but two." Le Bossu had already pointed out that the outcome of the epic, in contrast to that of tragedy should be pleasant, an idea derived from Aristotle.

Addison starts his discussion of *Paradise Lost* by waiving this discussion.[32] But he proceeds to examine it by other "rules" for the epic.[33] He takes up the fable first, in the best

[30]The historical estimate of a work of art may not be the ultimate estimate, as Matthew Arnold says, but it is an important element of our ultimate estimate. The "high seriousness" of Homer belongs, in part, to his age and not to ours. Much of the criticism of the period in which John Dennis lived went wrong because of the failure of the critics to include the historical estimate in their judgment of Homer and Virgil.

[31]Dryden, *Essays, Original and Progress of Satire,* vol. II, p. 29.

[32]Addison opens his discussion in Spectator, No. 267, with these words: "There is nothing in nature so irksome as general discourses, especially when they turn chiefly upon words. For this reason I shall waive the discussion of that point which was started some years since, whether Milton's 'Paradise Lost' may be called an heroic poem? Those who will not give it that title may call it, if they please, a divine poem."

[33]He may be a little inconsistent in this. If *Paradise Lost* is not a heroic poem, then it is perhaps useless to judge it by the rules for that kind of poem. But Addison seems less consistent than he is. He is judging Milton from the point of view of

neo-classical manner, and points out how the fable of *Paradise Lost* is single, entire, and illustrious. This may seem to be the wrong way of going about a piece of criticism—that is, trying to test a great poem by the light of rules which have been inferred from such poems. But, it seems to me, this is pretty much what one does in trying to study a work of art, not as a rhapsodical precieux, but as a fellow-craftsman. But to continue with Addison, Milton might have begun *Paradise Lost* with the heavenly powers in felicitous concord. But he does not; he plunges *in medias res*. Addison points out that this is in accord with the best epic practice, but implies that the best epic practice has a reason in that it insures unity of action. Whether the action of *Paradise Lost* takes place within the space of a year, as Le Bossu—and others—had claimed it should, Addison says it is impossible to judge because the action, taking place as it does largely in Chaos, is independent of time, but still it certainly preserves unity of time, place, and action, which the commentators on Aristotle had inferred for the epic from his statements about tragedy.

On the following Saturday—that is in *Spectator* Number 273—he takes up Milton's handling of character and manners, and shows that Milton adapted the rules to his subject satisfactorily. In Number 279, [34] Addison discusses Milton's sentiments and language. Homer had been criticised by certain writers for lack of decorum in his characters, such as, for example, his comparing Ajax to an ass. Le Bossu had defended Homer on a historical ground, namely, that, in Homeric times, asses were more highly esteemed than in later times.[35] Addison takes the same position regarding Homer, saying: "It was the fault of the age, and not of Homer, if there wants that delicacy in some of his sentiments, which appears in the works

structure, the manipulation of events of epic sweep, and *tone,* the sense of grandeur and importance in those events.

[34]This paper contains a very interesting comparison of Homer and Virgil with each other as well as with Milton, and an illuminating discussion of Virgil's *Aeneid.* Addison is quite aware of Virgil's greater sophistication as compared with Homer, and of Dryden's as compared with Virgil.

[35]See Le Bossu, op. cit., tom. II, Liv. IV, ch. III.

of men of a much inferior genius. Besides, if there are blemishes in any particular thoughts, there is an infinite beauty in the greatest part of them. In short, if there are many poets who would not have fallen into the meanness of some of his sentiments, there are none who could have risen up to the greatness of others. Virgil has excelled all others in the propriety of his sentiments. Milton shines likewise very much in this particular. Nor must we omit one consideration which adds to his honor and reputation. Homer and Virgil introduced persons whose characters are commonly known among men, and such as are to be met with either in history or in ordinary conversation. Milton's characters, most of them, lie out of nature, and were to be formed purely by his own invention. It shows a greater genius in Shakespeare to have drawn his Caliban, than his Hotspur or Julius Caesar[36] . . . It was much easier therefore for Homer to find proper sentiments for an assembly of Grecian generals, than for Milton to diversify his infernal council with proper characters, and inspire them with a variety of sentiments . . . Adam and Eve, before the Fall, are a different species from that of mankind, who are descended from them; and none but a poet of the most unbounded invention, and the most exquisite judgment, could have filled their conversation and behavior with such beautiful circumstances during their state of innocence."

In Number 285, Addison discusses Milton's language. There is nothing in this which need detain us here, but his general remarks on the uses of criticism in the paper for the following Saturday, Number 291, are interesting. He says: "It is in criticism, as in all other sciences and speculations; one who brings with him any implicit notions and observations which he has made in his reading of the poets, will find his own reflections methodised and explained, and perhaps several little hints that had passed in his mind perfected and improved in the works

---

[36]This is an interesting aspect of the problems of imitation and of verisimilitude. Addison, a neo-classicist, thinks Shakespeare a greater genius for having drawn Caliban than for having drawn Hotspur or Julius Caesar. The word "imitation" has come to have a very broad meaning. To be sure, Addison does not use the word here, but he elsewhere has it in his critical vocabulary.

of a good critic; whereas one who has not these previous lights is very often an utter stranger to what he reads, and apt to put a wrong interpretation upon it . . .

". . . The truth of it is, there is nothing more absurd than for a man to set up for a critic without a good insight into all the parts of learning . . A few general rules extracted out of the French authors, with a certain cant of words, has sometimes set up an illiterate heavy writer for a most judicious and formidable critic."[37]

And so, on each Saturday, he continues to take up some aspect of Milton's poetic qualities, always preserving an admirable balance between tradition and change. Another example of this may be seen in Number 315, where he has something to say of the allegorical in the fable.

"Aristotle observes, that the fable of an epic poem should abound in circumstances that are both credible and astonishing; or, as the French critics choose to phrase it, the fable should be filled with the probable and the marvellous . . . .

". . The great secret therefore of heroic poetry, is to relate such circumstances as may produce in the reader at the same time both belief and astonishment . . . .

". . . I know that many critics look upon the stories of Circe, Polypheme, the Sirens, nay the whole *Odyssey* and *Iliad* to be allegories; but allowing this to be true, they are fables which, considering the opinions of mankind that prevailed in the age of the poet, might possibly have been according to the letter. The persons are such as might have acted what is ascribed to them, as the circumstances in which they are represented might possibly have been truths and realities . . . . In a word, besides the hidden meaning of an epic allegory, the plain literal sense ought to appear probable. The story should be such as an ordinary reader may acquiesce in, whatever natural, moral or political truth may be discovered in it by men of greater penetration."

[37]One of the points most strongly insisted upon by all epic theorists was that Homer and Virgil, Aristotle and Horace, were masters of the learning of their time. Fielding is following the same tradition, here expressed by Addison, when he invokes learning in the invocation to Book XIII of *Tom Jones*.

This attitude toward the fable is sane. Addison does not challenge the authority of Le Bossu here. (He does so, however, in Number 369, when he says: "Though I can by no means think . . that an epic writer first of all pitches upon a certain moral as the ground-work and foundation of his poem, and afterwards finds out a story to it: I am, however, of opinion that no just heroic poem ever was or can be made from whence one great moral may not be deduced.") But, even if there is a hidden meaning, the outer meaning must be credible.

Addison was not a theorist. I sometimes wonder if, when he set out to write his analysis of Milton, he knew just what would be his critical termini. But the cool rationality of his temper, and his very genuine interest in concrete, tangible realities led him to challenge the theory of the fable as pure allegory, and to demand that the external story be credible. He did not depart from the conception that a great epic must teach a moral—that is the nature of the poem as conceived by traditional criticism. But the making of the moral need not be its beginning. Dryden, who defended the theory of the allegorical fable, did so, it seems to me, not so much because of the allegory in itself as because the unity of idea in the allegory gives the writer his artistic pattern. Dryden works as a craftsman, a fellow poet, interested in what it is that makes a poem a unit, just as a painting is a unit. Addison writes less from the craftsman's point of view and more from the reader's. His criticism is less likely to lead the Blackmores of life astray, I fancy, but Dryden's, whether wrong or right, is probably more useful to a great writer.

The last critic to be considered before we come to Fielding is Pope. Pope was perhaps too clever to be as well-balanced a critic as either Dryden or Addison, though this may be "damning with faint praise,"—a thing which is not intended. Pope was helped, however, by being associated with Swift. Swift was, of course, more concerned with crucifying dullness than with working out critical theories, but, even so, the results were amusing, not only in Swift's own *Tale of a Tub* and the *Battle of the Books*, but in Pope's *Dunciad* and in the prose treatise, περι βάθους, a burlesque of epic theory corresponding to Longinus' serious treatise, πsρι ὕψους. In 1723, when Pope published his translation of the *Iliad*, he wrote the usual preface setting forth the virtues of the heroic poem in general and the epics of Homer in particular. There is also the usual comparison of the respective merits of Virgil and Homer, the recognition that Virgil is more correct, while Homer has greater poetic fire. This whole *Preface* is little more than a condensation of Le Bossu's *Traité*. Indeed, Pope says explicitly:

"That I would farther recommend to him is to study his Author rather from his own Text than from any Commentaries, how learned soever, or whatever Figure they make in the Estimation of the World. To consider him attentively in Comparison with Virgil above all the Ancients, and with Milton above all the Moderns. Next these the Archbishop of Cambray's *Telemachus* may give him the truest Idea of the Spirit and Turn of our Author,[38] and Bossu's admirable *Treatise of the Epic Form* the justest Notion of his Design and Conduct."

His conception of the Fable, the allegorical fable, is altogether that of Le Bossu, with Boileau's idea of the "machines" as personifications, that is, neither pagan nor Christian, but "epic." In fact, the whole thing is in the Le Bossu-Boileau tradition.

In the *Dunciad*, (1729), however, and in the burlesque of Longinus, Pope—with Swift's inspiration—has a shot at the stodgy treatises. It is highly amusing, and rather appalling as well, for the burlesque—like the burlesque of *Pamela* in *Shamela*—is achieved by making very few changes in what was written in sober earnest. For instance, Warburton says

---

[38]*Télémaque* is definitely allegorical. Pope reveals his interpretation of Homer as allegory in thus saying that *Télémaque* can give the "truest idea of the Spirit and Turn" of Homer.

in the remarks of Ricardus Aristarchus[39] which preface the *Dunciad*:

"But when he cometh to speak of the person of the hero fitted for such poem, in truth he miserably halts and hallucinates. For, misled by one Monsieur Bossu, a Gallic critic, he prateth of I cannot tell what phantom of a hero, only raised up to support the fable. A putid conceit! As if Homer and Virgil, like modern undertakers, who first build their house, and then seek out for a tenant, had contrived the story of a War and a Wandering before they once thought either of Achilles or Aeneas."

And, in περι βάΘους, of *The Art of Sinking in Poetry*, Pope gives a *Receipt to Make an Epic Poem* which is a *reductio ad absurdum* of the many recipes for making an epic which had been put forth.

"An epic poem, the critics agree, is the greatest work human nature is capable of." This was the accepted opening. "I shall here endeavour (for the benefit of my countrymen) to make it manifest, that epic poems may be made without a genius, nay without learning or much reading . . . Molière observes of making a dinner, that any man can do it with money, and if a professed cook cannot do it without, he has his art for nothing; the same may be said of making a poem, 'tis easily brought about by him that has a genius, but the skill lies in doing it without one."

The recipe which follows does not follow Le Bossu exactly, for it advises getting the story first and the moral last, but otherwise the whole thing is an excellent burlesque of the methods of all the treatises on epic poetry at the time.[40]

[39]A footnote in Elwin and Courthope's edition of Pope, vol. IV, p. 93. says: "The Prolegomena of Aristarchus appears from Pope's letter to Warburton of the 28th of December, 1742, to have been written by the latter."

[40]The receipt, in part, runs thus:

"For the Fable.

"Take out of any old poem, history-book, romance, or legend . . . . those parts of story which afford most scope for long descriptions: put these pieces together, and throw all the adventures you fancy into one tale. Then take a hero, whom you may chuse for the sound of his name, [Note Boileau's criticism of the name of *Alaric*] and put him into the midst of these adventures. There let him work for twelve books; at the end of which you

The history of the epic theory from Dryden to Fielding has no central subject of conflict such as we found in France over Christian and Pagan epic. English epic theory reflects the French somewhat, but, by and large, the great men left the question of the Christian epic alone. After all, Milton had justified the theory of the French modern group, and it remained for the champions of Boileau in England to square Milton's practice with Boileau's strictures on the subject. They did it satisfactorily, if not altogether logically. In the meantime, interest in writing the epic more or less died down in England after Milton. In France, the attempt went on into the eighteenth century, each four or five years witnessing another trial. Even Voltaire put his hand to the plow and wrote the *Henriade,* an effort which elicited from Voltaire's friend, M. Malezieux, the sad remark: "Les Francais n'ont pas la tête épique." In the midst of all the discussion of the heroic poem, however, there was developing the popular literature represented by Defoe's narratives, by the verisimilar sketches of contemporary life in the *Spectator Papers.* The long-winded heroic romances still held on. Fielding read some of them. I suspect that Richardson read a great many. Cervantes, Le Sage, Scarron, various writers of the anti-romance of one sort or another flourished. The world of readers had become urban and bourgeois, and the day of the heroic epic had passed.

may take him out, ready prepared to conquer or to marry; it being necessary that the conclusion of the epic poem be fortunate."

"For the Moral and Allegory.

"These you may Extract out of the fable afterwards, at your leisure: be sure you strain them sufficiently."

"For the Machines.

"Take of Deities, male and female, as many as you can use, separate them into two equal parts, and keep Jupiter in the middle: let Juno put him in a ferment, and Venus mollify him. Remember on all occasions to make use of volatile Mercury. If you have need of devils, draw them out of Milton's Paradise, and extract your spirits from Tasso. The use of these machines is evident; since no epic poem can possibly subsist without them, the wisest way is to reserve them for your greatest necessities: when you cannot extricate your hero by any human means, or yourself by your own wit, seek relief from heaven, and the gods will do your business very readily . . . . . ."

CHAPTER VI

THE DEFINITION OF THE COMIC PROSE EPIC
JOSEPH ANDREWS

When *Joseph Andrews* appeared in 1742, the state of English letters was by no means happy.[1] In certain periods of literary history, one can detect tendencies and establish norms. Diverse as is the literature of Elizabeth's time, one can see clearly enough the influence of the revival of the Greek and Latin classics; one can say that the drama was the dominant literary type; or one can trace the effects of Puritanism on the life and thought of the times. Even in the more chaotic times of the Restoration, one can understand a great deal of what happened in the light of the struggle over the Ancients and Moderns; or of the imported French influence at war with the English tradition; or of the efforts of the new scientific spirit to reform the language of prose and poetry.

The mid-eighteenth century world, however, was, as Fielding later said in his *Covent Garden Journal* just quoted, in a state of anarchy. The theatre was very popular and had some very great actors and actresses and was soon to enjoy David Garrick. But the plays which were being written were, for the most part, unbelievably puerile, or stiff and bombastic. It was the age of "genteel" comedy, whose comedy excited the in-

---

[1] In the second paper of *The Covent Garden Journal*, dated Jan. 7, 1752, Fielding makes this statement: "Before I had fully resolved to draw my Pen, and to take the Field in the Warfare of Writing, I duly considered not only my own Strength, but the Force of the Enemy. I am therefore well apprized of the Difficulties I have to encounter: I well know the present dreadful condition of the great Empire of Letters: the State of Anarchy that prevails among Writers: and the great Revolution which hath lately happened in the Kingdom of Criticism; that the Constitutions of Aristotle, Horace, Longinus, and Bossu, under which the State of Criticism so long flourished, have been entirely neglected, and the Government usurped by a Set of Fellows, entirely ignorant of all those Laws."

Later in this paper, he makes the admission, "but though some of the Enemy have been taken dabbling with these, I am well assured they are not likely to come to a perfect good Understanding with them."

telligent to rage or futile tears and whose gentility was as prudent as Pamela's own. The old ranting tragedy, like Thomson's *New Sophonisba,* so frequently provoked the audience to laughter, as Fielding points out in the *Preface* to *Tom Thumb,* that Fielding's remedy was to write *Tom Thumb,* or the *Tragedy of Tragedies,* whose plain intent was to provoke mirth.[2]

In the field of narrative fiction, the old heroic romances still persisted. The list which Addison gives of Leonora's library[3] (as early as 1711, of course) contains the high-minded *Clelie,* whose *Carte du Tendre* surveys the field of amorous encounter. Besides romances, there were numerous translations of the *Iliad,* the *Odyssey,* and the *Aeneid.* And the anti-romances, such as Scarron's *Roman Comique,* Le Sage's *Gil Blas,* Marivaux's *Le Paysan Parvenu,* Defoe's *Moll Flanders,* were likewise extremely popular.

The fact is that the best work in either the drama or in narrative fiction was being done by the satirists and writers of burlesque. And, of the satirists, Fielding, because of his political satires in his plays *Pasquin* and *The Historical Register,* was the best known and most hated. (Pope had, of course, greater prestige, but he was less in the thick of the fray than his younger rival and admirer, Fielding. And by 1742, Swift was already insane.)

Politically, England seemed a world of corruption, bribery, and stagnation. This was on the surface.[4] Opposed to this world, however, was the vigorous Liberal Whig party, now united with the Tories against Sir Robert Walpole, the "Great Man" of so many satiric attacks, and especially of Fielding's. Fielding had, by this time, got into trouble with the authorities and his theatre had been closed. His parody of the frigid tragedies in *Tom Thumb,* and his political attacks in *Pasquin*

[2]The preface to the printed edition of *Tom Thumb* is a parody of a Dutch commentator, Burmann, and of John Dennis. And the notes are as amusing burlesques of the pedantic sort of "editing" as can be found.

[3]*Spectator,* April 12, 1711.

[4]For an excellent discussion of the eighteenth century world, see Turberville's *English Men and Manners of the Eighteenth Century.*

and other plays had been the most lively events in the drama of the time, with the exception of Gay's *Beggar's Opera*. But they had earned him a multitude of enemies, who would be unlikely to see very much good in anything he might write.

The necessity of earning a living for himself and Charlotte and their children forced him, when the theater was closed to him, to turn elsewhere for a medium for his keen wit and clever pen. The result was *Joseph Andrews*, first of all a parody of *Pamela*, but, as time has proved, a great novel. *Joseph Andrews* came out anonymously in 1742. The author announced on the title page that it was written in the manner of Cervantes, and readers could easily see the spiritual kinship between the ridiculous and lovable Parson Adams and the equally ridiculous and lovable Don Quixote.

In the *Preface* to *Joseph Andrews*—it had a preface, of course!—Fielding gave an account of the sort of thing he was endeavoring to write. The main outlines of this theory are well-known, and form, indeed, one of our fundamental conceptions of the modern novel, or at least, such novels as are in the Fielding tradition. Later commentators on Fielding, recognizing the truth of his vigorous statement that he was doing a "kind of writing, which I do not remember to have seen hitherto attempted in our language", have not always seen how close the ideas of this preface are to the Renaissance tradition in criticism. Of course, *Joseph Andrews* was a parody of *Pamela*, and because of that fact one might wonder if Fielding was not also parodying his critical predecessors. But, to say that *Joseph Andrews* is a parody is to say but half a truth. It is, basically, a reply of one ethical concept to another. Furthermore, Fielding repeats his definition of the thing he is writing in *Tom Jones*, which was not a parody. So it seems likely that from the first, he meant his statements about the kind of writing in his *Preface to Joseph Andrews* to be taken seriously. He says, first:

"The Epic, as well as the Drama, is divided into tragedy and comedy. Homer, who was the father of this species of poetry, gave us a pattern of both these, though that of the latter kind is entirely lost; which Aristotle tells us, bore the same relation to comedy which his *Iliad* bears to tragedy. And perhaps, that we have no more instances of it among the writers of antiquity, is owing to the loss of this great pattern, which, had it survived, would have found its imitators equally with the other poems of this great original.

"And farther, as this poetry may be tragic or comic, I will not scruple to say it may be likewise either in verse or prose: for though it wants one particular, which the critic enumerates in the constituent parts of an epic poem, namely metre; yet, when any kind of writing contains all its other parts, such as fable, action, characters, sentiments, and diction, and is deficient in metre only; it seems, I think, reasonable to refer it to the epic, at least, as no critic hath thought proper to range it under any other head, or to assign it a particular name to itself."

The conception of the epic as divided, like the drama, into comedy and tragedy is to be found in Aristotle. "But Homer, who shared in both tendencies, was superior to the other poets of either class. As for his supremacy in the serious style, he stands alone, not only through the general excellence of his imitations, but through their dramatic quality as well; for he makes his personages live before us. So also was he superior in the comic vein, since he first marked out the general lines of Comedy, by rendering the ludicrous—and not personal satire—dramatic; *for his mock-heroic Margites stands in the same relation to Comedy as the Iliad and Odyssey to Tragedy.*"[5] This idea forms one of the fundamental concepts of the whole of Renaissance criticism. *The Battle of the Frogs and Mice,* long ascribed to Homer, was referred to as the traditional example of the comic poetic epic. James Ralph, who was associated with Fielding in his Grub Street days, was one translator of this work, so that Fielding had almost certainly had his attention called especially to it.

[5]Aristotle, *Poetics,* edited by Lane Cooper, pp. 11-12.

The comic epic was, then, a commonplace of critical theory. Congreve, for example, in the *Preface* to his prose narrative *Incognita*—which Fielding may or may not have read, the edition of Congreve in his library not containing this novel—defines his own novel in these terms:

"Romances are generally composed of the Constant Loves and invincible Courages of Hero's, Heroins, Kings and Queens, Mortals of the first Rank, and so forth; where lofty performances, elevate and surprize the Reader into a giddy Delight, which leaves him flat upon the Ground whenever he gives off, and vexes him to think how he has suffer'd himself to be pleased and transported, concern'd and afflicted at the several Passages which he has Read, viz. these Knights Success to their Damosels Misfortunes, and such like, when he is forced to be very well convinced that 'tis all a lye. Novels are of a more familiar natures; Come near us, and represent to us Intrigues in practice, delight us with Accidents and Odd Events, but not such as are wholly unusual or unpresidented, such which not being so distant from our Belief bring also the pleasure nearer us. Romances give more of Wonder, Novels more Delight. And with reverence be it spoken, and the Parallel kept at due distance, there is something of equality in the Proportion which they bear in reference to one another, with that between Comedy and Tragedy."

Incognita is not a novel in the modern sense, nor the comic prose epic of Fielding, but rather a Congrevian version of the *novella*. Still, this distinction which he makes between novel and romance serves to show how the ideas of Aristotle were applied.

Le Bossu, in his elaborate analysis of the epic, while he confines himself chiefly to the technique of the serious epic, nevertheless has something to say on the subject of the relation of comedy, tragedy and the epic to each other. In discussing the way in which the fable is made in comedy, he says: "Cette Fable est raisonnable & vrai-semblable; mais parce-que les noms

sont feints aussi-bien que les choses, & que l'action n'est que particuliere, & de familles communes; elle n'est ni Epique ni Tragique: Elle peut seulement être emploiée en une Comédie.   Aristote nous apprend que les Poëtes Comiques inventent & les
choses & les noms."[6]   The comic fable, according to this statement of Le Bossu, differs from the fable in tragedy or in the
epic, through having its names invented. Otherwise, the method
of making a comic fable is practically the same as that for making an epic fable. Later, in Chapter XIII of Book I, he elaborates the distinction: "En cette Doctrine, nous trouverons avec
Aristote trois sortes d'Actions que les Poëtes emploient.   Dans
la prémiere, les Choses & les Noms des Personnes sont singuliers & véritables, & non feints ou inventez par le Poëte.   Les
Satyriques en usent ainsi.   Dans la seconde, & Les Choses & les
Noms sont feints & inventez par le Poëte.   C'est le stile des
Comiques.   Nous en avons donné un exemple dans la Fable
que nous avons mise sous les Noms d'Oronte, de Pridament, &
de Clitandre.   Dans la troisieme espéce, les Choses sont inventées, mais les Noms ne le sont pas.   Ils sont connus par
l'Histoire, ou par quelque Tradition.   Cela se voit en la Fable
que nous avons mise sous les Noms de Robert d'Artois, &
de Raoul de Nesle.   On en peut dire autant de l'Iliade, de
l'Odyssée, & de l'Eneïde.   Cette troisieme espéce d'Action est
pour le Tragédie, & pour l'Epopée."[7]   All this says nothing, of
course, about the comic epic, but the differentation between the
"épopée", by which he refers to the serious epic, and comedy
does not deny Fielding's thesis.   And, finally, Le Bossu, in
Chapter XVI of Book I, ascribes the *Batrachomyomachia (The
Battle of the Frogs and Mice)* to Homer.   "Cet autre Auteur (a
hypothetical author) aura lû aussi plusieurs aventures attribuées
au Rat, qui ne sont point dans la Batrochomyomachie
d'Homère."[8]

[6]Le Bossu, *Traité du poëme Epique*, tom. I, p. 39.
[7]*Ibid.*, tom. I, p. 88.
[8]Le Bossu. *op. cit.*, tom. I, p. 109.

Another illustration of the interest of seventeenth and eighteenth century critics in the comic epic of antiquity is given in the comments of Martinus Scriblerus on the *Dunciad* (1729), where this statement is made:

"This poem, as it celebrateth the most grave and ancient of things, Chaos, Night, and Dulness; so is it of the most grave and ancient kind. Homer (saith Aristotle) was the first who gave the Form, and (saith Horace) who adapted the Measure, to heroic poesy. But, even before this, may be rationally presumed from what the Ancients have left written, was a piece by Homer composed, of like nature and matter with this of our poet. For of Epic sort it appeareth to have been, yet of matter surely not unpleasant, witness what is reported of it by the learned Archbishop Eustathius, in Odyss. X. And accordingly, Aristotle, in his *Poetic*, Chap. iv., doth further set forth, that as the *Iliad* and *Odyssey* gave example to Tragedy, so did this poem to Comedy its first idea.[9]

". . . And thus it doth appear, that the first *Dunciad* was the first Epic poem, written by Homer himself, and anterior even to the *Iliad* or *Odyssey*.

"Now, forasmuch as our poet had translated those two famous works of Homer which are yet left, he did conceive it in some sort his duty to imitate that also which was lost; and was therefore induced to bestow on it the same form which Homer's is reported to have had, namely that of Epic poem; with a title also framed after the ancient Greek manner, to wit, that of *Dunciad*."[10]

This is not written seriously, of course. Martin Scriblerus is pretending to prove that Homer wrote a *Dunciad* of which Pope's is an imitation. But it is obvious that the idea of the comic epic of Homer is something with which the writer knows his readers are well acquainted.

Other examples of the theory of the comic epic might be adduced, but with the quotation from Aristotle himself, it is

[9] He refers here to Aristotle on the comic epic, quoted above, p. 98.
[10] Pope, *Works*, vol. IV, p. 77.

sufficient merely to indicate that this was taken for gospel along with the rest of the *Poetics*. Most of the treatises upon the epic did not, to be sure, take the comic epic into account. Authors wished to write the serious epic. But the existence of the comic epic was pretty generally admitted. There were mock heroic poems in plenty, but Fielding's comic epic is *not* mock-heroic. This distinction is a corollary of the Aristotelian definition of serious and comic epic. The comic epic is the treatment of persons and deeds not of heroic proportions. The mock-heroic is an account of trivial deeds done in a burlesque of the heroic style.

So far as the *prose* epic is concerned, there is not the explicit sanction for it in Aristotle. Aristotle nowhere says that epics may be written in prose or in verse. In fact, inasmuch as his treatment is essentially empirical and verse was the medium of the epic he is discussing, he certainly speaks of the epic as the poetic—that is, the versified—epic. On the other hand, he makes it clear that verse is not the distinguishing element of the epic, but rather imitation and structure. Thus, versified history is *not* an epic, but history.

Renaissance commentators upon Aristotle, however, speedily assumed that the epic might be in prose.[11] The assumption was by no means universal, however. Most of the Italians assumed it, many of the French did, Sidney in England did, but there were dissenting voices. Huet, for example, in his *Lettre sur l'Origine des Romans* speaks of the *poetic* epic and of the *prose* romance, though his decision is not clearly against the conception of the prose epic. He makes the distinction between epic and romance on the basis of love as the characterizing quality of the romance and of military and political action as the essential quality of the epic, pointing out, of course, that there are poetic romances. "Ie ne parle donc point icy des Romans en Vers, & moins encore des Poëmes Epiques, qui outre qu'ils sont en Vers, ont encore des differences essentielles

[11] See discussion of this in Spingarn, *Literary Criticism in the Renaissance*, p. 31. *passim*.

qui les distinguent des Romans . . Enfin les Poëmes ont pour sujet une action militaire ou politique, & ne traittent l'amour que par occasion: Les Romans au contraire ont l'amour pour sujet principal, & ne traittent la politque & la guerre que par incident."[12]

On the whole, however, most of the weight of opinion was in favor of the idea that the epic might be written either in verse or in prose. Many of the heroic romances called themselves prose epics. [13] The passage from Le Bossu in which he says that the epic may be written in prose has already been noted. And, more important still, so far as Fielding is concerned, is the statement which Cervantes puts into the mouth of the canon in Chapter XLVII of the First Part of *Don Quixote,* that "epics may be as well writ in prose as in verse". This passage occurs in the discussion of the romances which Don Quixote's friends had burned and the few which they had spared. Cervantes is here repeating what was, as I had said, very frequently stated as a critical principle. And he observes in a great many ways the technical principles for constructing an epic—as these were then understood. He uses interpolated stories,[14] he describes the arming of the hero,[15] he gives us an elaborate discussion between Don Quixote and Sancho Panza about the matter of time taken for the adventures to prove that the unity of time has been observed. These technical principles for the epic were, however, held to be just as important for the romance as for the epic. (The line between epic and romance was not always clearly determined, and, in fact, constitutes one of the vital issues in Renaissance criticism. In any event, the later writers of romances applied the principles

---

[12]Huet, *Lettre à M. Segrais sur l'Origine des Romans,* prefixed to the romance *Zayde,* tom. I, p. 6.

[13]Roger Boyle, Earl of Orrery, in the *Preface* to his romance, *Parthenissa,* compares his work to Virgil. Ml'e. de Scudéry, in the *Preface* to *Ibrahim, ou l'Illustre Bassa,* quoted above, p. 44, compares her romance to an epic.

[14]The idea of the interpolated story in the extended narrative to fill up pauses of action is very old, and appears both in epic and romance.

[15]The arming of the hero is an event of major importance in the romance as in the epic, of course.

of construction for the epic to their own work.)[16] Cervantes, therefore, need not necessarily have considered his book a comic prose epic, except insofar as he obviously considered it the opposite of a romance. It was an anti-romance in that it poked fun at most of the romances. But Cervantes was not wholly opposed to the romances. Some of the romances escaped the fire to which Don Quixote's library was consigned, and there are romantic elements in the stories of the Don himself, such, for example, as the episode of the Cave of Montesinos in the Second Part. And, indeed, Don Quixote's character itself is the final justification of the romantic attitude.

That Fielding had *Don Quixote* in mind in writing Joseph *Andrews* can not be doubted. He says explicitly that it is written in imitation of Cervantes; and Parson Adams is obviously the English brother of the Spanish Don. Moreover, both are tales of adventures along the road, with this difference, however: Don Quixote is out in search of romantic adventure, whereas Parson Adams, Joseph, and Fanny are going about the sensible business of getting home. In a sense, then, Parson Adams is comparable to Odysseus in a way that Don Quixote is not; in fact, Don Quixote is a hero of the "heroic" romance, and is closer to Orlando than to Odysseus. On the one hand, both Odysseus and the parson are respectable married men going home to their wives, whereas Orlando and Don Quixote are two romantic gallants following incredible adventures for the greater glory of their ladies fair.[17]

When Fielding first published *Joseph Andrews,* I do not think he had in mind the distinction between romance and epic

---

[16]Tasso's theory of the romantic epic accounts for some of the confusion. And, then, they have much in common. But the epic is an account *of this world*, matter-of-fact, even though heroic. There were "romanesque" qualities in the epic, as even the neo-classicist, Le Bossu, recognized. (tom. II, p. 166). "Or les Episodes de Circé, des Sirénes, de Polyphême, & semblables, sont nécessaire à l'Action de l'Odyssée, & néanmoins elles ne sont pas humainement Vrai-semblables. Homère les fait adroitement r'enterer dans la Vrai-semblance humaine, par la simplicité de ceux devant qui il fait faire ces récits fabuleux. Il dit assez plaisamment, que les Phéaques habitoient dans une Isle éloignée des lieux ou demeurement les hommes qui ont de l'esprit. Ulysses les avoit connus avant que de se faire connoître à eux; & aïant observé qu'ils avoient toutes les qualitez de ces fainéans qui n'admirent rien avec plus de plaisir que les aventures Romanesques; il les satisfait par ces récits accommodez à leur humeur".

[17]This difference between Parson Adams and Don Quixote is a very great one. Parson Adams is entirely a part of this everyday world. Don Quixote is riding away from it out into the world of his dreams.

just suggested. He says, in fact, in his preface: "Now, a comic romance is a comic epic poem in prose; differing from comedy, as the serious epic from tragedy." He thus does not make a distinction between the comic romance and the comic epic. He opposes his comic prose epic to the heroic romances and to the serious epic.

"Thus the Telemachus of the archbishop of Cambray appears to me of the epic kind, as well as the Odyssey of Homer;[18] indeed, it is much fairer and more reasonable to give it a name common with that species from which it differs only in a single instance, than to confound it with those which it resembles in no other. Such as those voluminous works, commonly called Romances, namely, Clelia, Cleopatra, Astrea, Cassandra, the Grand Cyrus, and innumerable others, which contain, as I apprehend, very little instruction or entertainment."[19]

He is here arguing in behalf of the epic in prose. But his argument is not complete. He should have said that there are serious epics and comic epics, serious romances and comic romances, all of them in prose or in verse. That he did not seems to show that he had not clearly formulated his theory as yet, and had not differentiated the anti-romance and the comic prose epic. But, at this stage, he seems to have had Cervantes chiefly in mind and to have conceived of his own novel in terms of *Don Quixote*. I do not wish to be understood in all I have here said as implying any less of reality (in the deepest sense) in Cervantes than in Fielding. In fact, *Don Quixote* is much more profoundly true than *Joseph Andrews*. But, whereas *Joseph Andrews*, and, later, *Tom Jones*, definitely are of this world as much as the *Odyssey* was, *Don Quixote* had been created by a new and more profound philosophical treatment of the old materials of the romance and is not quite of this world.

Fielding thus defined *Joseph Andrews* as a prose epic in

[18]See Ramsays', *Preface to Télémaque*. The edition of *Télémaque* in Fielding's library contained this *Preface*, which, as I have pointed out, is based on Le Bossu.

[19]It would be interesting to know whether Fielding identified Richardson's *Pamela* with such works as *Clélie*, with which, in its preoccupation with the point of honor, it has much in common.

terms which were pretty generally accepted as part of epic theory. But what is even more interesting is the evidence that he sought to apply the principles of epic structure to his novel. The only extended treatise on the epic in Fielding's library was Le Bossu's, but the edition which he owned was that of 1742. Whether Fielding had read Le Bossu before he purchased this edition one cannot say. I have not been able to find any explicit references to the work in Fielding's writings before this time, though *Tom Jones* (1749), and The *Covent Garden Journal* (1752), both have a number of references. The chances are that he knew pretty well what was in the book at least, for practically no author discussed the subject of the epic without referring to Le Bossu. The discussion of prose as a medium for the epic might have come from almost any commentator on Aristotle, or, of course, Aristotle himself. But the analysis of epic structure in the quotation from the *Preface to Joseph Andrews*, already quoted: "For though it wants one particular, which the critic enumerates in the constituent parts of an epic poem, namely metre; yet, when any kind of writing contains all its other parts, such as fable, action, characters, sentiments, and diction," etc., is too close to that of Le Bossu to be entirely accidental. Compare this with the divisions in Le Bossu, whose first book discusses the fable; the second, the action; the third, the narration (really an elaboration of the action); the fourth, manners (but "manners" involved characterization in criticism of this time); the fifth, machines (Fielding throughout his criticism abandons the use of machines, though he says he uses the marvellous, in the comic prose epic); the sixth, sentiments and expression.

The prefatory chapter of Book I of *Joseph Andrews* continues the analysis of the epic in the traditional terms of epic criticism. The first statement runs:

"It is a trite but true observation, that examples work more forcibly on the mind than precepts:[20] and if this be just in

[20]There was at this time almost no discussion, either of the epic in particular or of poetry in general, which does not state, or imply, the idea that it is the function of

what is odious and blameable, it is more strongly so in what is amiable and praiseworthy . . . A good man therefore is a standing lesson to all his acquaintances, and of far greater use in that narrow circle than a good book.

"But as it often happens that the best men are but little known, and consequently cannot extend the usefulness of their examples a great way; the writer may be called in aid to spread their history farther, and to present the amiable pictures to those who have not the happiness of knowing the originals."

Here we have Fielding's statement of the moral purpose of art, a thesis which is not in Aristotle, but has full classical authority, of course. In Renaissance criticism, the thesis derives its authority chiefly from Horace's dictum, "aut prodesse volunt aut dilectare poetae". In this particular chapter, Fielding certainly goes on to ridicule the special kind of virtue in the biographies he is parodying, those of Colley Cibber and of Pamela, but that he held the didactic theory is certain from everything he wrote, and especially from his repudiation of Rabelais and Aristophanes, for instance, as using the spirit of laughter for immoral ends.[21]

In *Joseph Andrews*, Fielding sketched in the outlines of his theory of the new literary genre which he was creating. He elaborated this in *Tom Jones*. In *Joseph Andrews*, Fielding pays less attention to plot structure than he later does in *Tom Jones*, where the plot is very closely knit. The adventures of Joseph and Fanny and Parson Adams are frequently not related to the central theme of the story very closely,[22] although, even in this early work, Fielding shows a greater interest in binding the episodes together than Cervantes had in *Don Quixote*, where the episodes are for the most part not bound to-

literature to teach by example. This idea is not in Aristotle, though he thinks art should, in its final effect, be moral. The idea of teaching by example is mediaeval. reenforced by Horace, Seneca (longum iter per praecepta, breve per exempla), and various others. But see the Prefaces to *Gondibert* and to *Prince Arthur*, Le Bossu's *Traité du Poëme Epique*, Ramsay's *Preface* to *Télémaque*.

[21]*Covent Garden Journal*, No. 10, February 4, 1752.

[22]Parson Trulliber, for instance, plays a brief part. And the battle with the hounds is simply an incident, not, as in Molly's battle in *Tom Jones*, closely knit to the narrative as a whole.

gether at all except by the unity of having the same hero. Still, Fielding had his artistic pattern in mind, even here, although he had not fully worked it out. Other stories of wandering and adventure— *Robinson Crusoe, Gulliver's Travels,* even *Don Quixote*—had justified their claims to being taken for accounts of actual facts by announcing that they were based on journals, or upon well-known biographies. Fielding deliberately manipulates his plot himself. And the central plot does determine a very great many of the incidents. Thus, if Joseph had not been with Lady Booby, he would not have set out. If he had not incurred Lady Booby's displeasure, he would not have had certain difficulties at the end. Lady Booby and Mrs. Slipslop and the complications brought about by their pursuit of Joseph govern many of the minor episodes of the book. Aristotle had reduced the plot of the *Odyssey* to a very simple struggle. A man, having incurred the displeasure of Poseidon, has great hardships in getting home to his demoralized land. Similarly, *Joseph Andrews* might be reduced to such a skeleton plot. A man, having incurred the displeasure of a lady, his superior in rank and power, tries to go home, meets with many misfortunes on the way, and at last arrives home, only to find, before he is happily brought out of his difficulties, that the lady and her relations try to thwart his efforts. Now, *Don Quixote* does not have such a plot. There is no single thwarting force in the whole narrative. Nor do other prose narratives of the comic sort such as *Gil Blas* or *Le Roman Comique* have such unity. All of Joseph Andrews' adventures have an end in view, as have Ulysses', and this struggle of a man against adverse circumstances which prevent him from achieving his purpose constitutes the principle of coherence in the story.

In still other ways does *Joseph Andrews* follow the principles of epic structure as Fielding knew them. There is, for instance, the famous battle between Joseph and Parson Adams on the one side, and the hounds on the other. The battle is described in terms of broad comedy, but with the form of a serious conflict in which our sympathies are engaged. At one point, Parson Adams flees. Here Fielding says: "If there be any modern so outrageously brave that he cannot admit of flight in any circumstance whatever, I say (but I whisper that softly, and I solemnly declare without any intention of giving offence to any brave man in the nation), I say, or rather I whisper, that he is an ignorant fellow, and hath never read Homer nor Virgil, nor knows he anything of Hector or Turnus." In other words, he virtually states that he has adapted a great scene from the *Iliad* and from the *Aeneid* to the purposes of his comic epic. The interesting thing, of course, is that though it is clear enough that he has the epic formula in mind, he has so completely mastered the material that the form is but the perfect way of revealing the material, and one is scarcely aware of the formula.

Another place in which he uses a traditional epic formula is in the interpolation of irrelevant tales, such as that of the story of Leonora. This was a practice followed by every narrator of the time. The authors of the picaresque tales made frequent use of the device. Cervantes uses the interpolated tale very often. The heroic romance seems at times to be built upon a pattern of maximum interpolation in a minimum of action. But the practice is of great antiquity. One of the most beautiful portions of Apuleius is the interpolated tale of Cupid and Psyche. And, finally, it is the practice of the epic. Ulysses, at the court of King Alcinous, hears the tale of Ilium, tells his own story, hears other great tales about gods and men. The spirit of Homeric interpolations is slightly different from that of later authors. The story of Leonora in *Joseph Andrews* has almost nothing in keeping with the central conflict of the whole novel, whereas the tales of great deeds and heroes in the *Odyssey* have much to do with Ulysses, the tale of the fall of Troy indeed bringing forth Ulysses' own story, and all of them being cast into the spirit of the naive and heroic world of the central theme. Whenever Fielding uses this device again, as in Mr. Wilson's story or, in *Tom Jones,* in the story of the Man of the Hill, he works them into the pattern of his central story by making them have an ethical bearing upon the problem of the hero's own life.

In making use of the interpolated tale, therefore, Fielding is using a device common to all narratives of the time, but in doing so, he had the sanction of epic usage and so may be said to have followed the epic tradition, a tradition, indeed, which has the sanction of the use of such tales in all extended narratives.

Finally, Fielding uses the formula of Discovery as outlined by Aristotle and made much of in the work of epic theorists. "A Discovery", says Aristotle, "as the word itself implies, is a transition from ignorance to knowledge, and hence a passing into love or hate on the part of those agents who are marked for happiness or misfortune."[23]   He then elaborates the various kinds of discovery, and subsequently, discusses the kind of discovery used in the scene of Ulysses in his bath.   In the scene in which the mystery of Joseph's and Fanny's parentage is being straightened out, Fielding makes use of this sort of discovery, Joseph being recognized as the child of Mr. Wilson by the strawberry mark which he bears on his chest.   At this point in the story Fielding refers specifically to Oedipus under similar circumstances.   "They felt, perhaps, little less anxiety in this interval than Oedipus himself, whilst his fate was revealing." The author obviously has the Greek sources of this practice clearly in mind when he makes use of a very old device for bringing about a reversal of fortune.

These are perhaps minor points.   The really important thing for Fielding's conception of the comic prose epic is that he managed to give an epic sweep to the material of his own age, to combine modern material with the form of the Greek epic.   But the study of these small details is interesting as revealing that Fielding had studied the whole problem, and was consciously following the "rules".   We are not conscious of the rules, as we are in the work of the French writers of epics

[23]Aristotle, *Poetics*, edited by Lane Cooper, p. 36.

of the seventeenth century. But this arises from the fact that Fielding is an artist. The formal principles give unity to his materials without our being aware of them. Here is the art which conceals art, but it is the art of a conscious artist.

CHAPTER VII.

DEVELOPMENT OF PRINCIPLES OF EPIC STRUCTURE
TOM JONES

By the time that *Tom Jones* appeared in 1749, Fielding had assuredly read Le Bossu. For one thing, he refers explicitly to Le Bossu in the prefatory chapter of Book XI. "For I can never be understood, unless by the very persons here meant, to insinuate that there are no proper judges of writing, or to endeavor to exclude from the commonwealth of literature any of those noble critics to whose labours the learned world are so greatly indebted. Such were Aristotle, Horace, and Longinus, among the ancients, Dacier[1] and Bossu among the French. and some perhaps among us; who have certainly been duly authorized to execute at least a judicial authority in *foro literario*." When Fielding refers thus explicitly to some author, it may generally be taken for granted, I think, that he has read that author, for Fielding is very frank about himself, and being a wide reader, would have no reason for referring to authors whom he has not read. Furthermore, the internal evidence of *Tom Jones* bears this out.

The definition of his novel as the comic prose epic already made in *Joseph Andrews* is implied throughout the critical discussions of *Tom Jones*. The only place where he refers definitely to it is in the prefactory chapter of Book V. Here he says: "For this our determination we do not hold ourselves strictly bound to assign any reason;[2] it being abundantly sufficient that we have laid it down as a rule necessary to be observed in all

[1]He may refer here either to M. Dacier, who wrote a treatise on satire, or to Mme. Dacier, who translated Homer, with a preface on the epic.

[2]That is, to write prefaces for each book. He does not have these prefaces in *Amelia*. Does this mean that he did not consider *Amelia* a comic prose epic? Or was he simply sure by then that he had established his critical principles?

prosai-comic-epic writing." The determination to which he refers is that of writing the critical prefaces to each book. The
point is of relatively little importance, but one wonders if this
necessary rule was got from the universal custom in Fielding's
time of writing prefaces to all epics, original or translations,
serious or mock-epic.

Although he thus lays down this rule for his comic prose
epic, he sets very definite limits to the critic's rôle. Critics,
he says, are clerks whose office it is to transcribe the rules
which the masters of a science have determined. But, unfortunately, the clerks have invaded the prerogatives of the masters,
and have attempted themselves to legislate. "Hence arose an
obvious, and perhaps an unavoidable error; for these critics
being men of shallow capacities, very easily mistook mere form
for substance. They acted as a judge would, who should ad-
here to the lifeless letter of the law, and reject the spirit.
Little circumstances, which were perhaps accidental in a great
author, were by these critics considered to constitute his chief
merit, and transmitted as essentials to be observed by all of
his successors."[3]

That Le Bossu was not, in the opinion of Fielding, one of
the critics who had encroached upon the domain of the masters
of the art of writing, we have his explicit statement for, in the
passage from Chapter I of Book XI, cited above. It is, indeed,
evident in *Tom Jones* that Fielding had studied Le Bossu with
especial care. Le Bossu was, as I have said, valuable not for
his theories about the nature of the epic, but for his analysis of
the technique and structure of the epic.[4] He analyzes the fable,

[3]This criticism of the critical opinions of men of shallow capacities—that is, that
they mistook form for substance—is very like later criticism of the whole body of
criticism of the period. The fact that Fielding makes an exception of Le Bossu should
have some weight in our estimate of the French critic, even when he seems absurd.
Fielding saw clearly the absurdity of the criticism written by little men. That he
finds Le Bossu worthy a place beside Aristotle shows that Le Bossu had something to
offer to the men of that age at least. One cannot dismiss altogether a man highly
esteemed by a great creative artist—as does M. Duchesne, for instance, (see pp. 269,
seq. of his *Histoire du Poeme Epique*) when he says of Le Bossu: "Telles sont les
visions bizarres, qui en 1675, succédèrent aux théories parfois erronées, mais sensées
et généreuses, de 1650."

[4]Thus, one thing which M. Duchesne finds absurd is Le Bossu's reducing the story
of the *Iliad* to a fable comparable to a fable from Aesop. This may be absurd from
the point of view of the reader, who is interested in the effect, but it might be useful

the action, the characters, etc. His section on machines is much the smallest of his six books, taking up only forty-four pages, whereas the length of the other books ranges from sixty-nine to one hundred and forty-eight pages. Thus his interest in what was for neo-classical critics the most difficult aspect of the primitive epic, the supernatural, was not marked. The real center of interest in Le Bossu is in the structural principles for extensive narratives.

The unities had been so universally accepted for the drama in Renaissance criticism that critics decided the epic must have unities as well.[5] Unity of action the epic obviously has, and unity of action Aristotle stressed in his discussion of the epic. But he says, of course, nothing about unity of time or unity of place. Renaissance critics worried over this problem for years without arriving at unanimity, but there was a substantial body of criticism which set the space of a year for the duration of the epic action. Le Bossu does not dogmatize on the subject. He studies the three epics from which he is endeavoring to elaborate his principles—that is, the *Iliad*, the *Odyssey*, and the *Aeneid*. He would obviously like to get the epic action into one year, for he has an elaborate discussion of equinoctial storms to prove that the *Aeneid might* be brought within a year. But he is willing to admit that one cannot be dogmatic about it.

"Je me suis insensiblement trouvé engagé en l'éxamen de cette question particuliere. [He refers to the duration of the epic narrative.] Je l'ai trouvée beaucoup plus ample que je ne me l'étois imaginé; & j'en ait fait un assez gros traité, où l'on pourra voir plusieurs choses qui me semblent pas inutiles pour l'intelligence de l'Enéïde. J'y propose la question du temps d'une mainere problematique & je laisse volontiers aux autres, à croire & à décider ce qui leur plaira."[6]

He believes that it was the practice of Homer to confine his epic action to a short time, certainly no more than a year.

to a writer who wants to learn how to have many episodes without destroying the unity of the central pattern.

[5]See Springarn, *Literary Criticism of the Renaissance*, p. 206 seq. for a discussion of unity of time in the epic.

[6]Le Bossu, *op. cit.*, tom. I, p. 387.

The action of the *Odyssey*, as Le Bossu reckons it, is fifty-eight days, that of the *Iliad* forty-seven days. The practice of Virgil is less clear, but he believes, as I have said, that the action of the *Aeneid* may be comprised within a year.[7] A great deal of antecedent material is, of course, worked into these narratives, but Le Bossu shows how the authors managed to give the whole background of antecedent material in the course of the action.

This analysis is certainly no more formal than—let us say— an analysis of the practice of representative novelists which we might make today in order to determine some principles of narrative technique. It is interesting to note how Fielding calls attention to the time consumed by the main action of *Tom Jones*. The titles of the chapters of *Joseph Andrews* had followed the manner of Cervantes, the titles being slightly ironical and gracefully secretive. The chapter headings in *Tom Jones* give us more information about their contents than do those in the earlier novel. And the descriptions of the books contained in the analytical titles call explicit attention to the time.

Book One contains "as much of the birth of the foundling as is necessary . . . to acquaint the reader . . ." Books Two and Three summarize events until Tom is arrived at the age of seventeen. Book Four is described as "containing a year"; Book Five, as "containing a portion of time somewhat longer than half a year"; Book Six, three weeks, etc. In other words, once the antecedent material is given in the first four books, the action is made to come well within a year. While this does not follow the rule about limiting the action to one year and work- ing in the antecedent material in the course of the action, it nevertheless does announce quite definitely the fact that once the stage is set, the principle of duration of epic action is strictly observed.

There are several points to be noted here. The action of the novel is unified far more organically than simply by bringing the major action within certain time limits. This is more important than unity of time. For one thing, this dramatic structure is

[7] Le Bossu, *op. cit.*, tom. I, liv. iii, ch. xii.

the one kind of unity which Aristotle had emphasized. In discussing the structure of the epic as a whole, Le Bossu follows Aristotle, when he says:

"Dans l'idée que j'en ai conceuë par la lecture de nos Auteurs, je croirois que trois choses y sont nécessaires. La prémiere est, de n'emploier aucun Episode qui ne soit tiré du plan & du fond de L'Action, & qui ne soit un membre naturel de ce corps. La seconde est, de bien lier ces Episodes, & ces membres les uns avec les autres. Et la troisieme, de n'achever aucun Episode, de telle sorte qu'il puisse paroître une Action entiere; mais de laisser toûjours voir chacun en particulier dans sa nature de membre d'un corps, & de partie non achevée."[8]

These principles are fundamental in the structure of *Tom Jones*. One example will suffice to illustrate what I mean. Jenny Jones is supposed to be the mother of Tom, and is sent away from Squire Allworthy's. Had Fielding not had the structure of the epic as expounded by Le Bossu—or, for that matter, as practiced by Homer—clearly in mind, he would have let her drop out of the story. But she reappears, though we do not at first know that she has reappeared, as Mrs. Waters, one of Tom's inamoratas. When he discovers, later in the story, that Mrs. Waters is Jenny Jones, Tom is led to think that he has committed incest. And finally, Mrs. Waters unravels the mystery of Tom's birth. Thus, what might have been treated as a series of unrelated amatory episodes becomes one thread of a closely-knit plot, each episode drawn from one preceding it and bringing about another complication and finally the unravelling.[9]

Here is another point wherein Fielding's conception of his work as epic is clearly differentiated from the work of those predecessors and contemporaries with whom he has so often been compared. No episode in *Don Quixote* necessarily leads into another episode. In fact, much of the action is a series of unrelated events, bound together by the unity of the hero—not, as Aristotle and his commentators all agree, sufficient to consti-

---

[8] Le Bossu, op. cit., tom. I, p. 171.

[9] Other examples are to be found in the parts played by Mr. Dowling, by Mrs. Fitzpatrick, by Black George, by Partridge himself.

tute unity of action.   The unity of *Don Quixote,*—for it has unity—lies in its underlying cosmic irony, not in its structure. The episodes in such anti-romances as *Le Roman Comique,* or *Gil Blas,* or *Le Roman Bourgeois* of Furetière, are even more unrelated to each other than those of *Don Quixote.   Tom Jones* is, in this respect, an entirely different kind of narrative.   It is a unified piece of action, not a chronicle.   *Joseph Andrews* had followed the epic principles, on the whole, superficially.   It is an Odyssey of the road, a very superior one, to be sure, but still in part a series of disconnected events, bound together more closely than other such Odysseys of the road by the sense of purpose behind the events—the efforts of the three involuntary adventurers to get home.   But the persons, other than Joseph, Fanny, and Parson Adams, who take part in one adventure need not necessarily turn up in another to offer some further complication of plot, or to unravel some knot already sufficiently complicated.   Some of the adventures exist entirely independently of the others.

This is not true of *Tom Jones,* whose incidents are worked into a complex and neatly articulated plot.   Part of this structural sense in plot, Fielding undoubtedly got from his dramatic technique.[10]   *Joseph Andrews,* with its four books, has something of the quality of a play.   And the neatness of complication of unravelling in *Tom Jones* smacks a bit of the well-made play of that period, especially in the end where all sorts of persons are rushed forward to bring about a happy denouement.[11] It is not for nothing that Coleridge classed the plot of *Tom Jones* with the plots of the two plays, *Oedipus* and *The Alchemist,* as being perfect plots.   Even allowing for the influence of his experience in writing plays, however, it seems obvious that between the time of writing *Joseph Andrews* and that

[10]Mr. Cross, in his *Life of Fielding,* and M. Digeon, in his *Novels of Fielding,* make much of the influence of Fielding's dramatic technique upon the structure of the novels.

[11]It may be urged that the action at the end is so swift as to give the impression that the author has done what he elsewhere (see his preface to Book VIII of *Tom Jones*) condemns—hastily changed his rogue into a good man at the very end.   But this change in Tom has always been a possibility and his ultimate mastery of his impulses has been throughout suggested.

of *Tom Jones*, Fielding made a serious study of epic structure. Aristotle and Le Bossu both emphasize the dramatic structure.

To come back from unity of action, then, to unity of time—although I have compared it to the *Odyssey*, *Tom Jones* differs from the *Odyssey* in one very important way. The *Odyssey*, as Le Bossu had pointed out, although it covers an action of many years, actually, in the telling, is reduced to a space of forty-eight days. All of the ten years of wandering up to the time when the narrative of the *Odyssey* opens is told to the reader in Ulysses' account of his experiences, and in the information given Telemachus in the first four books. *Tom Jones*, on the other hand, is the tale of a young man from birth until he is settled in life. In this way, it resembles such a book as *Gil Blas*, which also starts with the birth of the hero and ends with his settling down. *Tom Jones*, then, is like *Gil Blas*, in that it is the history of a youth from birth to maturity, whereas the *Odyssey* is the account of the difficulties a mature man has in getting home from war. *Joseph Andrews* is closer to the *Odyssey* here than is *Tom Jones*.

It may be felt that Fielding has here abandoned epic structure for a chronicle. There can be no doubt, that Fielding's conception of his novel was, in part, influenced by the sort of thing which was done in various tales of the picaresque sort, of which *Gil Blas* is the most nearly similar. The amount of space devoted to the hero's childhood is very short in *Gil Blas*,—one chapter—and comparatively long in *Tom Jones*—the first three books. In this way, the narrative of *Tom Jones* is even more extended than that of *Gil Blas*. The similarity of these two tales is, however, not so great as at first appears. Fielding has made one major change in the form—he has made his plot dramatic by connecting the incidents. Fielding takes the central situation of such a novel as *Gil Blas*—that is, he places a young man in the world and has him drawn down by certain forces, lifted by others—and brings all these forces to a focus, so that all of the incidents work toward a central dramatic point, and so develops his conflict. But in saying that this is what Fielding has done, one must consider what change in kind of narrative this dramatic concentration effects. Concentration of plot is precisely what Fielding—and other critics—held was the difference between the epic structure and simple chronological narrative. This is the distinction as made by Aristotle, who says:

"In the Epic, as in Tragedy, the story should be constructed on dramatic principles: everything should turn about a single action, one that is a whole, and is organically perfect—having a beginning, and a middle, and an end . . . . Putting the thing negatively, we may say that the plot of an Epic must be unlike what we commonly find in histories, which of necessity represent, not a single action, but some one period, with all that happened therein to one or more persons, however unrelated the several occurences may have been. For example: The Battle of Salamis took place at the same time as the defeat of the Carthaginians in Sicily: but the two events did not converge to the same end. And similarly, one event may immediately follow another in point of time, and yet there may be no sequence leading to one issue. Nevertheless, one may venture to say, most of the epic poets commit this very fault of making their plots like chronicles."[12]

The difference between Homer and Statius, says Le Bossu, is that Statius has written a chronicle, and Homer a narrative with a plot. The difference betwcen *Gil Blas,* or *Lazarillo de Tormes,* or *Le Roman Comique,* and Fielding's novels is that the former are chronicles and the latter have a dramatic plot. *Tom Jones* does indeed open with the birth and childhood of the hero, but there is not a single incident of any importance in even these first three books, which does not bear upon the central plot. Molly Seagrim is not merely an amorous episode. Through her Tom is kept from Sophia, is brought into disgrace in the eyes of Mr. Allworthy, gets involved in the affairs of Black George's family. But, one may say that had Fielding followed the practice of Homer exactly, he would have introduced

[12]Aristotle, *Poetics,* p. 77.

these early years as antecedent material in the course of the narrative.

There may be several reasons why he does not do this. For one thing, the theory of unity of time for the epic was not universally held by Renaissance critics. Le Bossu thinks that Homer and Virgil limited their action to a period within a year, but he is not dogmatic about the necessity that the time covered by the narrative proper should be confined to a year. Thus, according to Le Bossu, though Homer and Virgil had confined their direct action within a year, it might be possible to extend the time and still keep the structure. There is an even more important reason, however. Virgil and Homer were writing about persons and events well-known to their audiences, and hence could speak of Achilles or of Ulysses, or of Aeneas without having to tell us who they are. But the heroes of the comic prose epic have fictitious names and are not widely known. Hence if one starts telling about a young man named Tom Jones, who is found on the road leading from the West of England to London, one must tell who Tom Jones is, and how he happened to be there. Once Fielding has told us who his hero is and what is the transaction in which his fortunes are involved, he starts the narrative in which the conflict of forces for and against the hero is concentrated, and develops this within a single year. Nor does he altogether depart in this from the technique of the *Odyssey,* where, before the main action is started, the first four books give an account of the Council of the Gods and of Telemachus' attempts to find out what has become of his father, all of which gives us most of our necessary antecedent material, to be supplemented later by Ulysses' own account of his wanderings. In other words, to go back to Aristotle's distinctions— whither Fielding went—*Gil Blas* is a *Little Iliad,*[13] or, if there

---

[13]Aristotle, *Poetics,* p. 78. "In precisely this respect, therefore, Homer, as we have already said (p. 30), manifestly transcends the other epic poets. Far from taking all the legend of Ilium for his theme, he did not attempt to deal even with the War in its entirety, although this had a definite beginning and end. Very likely he thought that the story would be too long to be easily grasped as a whole—or, if it were not too long, that it would be too complicated from the variety of the incidents. As it is, he has selected a single phase of the war for his main action, and employs a number of the other incidents by way of episode; for example, he diversifies his narrative with the *Catalogue of the Ships,* and so forth. Of the other epic poets, some take for their subject all

had been such, a *Little Odyssey,* whereas *Tom Jones* is a Homeric *Odyssey.* With certain modifications, necessary for informing the reader about the situation, Fielding observes the principle of unity of time in the main action of his story, and not only observes it, but, by his chapter headings, calls attention to the fact that he is doing so.

Another principle of epic construction which seems to have interested him has to do with the outcome of the action. Here again he follows Aristotle and his Renaissance interpreters. In contrast with the action of most tragedies, the action of even a serious epic should end favorably. Not only does Fielding observe this principle in his own novels, but it is said that he did not think that *Clarissa* should have had a tragic outcome. In a letter of November 7th, 1748, written by Richardson to Aaron Hill, Richardson says, plaintively: "These will show you, Sir, that I intend more than a novel or romance by this piece; and that it is of the tragic kind. In short, that I thought my principal characters could not be rewarded by any happiness short of the heavenly. But how have I suffered by this from the cavils of some, from the prayers of others, from the entreaties of many more, to make what is called a happy ending, Mr. Lyttleton, the late Mr. Thomson, Mr. Gibbes, and Mr. Fielding have been among these."[14]

M. Digeon, in commenting upon this letter, says that he wishes we might know what were the arguments Fielding used. It is a wish we all can echo. Did they consist in pointing out that there was really no reason, inasmuch as both Clarissa and Lovelace ultimately came to desire it, why those two self-analysts should not marry? Or, did he base his arguments upon some theory about the kind of ending an epic should have?

the deeds of one hero; others all the events in one period; and others a single action, but one with a multiplicity of parts. This last is what was done by the author of the *Cypria,* and by the author of the *Little Iliad.* The consequence is that the *Iliad* and the *Odyssey* each furnished materials for but a single tragedy, or at most for two; while the *Cypria* supplies subjects for a number; and the *Little Iliad* for eight or more: an *Award of the Arms,* a *Philoctetes,* a *Neoptolemus,* a *Eurypylus,* a *Mendicant Odysseus,* a *Spartan Women,* a *Sack of Ilium,* a *Sailing of the Fleet*—one might add a *Sinon* and a *Trojan Women.*"

[14]Quoted in Digeon, *Novels of Fielding,* p 131.

M. Digeon seems to imply that he guesses it is the latter. I am not sure, for Fielding obviously did not think that Richardson's novels were epics, and hence the rules of epics need not apply to Clarissa. It is, nevertheless, interesting to consider the problem. Here is what Le Bossu has to say on the subject of the fortunate outcome to the epic:

"Aprés avoir vû ce que c'est que l'Achévement de l'Action, & quand il le faut faire; il reste encore une troisieme question: c'est de savoir si l'Achévement doit laisser le Héros dans une tranquilité heureuse; ou s'il est libre de laisser malheureux.

"Nos poëtes ne nous one point donné d'exemples d'un Héros qui demeure misérable, & qui succombe. Les fins tristes sont bonnes pour la Tragédie. Elles y étoient beaucoup mieux receuës autre-fois, qu'elles ne le sont aujourd'hui: parce-que dans les Etats Populaires des Grecs, où la Monarchie étoit odieuse, on n'écoutoit rien avec plus de plaisir, & avec plus d'avidité que les malheurs des Rois. Aristote avoit encore une autre raison de préférer cette catastrophe à une plus heureuse. La Scéne Tragique est le trône des passions; la terreur & la pitié y doivent regner entre toutes les autres. Or ces deux passions naissent avec plus de facilité des tristes évenemens: . . . .

"Mais ces raisons ne sont pas pour l'Epopée, puisqu-elle est moins pour purger les passions que pour faire quitter les mauvaises habitudes, & pour en faire prendre de bonnes."[15]

So far as one can judge from Fielding's practice, he subscribed to this doctrine, but, in making this statement, one has to remember that Fielding, in his dramatic compositions, was always interested in comedy, and hence, the happy ending. Therefore, his practice in his novels may arise solely from the fact that he was not interested in depicting tragic passions. I doubt, however, if this is the whole truth. The dedication of *Tom Jones* to Lord Lyttleton sounds more like a statement for the comic prose epic as designed to "make men quit their evil habits" than a mere accidental happy ending. This may certainly be further confirmed from the conclusion to *Tom Jones.*

[15]Le Bossu, *op. cit.*, tom I, pp. 260-262.

In the first chapter of Book XVII—the next to the last book—Fielding points out that Tom's situation is undoubtedly very complicated and that the outcome may be either happy or unhappy. In thus calling attention to the situation, Fielding seems to wish the reader to observe that the ending is at last happy.

He grants that the bringing about of a happy ending is not the easiest thing in the world. "In this", he says, "the antients had a great advantage over the moderns. Their mythology, which was at that time more firmly believed by the vulgar than any religion is at present, gave them always an opportunity of delivering a favourite hero".[16] In spite of all difficulties, however, Fielding brings about this happy ending—and with considerable versimilitude, although the action is so swift at the end that the outcome seems at first less convincing than other sections of the novel. But it is prepared for by innumerable hints, episodes, suggestions of moral purpose, and so on, throughout the whole novel. And already in the preface to Book VIII, where Fielding is discussing the marvellous, he has suggested his principle in this matter.

"Our modern authors of comedy" he announces, in that book, "have fallen almost universally into the error here hinted at ; their heroes generally are notorious rogues, and their heroines abandoned jades, during the first four acts; but in the fifth, the former become very worthy gentlemen, and the latter women of virtue and discretion: nor is the writer often so kind as to give himself the least trouble to reconcile or account for the monstrous change and incongruity.[17] There is, indeed, no other reason to be assigned for it, than because the play is drawing to a conclusion."

Throughout *Tom Jones*, however, the hero is described as a young man of good impulses who falls from grace because

---

[16]Comment on the reference to the problem of machines in this passage is reserved for later discussion. The question of a fortunate outcome is more or less bound up with that of the marvellous.

[17]In his translation of Moliére's *L'Avare*. Fielding made an attempt to have the ending more credible in this respect than Moliére's own by shifting the emphasis in the plot from a study of miserliness to an intrigue to rob a miser. (See Digeon, *The Novels of Fielding*, pp. 12-15).

he has not learned to direct his impulses intelligently. And the whole of the novel is little more than the tale of how he at last learns the lesson of directing his impulses wisely. His example thus affords the reader an illustration of a moral which will lead him to quit evil ways and take good ones.[18]

The hero of such a story does not have to be possessed of all known virtues—he does not, that is, have to be an "honnête homme", to use the French phrase of the period. Richardson, in *Sir Charles Grandison*, attempted to create such a character, in this following the practice of the writers of the heroic romance.[19] But Fielding, following the lessons of life itself and reinforced in his doctrine by what Le Bossu points out about the characters of the ancient epic, depicts his hero as good, but not perfect.

In the first chapter of Book X, he thus describes his hero: "In fact, if there be enough goodness in a character to engage the admiration and affection of a well-disposed mind, though there should appear some of those little blemishes, quas humana parum cavit natura, they will raise our compassion rather than our abhorrence. Indeed, nothing can be of more moral use than the imperfections which are seen in examples of this kind; since such form a kind of surprize, more apt to affect and dwell upon our minds than the faults of very vicious and wicked persons. The foibles and vices of men, in whom there is a great mixture of good, become more glaring objects from the virtues which contrast them and show their deformity; and, when we find such vices attended with their evil consequences to our favourite characters, we are not only taught to shun them for our own sake, but to hate them for the mischiefs they have already brought on those we love."

[18]This belief in the need for intelligence in morality was a central doctrine of the conception of art as didactic. It was also part of the philosophy of the time. Fielding believes in the necessity for good impulses first. Square, Thwackum, Blifil, are all intelligent after a fashion. But the sane and balanced life involves both good impulses and reason. Fielding was a believer in the moral precepts of Christianity, but his belief was a combination of the Socratic "Know thyself", the traditional Greek and Roman belief "mens sana in corpore sano", and the necessity for good works and a feeling of human brotherhood of Christian doctrine.

[19]Amelia is perhaps a feminine version of the "honnête homme". Yet, even here, the story has a matter-of-factness which makes the action *not* romantic.

The conception of the moral purpose of the epic is here clearly implied, in much the same terms as those in which Le Bossu defines the purpose of the *Iliad*, for example. And the conception of character portrayal within the whole story likewise bears a close similarity to the words of Le Bossu on the subject. There are numerous passages in the *Traité du Poëme Epique* which betray the same point of view about manners that Fielding has. For instance:

"De-même, en une Epopée, les Moeurs sont Bonnes, quand on reconnoit la vertu ou le vice, les bonnes ou les mauvaises inclinations de ceux qui parlent ou qui agissent: & elles sont Mauvaises, quand un homme de bien paroit vicieux, ou qu'un méchant homme fait voir de bonnes inclinations."[20]

"Ce doute paroîtra peu raisonnable à ceux qui n'ont qu'une seule idée des Héros, & qui sous ce nom ne connoissent que ces excellens hommes à qui il ne manque aucune vertu, qui sont les maitres de leurs passions & de tous leurs mouvemens, & qu'une nature excellente & divine éléve au-dessus du reste des hommes. Mais les Poëtes anciens ni les Maitres de l'Art, n'ont jamais pensé à placer leurs Héros dans un rang si relevé, sans qu'il leur fut permis d'en descendre."[21]

"Ce que nous disons ici n'est pas pour exclure du Poëme, ce que la Morale condamne. Une Poëte ne doit jamais donner de mauvais exemples: mais il y a bien de la différence entre un mauvais exemple, & l'example d'une mauvaise action, ou d'une mauvaise personne."[22]

By the time that Fielding had worked out his technique of the comic epic in *Tom Jones*, he was beginning to be independent of Cervantes. He never ceased to class Cervantes as one of the great writers of the comic, but he had ceased to be under Cervantes' influence. He certainly has ceased to compare his work with that of Cervantes, and he is obviously concerned with the large structural problems of the epic,— a thing

[20]Le Bossu, *op. cit.*, tom II, p. 29.
[21]*Ibid*, tom. II, p. 36 .
[22]*Ibid.*, tom. II, p. 121.

which did not concern Cervantes. By 1752, we know that Fielding had ceased to feel Cervantes was his master, for in an analysis of Mrs. Charlotte Lennox's *Female Quixote* in the *Covent Garden Journal*,[23] Fielding points out as one of the superiorities of the latter over its prototype the fact that it has an epic structure. Here is what he says: "Fourthly, here is a regular Story, which, tho' possibly it is not pursued with that Epic Regularity which would give it the Name of an Action, comes much nearer to that Perfection than the loose unconnected Adventures in *Don Quixote*; of which you may transverse the Order as you please, without any Injury to the whole."

In this same passage, Fielding has further comment to make upon Cervantes' performance, which indicates that he has, by now, distinguished between the genre in which Cervantes was working and his own.

"Fifthly," he says, "the Incidents, or, if you please, the Adventures, are much less extravagant and incredible in the English than in the Spanish Performance. The latter, in many Instances, approaches very near to the Romances which he ridicules. Such are the stories of Cardenio and Dorothes, Ferdinand and Lucinda, etc.[24] In the former, there is nothing except the Absurdities of the Heroine herself, which is carried beyond Common-Life; nor is there any Thing even in her Character, which the Brain a little distempered may not account for. She conceives indeed somewhat preposterously of the Ranks and Conditions of Men; that is to say, mistakes one Man for another; but never advances towards the Absurdity of imagining Windmills and Wine-Bags to be human Creatures, or Flocks of Sheep to be Armies."

He still loves *Don Quixote*, but he recognizes that there is a difference between it and his own novels.

As a writer, Fielding's methods were at once careless and careful. That he conciously followed epic structure in *Tom*

[23]Dated March 24, 1752. Number 24.
[24]These interpolated stories are like Fielding's Tale of Leonora in *Joseph Andrews*, Fielding's comment here shows that although he followed Cervantes' practice in *Joseph Andrews*, he later decided that such stories were unsuited to the comic prose epic.

Jones seems certain, but his theory of the comic prose epic is developed by flashes. For all the care with which the plot structure of *Tom Jones* is executed, there is reason to believe that Fielding did not always know just where his plot would lead him next. For instance, there is the famous slip[25] in the seasons which occurs between Books V and VI of *Tom Jones*. At the end of Book V, Tom is represented at thrashing Blifil one afternoon in early June, and according to the announcement made at the head of Book VI, three weeks later, it is autumn, the weather being described as cold. A curious slip in one who planned his work, in other respects, so carefully that it has been inferred that he consulted an almanac![26]

Furthermore, his prefatory chapters for each book have relatively little to do with the contents of the book which follows. It is more than possible that Fielding inserted these when his manuscript was in the hands of the printers. But these things do not negative the other theory—that he planned his book on the spacious scale of the *Odyssey*, and that, in writing, he had clearly in mind the technical analyses of narrative structure found in Le Bossu.

By the time he was ready to write *Amelia*, he had ceased to write these little essays upon the art of the comic prose epic, it may be because he had by then sufficiently established, or at least thought he had established, the principles on which he was working. On the other hand, *Amelia* has not a Homeric quality about it. It belongs to the same genre as *Tom Jones*, certainly, but it has a more sentimental tone—more tears than *Tom Jones*, less laughter. If *Tom Jones* is Homeric, *Amelia* may be said to have much in common with Virgil.[27] That is, the structure, the sweep of events are the same; the tone is different. I doubt if Fielding made any distinction between the

<hr />

[25]Most writers on Fielding have called attention to this. For a detailed discussion of the plot of *Tom Jones*, see Cross, *Life of Fielding*, vol. II, pp. 179 seq.

[26]Mr. Cross refers to a discussion of Fielding's probable use of an almanac by Mr. Frederick S. Dickson. See Cross, *op. cit.*, vol. II, p. 189.

[27]The affair between Captain Booth and Miss Mathews has much in common with the romance between Aeneas and Dido—something of the same forced quality and struggle against the claims of duty.

epic mood of Homer and of Virgil. There is certainly no evidence that he does. But it is a curious fact that in his three novels—*Jonathon Wild* is a little outside this discussion— he wrote both two *Odysseys* and a sophisticated epic like the *Aeneid*.

Besides the attention to the large epic structure in *Tom Jones*, as well as in *Joseph Andrews*, there is the same working out of epic formulae in small details. There is, for example, the Homeric battle of Molly Seagrim and her enemies in the churchyard. The chapter in which this battle is described is entitled: "A Battle sung by the Muse in the Homeric Style, and which none but the Classical Reader can Taste." The tale is told in terms of broad but not mock-heroic comedy. That is, the battle is serious for the participants and the importance of it is fitted to the importance of the characters. It involves the petty, but real jealousies and scandals of a whole community, not a trivial quarrel over a rape of a lock. In the epic style, Fielding invokes the Muse—not the Homeric Muse, however, but the muse of *Hudibras*.[28]

"Ye Muses, then, whoever ye are, who love to sing battles, and principally thou who whilom didst recount the slaughter in those fields where Hudibras and Trulla fought, if thou wert not starved with thy friend Butler, assist me on this great occasion. All things are not in the power of all."

Then follows an elaborate simile, worked out as a comic, or everyday, parallel to the heroic similes of Homer. Compare, for instance, the simile at the opening of the battle between Hector and Achilles in Book XXII of the *Iliad*. "As a falcon upon the mountains, swiftest of winged things, swoopeth fleetly after a trembling dove; and she before him fleeth, while he with shrill screams hard at hand still darteth at her, for his heart urgeth him to seize her" with "As a vast herd of cows in a rich farmer's yard, if, while they are milked, they hear their calves at a distance, lamenting the robbery which is then committing, roar and bellow," the simile with which Molly's battle

[28]A copy of *Hudibras* with Grey's annotations was in Fielding's library.

opens. The latter is obviously written with the other in mind. Yet Fielding's is scarcely a burlesque, for his simile precisely fits the situation in the Somersetshire churchyard that day. It is the comic version of the serious epic simile.

Parts of the descriptions of this battle are burlesques. The invocation to the Muse, given above, seems definitely a burlesque, especially as the Muse invoked is Butler's. But Fielding had already said, in the *Preface* to *Joseph Andrews*, that burlesque was to be admitted in the diction of the comic epic.

In his comic prose epic, Fielding could also use a serious invocation, such as the one to be found in Chapter II of Book IV of *Tom Jones*, when the author introduces Sophia. Here, Fielding makes use of the pagan deities of nature, using them as poetical explanations of natural phenomena, as Boileau and Le Bossu had stated they should be used.[29] The passage begins thus:

"Hushed be every ruder breath. May the heathen ruler of the winds confine in iron chains the boisterous limbs of noisy Boreas, and the sharp-pointed nose of bitter-biting Eurus. Do thou, sweet Zephyrus, rising from thy fragrant bed, mount the western sky, and lead on those delicious gales, the charms of which call forth the lovely Flora from her chamber, perfumed with pearly dews, when on the 1st of June, her birth-day, the blooming maid, in loose attire, gently trips it over the verdant mead, where every flower rises to do her homage, till the whole field becomes enamelled, and colours contend with sweets which shall ravish her most."

The rulers of the winds are here admitted to be heathen, but the invocation is cast in terms which do not demand literal faith in them. Zephyrus is a poetical name for the west wind, not a god in whose literal presence the author either believes or expects us to believe. But the invocation, though not literal, is nevertheless serious, and serves to cast something of the eternal glamor of beauty over the description of Sophia.

[29]See Chapter IV, of this study for a discussion of Boileau's and Le Bossu's views on the pagan marvellous.

Thus, Fielding used, as occasion demanded, the serious poetical invocation of the epic, as conceived by criticism of his time, a burlesque invocation to the Muse, and similes and descriptions of battle scenes done in terms of broad comedy.

So, too, with other smaller points. A pause in the narrative is filled up with the tale of the Man of the Hill. Ulysses, unavoidably detained among the Phaeacians, is entertained with songs about great and heroic deeds. Tom, unavoidably benighted with the Man of the Hill, listens to his tale, a tale having a spiritual kinship to Tom's own life. And, finally, at the end, the reversal of fortune is brought about by a discovery, in the best Aristotelian tradition.[30] The discovery in *Tom Jones* is not brought about by the finding of an identifying mark on the hero, but arises from the action itself.[31] Mrs. Waters, who, step by step, has become involved in Tom's fortunes, at last discovers and reveals the secret of Tom's birth and the foundling becomes Mr. Allworthy's heir.

In *Tom Jones*, then, Fielding worked out the technique of his whole plot more precisely than he had done in *Joseph Andrews*. Here, too, he gets away from the suggestion of the anti-romance which lingers in the earlier book,—in the unrelated adventures, in the touches of parody here and there, in the slightly picturesque descriptions of a world of wandering rogues. It is the fully developed comic prose epic—full of irony, full of broad comedy, full of "thoughtful laughter." Partridge is Cervantesque, but he is an integral part of the story now in a way that the greater Parson Adams was not. Parson Adams was Joseph's guide, philosopher, and friend, but he had no intimate connection with Joseph's career. Partridge, on the other hand, is one of the pivotal figures in bringing Tom's fortunes into their complication and then unravelling them. The action develops slowly, but, with one or two slight

[30] This ending by Reversal and Discovery, a fairly elaborate treatment of which is given in Aristotle, is made much of by most Renaissance epic theorists. See Le Bossu, *op. cit.*, tom. I, liv. iii.

[31] Discovery by identifying mark is a lower form of discovery, says Aristotle (*Poetics*, edited by Lane Cooper, pp. 53-57) than the kind which arises from the action itself.

errors, such as the mistake in the time of year, mentioned above, the entanglement of the action and its unravelling are beautifully proportioned. The first six books develop the entanglement in Somersetshire, ending with Tom's being turned out of doors. The next six books develop the action on the road, the complications probably reaching their height at the inn at Upton, where Mrs. Waters, the Fitzpatricks, Tom, and Sophia all turn up, and, ironically, Tom and Sophia, the avowed lovers, do not meet. The last six books take place in London, ending finally in the unravelling of all the entanglements of the preceding vast narrative. It is no wonder that Fielding, surveying the intricacy of his vast epic plot, so carefully bound together, said that he was founding a "new province of writing".

CHAPTER VIII.

The Verisimilar and the Marvellous

Fielding, in defining his novel as the comic prose epic, spoke the ambitions of his age. Thoughtful men looked upon the world of Homer with veneration as a world in which men were heroic and gave to life significance and dramatic stir, through the force of their personalities. That world had passed, and the vain attempts of the sophisticated French and English poets of the seventeenth century to recapture the spirit of the heroic age are at once pathetic and ludicrous.[1] The only author who could succeed in writing a national epic in the sense in which the *Iliad* was a national epic would have to grasp the difference between the heroic age of the *Iliad* and the new age. Fielding took this task seriously. I have already shown how full his library was of the ancients on the one hand and of the history of his own country on the other.[2] No man ever took a keener interest in the world in which he lived than did Henry Fielding. He attacked the abuses of his times in plays like *Pasquin, The Historical Register*, and even *Don Quixote in England*, where the Spanish hero is anglicized and made to take part in a political campaign. As magistrate, Fielding came to know about the people of London's streets, and to see clearly into some of the causes which brought them to Bow Street. He embodied the results of his reflections on this subject in his pamphlet,

[1]Leaving aside his genius, which cannot be defined, one of the reasons why Fielding had succeeded where others had failed was that he was so thoroughly a man of his age. He has the rationality and sentimentalism, the satiric sense and the humanitarian spirit, the love of city ways and joy in the country, which we find scattered here and there in his lesser contemporaries.

[2]Fielding's respect for history is very great. The creative genius, in his belief, interprets the veritable rather than creates something wholly fictitious. Here is one limitation of his genius. Fielding could not have created Caliban, though he may have recognized, with Addison, Shakespeare's imaginative power in depicting such a creature.

Some Causes of the Late Increase of Robbers. He knew and loved the English countryside. One of his happiest poems is the hunting song from *Don Quixote in England,* the first stanza of which runs:

> "The dusky night rides down the sky
> And ushers in the morn;
> The hounds all join in glorious cry,
> The huntsman winds his horn."

He was intensely patriotic, as were most of Sir Robert Walpole's opponents. His song, *The Roast Beef of Old England,* was for years a favorite patriotic piece. He had subjected himself thoroughly to the discipline of French drama, but he knew English drama intimately, and loved it. In an age when other men were "revising" Shakespeare, he invokes the spirit of Shakespeare to his aid in writing his great prose epic. He also satirized the gentlemen who were doing the revising.[3] He believed in the principles according to which the great works of the past had been written, but he was one of the first to recognize his own contemporary Lillo with his bourgeois tragedy. He had, in short, a comprehensive soul—not so comprehensive, of course, as Shakespeare's, but with a measure of the same large zest for the life around him.

He was thus equipped as few others were to attempt the troublesome problem of verisimilitude, about which so much had been written and so little clearly discerned. Certain half truths, such as that contained in Pope's dictum that nature and Homer are the same—a half truth because, no matter how eternal human passions may be, the manners by which they are revealed do change, and, after all, we know passions only through their expression—such half truths, then, had confused men's minds. The man whose epic theory was to count was the man

---

[3]One of his best burlesques is his own editing of Hamlet in the manner of eighteenth century editors. (*Covent Garden Journal,* No. 31 April 18, 1752.) For example,
    "To die, to sleep;
    To sleep, perchance to dream."
is amended to "To lie to sleep." For, says Fielding, "why to die first, and to go to sleep afterwards?"

who knew the manners of his own day, with a full appreciation of the eternal motives behind them.

Fielding saw his problem clearly. In this, he was assisted by the great men of the past, and of his own day. Both *Joseph Andrews* and *Tom Jones* are filled with references to the author's belief that direct observation of human nature is essential in giving the creator of characters acquaintance with the manners of mankind. *Tom Jones* starts out with this observation in Chapter I of Book I.

"The provision, then, which we have here made is no other than Human Nature.[4] Nor do I fear that my sensible reader, though most luxurious in his taste, will start, cavil, or be offended, because I have named but one article. . . .

"An objection may perhaps be apprehended from the more delicate, that this dish is too common and vulgar; for what else is the subject of all the romances, novels, plays, and poems, with which the stalls abound? Many exquisite viands might be rejected by the epicure, if it was a sufficient cause for his contemning of them as common and vulgar, that something was to be found in the most paltry alleys under the same name. In reality, true nature is as difficult to be met with in authors, as the Bayonne ham, or Bologna sausage, is to be found in the shops."

Human nature, then, is to be his subject. This is one of the fundamental doctrines of Renaissance criticism. Poetry is an imitation, the imitation of human nature. Aristotle had said, in defining the objects of poetry: "Accordingly, we may proceed to the Objects which the imitator represents. The primary objects of artistic imitation are human beings in action, men performing or undergoing something."[5] This mimetic theory of poetry aroused much discussion during the Renaissance. Aristotle had followed this statement that poetry imitates an action by the further statement that the poet, the epic or tragic

---

[4]Neither the ancients nor the Renaissance critics were interested in external nature in the way in which the Romantic poets were interested in it. Aristotle speaks of comedy, tragedy, and epic in terms of human action.

[5]Aristotle, *op. cit.*, p. 6.

poet, in contrast to the historian, imitates not what is, but what ought to be, not the particular, but the typical. Plato's use of the word "imitation" was easily comprehensible. An artizan makes a bed, imitating the divine prototype. The poet imitates the artizan's handiwork. But Aristotle's use of the word is far less simple. What exactly was meant by "imitating" what ought to be? The poet imitates human action. This is easily understood. Achilles killed Hector, and Homer tells us about it. But what if Homer changes the actual fact? The problem of ideal imitation provoked long discussions. On the whole, Renaissance opinion worked out the solution in this way. It is the function of the poet to instruct; therefore, the poet imitates those actions which delight and hence instruct by examples; the object of poetic imitation is human nature, but human nature idealized for purposes of instruction. Whether the idealization of human nature should mean that the poet should represent only good men—the *honnêtes hommes* of seventeenth century French criticism—raised another point. Le Bossu, as we have seen, points out that Achilles was not an *honnête homme*. Then, having decided whether one's hero is an *honnête homme* or not, one must decide whether one's imitation of human beings in action should be an imitation of the works of the ancients, or a direct "imitation" of human nature, as observed by the writer.[6] Pope expressed succinctly an easy harmonization of these two conflicting points of view when he said: "Nature and Homer were, he found, the same."

In saying, therefore, that he was going to serve his readers human nature, Fielding expresses the traditional point of view of Renaissance criticism. But on the question of where the author should get his material for imitating human nature, there was still need for definition, although Pope had expressed in his dictum, just quoted, a fairly generally accepted opinion. In Chapter I of Book IX, of *Tom Jones*, Fielding takes up this

---

[6] I deliberately use the word "imitation" here in two senses, as it was used in criticism. In the first sense, it means copying another's work. In the second, it means inventing according to an ideal conception.

question. The author, he says here, needs, first of all, genius, which Fielding defines as "that power or rather those powers of the mind, which are capable of penetrating into all things within our reach and knowledge, and of distinguishing their essential differences. These are no other than invention and judgment." But there is some misunderstanding, in Fielding's opinion, over the exact meaning of invention.[7] Some think it the faculty simply of creating new things. If this were so, the writers of romance would have that faculty in the highest degree. But "by invention is really meant no more (and so the word signifies) than discovery, or finding out; or to explain it at large, a quick and sagacious penetration into the true essence of all the objects of our contemplation. This, I think, can rarely exist without the concomitancy of judgment."

This definition of invention as discovery or finding out is another of the tenets of Renaissance criticism. The effort to define literary creation in terms which would not violate the Aristotelian definition of poetry as the imitation of human beings in action brought about many critical discussions. The poet does "create". In the very nature of Aristotle's definition, which was, in part, written in reply to Plato's adverse criticism of the arts as being an imitation of an imitation of a divine prototype, the fact that the poet "imitates" *directly* was stressed.[8] But the product of his imitation must seem convincing—must be verisimilar. A poet does not, therefore, bring into being something which never was, and never will be. He *creates* by plumbing more deeply than others the resources of our human nature. This theory of invention was, of course, necessary if the critics were to harmonize their (Artistotelian) conception of poetry as the imitation of an action with their other (Horatian) theory of the purpose of poetry being to instruct. Actions do not immediately reveal their hidden lesson.

[7] The definition of invention, in the light of a theory of imitation, was one over which there was great discussion in almost all critical works.

[8] Plato had thus accused the poet of copying a particular phenomenon, which was itself an imitation of the divine idea. Aristotle implies, in his *Poetics*, that the poet imitates directly from the divine idea.

The poet must discover them.   Thus, if the writer narrates facts, he must alter them so that he tells not what has happened, but what ought to have happened, the general, not the particular.   If he uses ficticious events, he has to invent these happenings on the basis of general human probability.   In either case, he does not make something out of nothing, but simply discovers the hidden meaning.   To use a Platonic phrase, the poet must imitate directly the divine idea.   His work must *seem* true—must be in accord with the phenomenal world.   But it must have its ethical source in the noumenal world.   Genius, this combination of invention and judgment, seeks the objects for its imitation in studying what other men have done and in observing directly the manners of men.   The necessity for observing the manners of men as one great source for a knowledge of human nature is thus expressed by Fielding, in this prefatory chapter to Book IX of *Tom Jones.*

"Again, there is another sort of knowledge, beyond the power of learning to bestow, and this is to be had by conversation.   So necessary is this to the understanding the characters of men, that none are more ignorant of them than those learned pedants whose lives have been entirely consumed in colleges, and among books; for however exquisitely human nature may have been described by writers, the true practical system can be learnt only in the world.   Neither physic nor law are to be practically known from books. . . .

"Now this conversation in our historian must be universal, that is, with all ranks and degrees of men; for the knowledge of what is called high life will not instruct him in low; nor *é converso*, will his being acquainted with the inferior part of mankind teach him the manners of the superior."[9]

Besides observing directly the manners of men, the writer must be a learned man.   In Chapter I of Book IX of *Tom Jones,*

[9]Molière emphasizes the necessity for the writer's knowing his own age directly. Cf Dorante's Speech in *La Critique de l'Ecole des Femmes*:
"Mais, lorsque vous peignez les hommes, il faut peindre d'apres nature.   On veut que ces portraits resemblent, et vous n'avez rien fait, si vous n'y faites reconnoitre les gens de votre siècle."

after Fielding has defined invention, he goes on to say that the writers of epics must have a share of learning:

". . . for which I could again cite the authority of Horace, and of many others, if any was necessary to prove that tools are of no service to a workman, when they are not sharpened by art, or when he wants rules to direct him in his work, or hath no matter to work upon. All these uses are supplied by learning; for nature can only furnish us with capacity; or, as I have chóse to illustrate it, with the tools of our profession; learning must fit them for use, must direct them in it, and, lastly, must contribute part at least of the materials. A competent knowledge of history and of the belles-lettres is here absolutely necessary; and without this share of knowledge at least, to affect the character of an historian, is as vain as to endeavor at building a house without timber or mortar, or brick or stone. Homer and Milton, who, though they added the ornament of numbers to their works, were both historians of our order, were masters of all the learning of their times."

This idea that the writer must be learned was insisted upon throughout Renaissance criticism. For instance, de Scudéry says in his *Preface* to *Alaric*: "Je tiens au contraire, que pour estre veritable Poëte, il faudroit ne rien ignorer: & que plus on voit de sçavoir dans un Poëme, plus l'Autheur en merite de louange". In fact, the writer of the epic, as conceived by the Renaissance, might say with Bacon: "I have taken all knowledge to be my province". Sometimes, one feels, indeed, that certain theorists think learning alone will suffice. Such appears to be the clear view of Vida in his *Ars Poetica*.[10] Fielding, then, in invoking the aid of learning was acting in accord with a well-established belief of his times.

Fielding frequently refers to his novels as biographies, or as histories, but he is careful to make it clear that they are biographies with a purpose, that is, that they are records which preserve the significant facts of his characters' lives. Thus, he says, in Chapter I of Book III of *Joseph Andrews*: "Now

[10]See Spingarn, *Literary Criticism in the Renaissance*, pp. 127 seq.

with us biographers the case is different; the facts we deliver
may be relied on, though we often mistake the age and country
wherein they happened." His characters are drawn from nature, and are not like the characters which are to be found in
the romances of the times, "who, without any assistance from
nature or history, record persons who never were, or will be, and
facts which never did, nor possibly can, happen; whose brains
are of their own creation, and their brains the chaos whence
all the materials are selected . . . .

"But to return to the former class, who are contented to copy
nature, instead of forming originals from the confused heap of
matter in their own brains; is not such a book as that which
records the achievements of the renowned Don Quixote more
worthy the name of a history than even Mariana's: for, whereas
the latter is confined to a particular period of time, and to a
particular nation, the former is the history of the world in
general, at least that part which is polished by laws, arts, and
sciences; and of that from the time it was first polished to this
day; nay, and forwards as long as it shall so remain?"

It is ideal truth which he is endeavoring to picture, according
to this statement. In thus defining his novels as histories, and
yet stating that they are ideal, Fielding uses the terms "history"
and "epic" in a sense somewhat different from the way in which
they were used by most critics. History was, according to
Aristotle, an account of what had happened. An epic—or a
tragedy—was an account of what ought to be. History differs
from either epic or tragedy in thus being a record of the particular, whereas epic and tragedy are a record of what ought to
have happened, or of ideal truth. One of the most persistent
sources of the debate among Renaissance critics is the discussion of whether epic material *must* be historical or fictitious.[11]
In thus calling his novels histories, but idealized histories,
Fielding apparently sides with the champions of historical
material for epics. But he uses the word history in a sense not
ordinarily used by other critics. What he seems to say is that

[11]See de Scudéry's discussion of this in his *Preface* to *Alaric*, quoted above, p. 40.

his novels are invented, or discovered, histories, in that they are "true to life" in the way that actual events are. It is clear from this use of the word that Fielding distinguishes history, as a chronicle of what has happended, from epic, not so much on the basis of material, but on the basis of form. That is, the epic may be equally true to specific occurences as a history, but the form is different. This distinction is implied in Aristotle. But the difference in form is very important, and Fielding, in using the word *history*, even though it is clear he uses it to indicate the verisimilitude of his tales, is using the word in a way which is confusing and outside of the usual critical usage of his time. The epic is a unit; a history is a record of all the events which happened at a given time, or at different times to a person or group of persons. Of course, this difference of form arises from a difference in material, and leads to a difference in temper. A historian cannot select his material in order to give a dramatic form to his chronicle. Only the writer of epic or drama can do this. For the latter has his fable— his artistic pattern—in mind, and his material is thus actually philosophical or general, and not particular. Fielding esteemed history greatly. And he was a realist in a way that many Renaissance critics were not. That is, he believed in telling *all sides* of a situation. But he told those sides with his *epic* principle of selection in mind—to show the manner in which his heroes adjusted themselves to the good life.

Thus, as a writer of epic, he has his fable, or general principle of selection in mind, but, as a historian, he studies what has happened. He gets his material from life. In his novels we see the English country life of the eighteenth century, charming, fresh, with its squires absorbed in their hounds and their drink; we see the life of the upper classes and of the lower classes in London; there is a picture of the army in the Upton scenes in *Tom Jones*, of the clergy in Parson Adams and Parson Trulliber; gamekeepers, young men of fashion, landladies, inn-keepers, lawyers, doctors—they are all here. Sometimes, Fielding gives each of these very minor characters a name; sometimes he does not. The characters come and go in a picture which has an amazing sense of thickness, of depth.

But, though the material comes from life, the purpose is general. His comic prose epic is an imitation of human beings in action, presented as idealized truth. The genius which enables man to do this is compounded of invention and judgment. In discovering what is true to universal human nature, genius employs learning and direct observation of the manners of men. His position in defining imitation is neither so extreme as Vida's[12] who thought translation of the ancients a high form of creative effort, nor as Molière's, speaking through Dorante, in *La Critique de l'Ecole des Femmes*:

"Il semble, à vous ouïr parler, que ces régles de l'art soient les plus grands mystères du monde; et cependent ce ne sont que quelques observations aisées, que le bon sens a faites sur ce qui peut ôter le plaisir que l'on prend à ces sortes de poémes; et le même bon sens qui a fait autrefois ces observations les fait aisement tous les jours, sans le secours d'Horace et d'Aristote."

Fielding's view is held by most of the greatest critics whom he knew, those men especially who had studied as craftsmen the problems of creative art. When Dryden says, in his *Apology for the Heroic Poem*: "Thus I grant you, that the knowledge of Nature was the original rule; and that all poets ought to study her, as well as Aristotle and Horace, her interpreters",[13] he is stating the traditional criticism of that time. Fielding's position is virtually the same, although as a writer of comedy, he *emphasizes*, with Molière, the necessity for understanding the manners of men of his own time. With Molière, he could laugh at the rules *as they were conceived by stupid men*. In Chapter I of Book V of *Tom Jones*, he says that "these critics being men of shallow capacities, very easily mistook form for substance". But the substance of criticism which Fielding accepted as es-

[12]See quotation of Vida *re* translation, quoted above, p. 58.
[13]Dryden, *Essays*, Vol. I, p. 183.

sential was the conversative tradition as it had gradually been worked out by critics of Aristotle's *Poetics*.

But the term "human nature" had been the source of considerable discussion. What was meant by imitating the actions of men as they ought to be? Must one's characters be schematized? For some of the critics it had meant the elaborate theory of "decorum".[14] Certain qualities belong to certain sorts of men, and to give other qualities to them is to violate decorum. Thus, a king must be kingly, an old man wise, and so on. But intelligent opinion, while agreeing that the manners of a man must suit him, did not insist upon a rigid definition of just what manners were suitable. Le Bossu, for instance, a conservative exponent of neo-classical opinion, makes it perfectly clear that the valor of Achilles is not the same sort of thing as the valor of Aeneas. Fielding expresses practically the same idea thus:

"Another caution we would give thee, my good reptile, is, that thou does not find out too near a resemblance between certain characters here introduced; as, for instance, between the landlady who appears in the seventh book and her in the ninth. Thou art to know, friend, that there are certain characteristics in which most individuals of every profession and occupation agree. To be able to preserve these characteristics, and at the same time to diversify their operations, is one talent of a good writer".

In other words, a character may be both typical and individual. He may be Tom Jones, but he has certain universal qualities, and most young men of the eighteenth century could find some sort of spiritual identity with him. Fielding, then, makes his characters and events seem verisimilar by choosing to portray characters who, in the best sense of the word, are typical, and by making such characters as are somewhat eccentric, Parson Adams and Partridge, not precisely eccentric in the sense of being departures from the usual, so much as eccentric in the sense that they do the very human thing of

[14]See Spingarn, *Literary Criticism in the Renaissance*, pp. 81-106.

mistaking the world of their own imagining for the world outside them. Fielding needs no miracles to make Parson Adams sane. He is never insane. But Cervantes had had to give his Don Quixote some miraculous adventures to effect his cure. Verisimilitude, for Fielding, is conceived in terms of the rationalistic world in which he lived, while verisimilitude for Cervantes is romantic, although it is romance whose glory is ideally true. Thus did Fielding solve the problem of verisililitude—a fairly easy problem on the whole. What he does with the marvellous is more ingenious.

Having grasped the fact that his comic prose epic must be created, in epic form, out of eighteenth century materials, Fielding discarded machines altogether. He does not, like de Scudéry, try to write a Christian epic with witches and demons and angels. Nor does he, like Fénélon, follow Boileau's conception of the marvellous as an "amas de nobles fictions", and write another Télémaque, in which Greek deities are allegorical symbols of abstract qualities. In Chapter I of Book VIII of *Tom Jones*, he gives us his views on the whole subject of the marvellous, views which are an admirable illustration of his common sense, of his artistic powers, and of his knowledge of critical theory of the time. His conclusions are summed up thus:

"But I have rested too long on a doctrine which can be of no use to a Christian writer: for as he cannot introduce into his works any of that heavenly host which make a part of his creed, so it is horrid puerility to search the heathen theology for any of those deities who have been long since dethroned from their immortality. Lord Shaftesbury observes, that nothing is more cold than the invocation of a muse by a modern; he might have added, that nothing is more absurd. . . .

"The only supernatural agents which can in any manner be allowed to us moderns, are ghosts . . . .

"As for elves and fairies, and other such mummery, I purposely omit the mention of them, as I should be very unwilling to confine within any bounds those surprizing imaginations, for whose vast capacity the limits of human nature are too narrow . . . .

"Man therefore is the highest subject (unless on very extraordinary occasions indeed) which presents itself to the pen of our historian, or of our poet; and, in relating his actions great care is to be taken that we do not exceed the capacity of the agent we describe."

Thus, he will not use Christian deities, because he agrees with Boileau that it is not fitting for a Christian to introduce his deities, which, by the dogmas of Christian theology, are essentially other-worldly. But he agrees with the champions of the Christian epic in thinking that it is horrid puerility for moderns to introduce pagan deities. The romantic paraphernalia of elves and fairies are suitable only for romances. Ghosts may be used, indeed, but sparingly. Man is the only agent to be introduced. He concedes that there may be occasions in which man may not be the highest subject, but such occasions are very extraordinary indeed. He himself, when introducing Sophia, uses pagan deities as "poetical" fictions. In virtually discarding machines, Fielding does what Davenant had already done, but he is probably not so much following Davenant's example as the rationalistic teachings of Hobbes and others.[15] The really interesting things in this chapter on the marvellous are the comments upon the use of the marvellous in the ancient epics, and his own definition of the marvellous, *for the comic epic, as the surprising.*

The ancient heathen deities are, he says, of poetical origin. This is Boileau's opinion, and Le Bossu's,—indeed, the opinion of a long line of theorists who see, in the Greek and Latin epics, poetical allegories. "The poet, being desirous to indulge a wanton and extravagant imagination, took refuge in that power, of the extent of which his readers were no judges, or rather which they imagined to be infinite, and consequently they could

---

[15]He owned Davenant's works, however, as well as Hobbes' and could have got the idea from either—or from neither.

not be shocked at any prodigies related of it. This hath been strongly urged in defense of Homer's miracles; and it is perhaps a defense; not, as Mr. Pope would have it, because Ulysses told a set of foolish lies to the Phaeacians, who were a very dull nation: but because the poet himself wrote to heathens, to whom poetical fables were articles of faith." Although the argument here is not altogether clear, it seems, on the whole, to advance the belief that the tales of the gods were allegories, believed, partly literally, partly symbolically, by the people. Fielding's further remarks in this connection are really among the most interesting of the whole critical discussion of machines in the ancient epics.

"I wish, likewise, with all my heart, that Homer could have known the rule prescribed by Horace, to introduce supernatural agents as seldom as possible. We should not then have seen his gods coming on trivial errands, and often behaving themselves so as not only to forfeit all title to respect, but to become the objects of scorn and derision. A conduct which must have shocked the credulity of a pious and sagacious heathen; and which could never have been defended, unless by agreeing with a supposition to which I have been sometimes almost inclined, that this most glorious poet, as he certainly was, had an intent to burlesque the superstitious faith of his own age and country."

The tales told in Homer did shock at least one pious and sagacious heathen, namely Plato, whose writings Fielding owned. But the theory that perhaps Homer was burlesquing the superstitious faith of his own age and country was not a canon of most seventeenth and eighteenth century critics whom Fielding knew, directly or by hearsay. Did Fielding have Lucian, his favorite Greek author, in mind when he developed this idea? It is interesting that Professor Ker, in his *Epic and Romance*, discusses the story of Ares and Aphrodite in somewhat the same terms.

"It is possible to take them in a light-hearted way and weave them into poetical stories, without much substance or solemnity:

enhancing the beauty that may be inherent in any part of the national legend, and either rejecting the scandalous chronicle of Olympus or Asgard altogether, or giving it over to the comic graces of levity and irony, as in the Phaeacian story of Ares and Aphrodite, wherein the Phaeacian poet disgressed from his tales of war in the spirit of Ariosto, and with an equally accomplished and elusive defiance of censure."[16]

Fielding undoubtedly had great fun out of Lucian's *Dialogues of the Gods*, which are certainly not unlike some of Ariosto in spirit. And Fielding's *Voyage from this World to the Next* treats various great persons of the past, whose names were almost sacrosanct, with a Lucianic—or Ariostan—levity.

But, in thus discarding machines, Fielding did not consider that he had altogether discarded the marvellous. He discarded the supernatural, but he retained the surprising. This is what he means by saying that an author "may very well fall into the marvellous, but not into the incredible". Thus, it is surprising that Tom should prove to be Miss Bridget Allworthy's eldest son and hence his patron's nephew, but the supernatural need not be invoked in order to bring to pass the fact itself, or the discovery of this fact. Whether one believes that Joan of Arc heard heavenly voices, or merely thought she heard them, it nevertheless remains a marvellous fact than Joan did what she did. In his chapter on the marvellous, which prefaces Book VIII of *Tom Jones*, Fielding analyzes his problem of the surprising combined with the verisimilar. He cites certain historical facts which are "marvellous",—the "successless armament of Xerxes described by Herodotus, the successful expedition of Alexander related by Arrian . . the victory of Agincourt obtained by Harry the Fifth, or that of Narva won by Charles the Twelfth of Sweden". The more one reflects upon these incidents, says Fielding, the more astonishing they appear. But, if such events do take place, it is the plain duty of the historian to record them.

16Ker, *Epic and Romance*, p. 42.

"Nor is possibility alone sufficient to justify us; we must keep likewise within the rules of probability. It is, I think, the opinion of Aristotle; or if not, it is the opinion of some wise man, whose authority will be as weighty when it is as old, 'That it is no excuse for a poet who relates what is incredible, that the thing related is really matter of fact'. This may perhaps be allowed true with regard to poetry, but it may be thought impracticable to extend it to the historian; for he is obliged to record matters as he finds them, though they may be of so extraordinary a nature as will require no small degree of historical faith to swallow them. . . . .

"Such facts, however, as they occur in the thread of the story, nay, indeed, as they constitute the essential parts of it the historian is not only justifiable in recording as they really happened, but indeed would be unpardonable should he omit or alter them . . . .

"To say the truth, if the historian will confine himself to what really happened, and utterly reject any circumstance, which, though never so well attested, he must be well assured is false, he will sometimes fall into the marvellous, but never into the incredible.[17] He will often raise the wonder and surprize of his reader, but never that incredulous hatred mentioned by Horace. It is by falling into fiction, therefore, that we generally offend against this rule, of deserting probability, which the historian seldom, if ever, quits, till he forsakes his character and commences a writer of romance. In this, however, those historians who relate public transactions, have the advantage of us who confine ourselves to scenes of private life . . . .

"But we who deal in private character, who search into the most retired recesses, and draw forth examples of virtue and vice from holes and corners of the world, are in a more

[17]The use of the word "historian" here is another example of Fielding's identifying his fiction with the temper of history. History and creative narrative alike test their data on the basis of credibility. Did Joan of Arc hear voices, or did she not? It would be a very bold historian of the twentieth century, save perhaps some Church apologist, who would assert that she did. This is an interesting point which Fielding contributes to the theory of verisimilitude.

dangerous situation. As we have no public notoriety, no con-
current testimony, no records to support and corroborate what
we deliver, it becomes us to keep within the limits not only of
possibility, but of probability too."

A thing may thus be possible, may even appear probable,
but still marvellous. And the historian must record it. But
these marvellous, or surprising occurrences should, says Fielding, "be such as may not only be within the compass of human
agency, and which human agents may probably be supposed to
do; but they should be likely for the very actors and characters
themselves to have performed; for what may be only wonderful
and surprizing in one man, may become improbable, or indeed
impossible, when related of another". Thus, Tom's magnanim-
ity towards Blifil at the end of the book may be surprising,
when one considers all that Blifil has done against Tom. But,
when one considers what Tom is like—that he is open-hearted
and generous and forgiving,—then the event, though surprising, is not improbable. If, on the other hand, Blifil had
suddenly turned magnanimous, such a reversal of a man's
whole nature would have appeared not merely surprising, but
incredible. Fielding thus affirms that faithfulness to the essential truths of human nature will permit the use of the
element of the marvellous which is within the limits of our
humanity. A character must always act in character. If he
is a mean hypocrite like Blifil, he cannot be made suddenly to
appear the opposite. This view of characterization—a liberal
treatment of the theory of decorum—is another important
Renaissance tenet. As I have pointed out, Le Bossu had
shown that Achilles could not be made to have the piety of
Aeneas, without violating the integrity of the characterization.
But an open-hearted man may be *surprisingly* magnanimous.
And, in the events themselves, unusual happenings may occur, which, though surprising, are not incredible, such as the
final solution of Tom's birth. Occasionally, Fielding may
strain coincidence, as when he has Tom, Partridge, and Mrs.
Waters meet together at the inn at Upton. But, even so, that

there is in human affairs an element of the marvellous which is not supernatural Fielding is perfectly justified in asserting. In fact, this quality of the marvellous in life is one of the reasons why men read and write tales. Coincidences and surprising turns of fortune do occur. Homer invoked the gods to account for them. We moderns say simply that chance has intervened. In asserting that his novels are histories, Fielding is really asserting that the surprising is probable. His events and his characters may be invented—as, according to the definition of comedy which was then held, they had to be; but they are true to human nature, and, as records of what might happen to a representative young man, they may contain, as does history, both the marvellous and verisimilar.

The problem for the writer of the modern epic has been, as I have stated, to combine modern material, conceived in a rationalistic spirit, with the form of the Greek and Latin epic. Fielding had studied the form, and he put the principles he had learned into practice. It is significant, I think, that both *Joseph Andrews* and *Tom Jones* are *Odysseys*, not *Iliads*. The *Iliad* is the tale of the heroic age far more than the *Odyssey* is. One could not write an *Iliad* without an Achilles and a Hector, mighty warriors of opposing camps. But one could write the story of a man's trying to get home after a long absence with a hero belonging to any age. In fact, Aristotle's summary of the *Odyssey*, barring the reference to Poseidon, might be the plot of a tale of any time and any country.

"A certain man has been absent from home for many years; he is dogged by Poseidon; and he is left companionless. Meanwhile, affairs at home are in evil case: his substance is being wasted by suitors to his wife, who have also formed a conspiracy to kill his son. Tempest-tossed, the man himself at length arrives, reveals who he is to certain persons, and attacks his enemies, the outcome being that he is preserved, and they perish."[18]

[18]Aristotle, *op. cit.*, p. 60.

That some of the escapes are marvellous is clear. They are equally marvellous in *Joseph Andrews* and *Tom Jones*. But in both the *Odyssey* and in Fielding's novels, the surprising seems, or is made to seem, probable.

CHAPTER IX

FIELDING'S THEORY OF COMEDY

Fielding had not only to adapt to his writing the principles of epic structure, but he had also to work out his theory of comedy,—or, if he did not have to work them out, he nevertheless did, for he was a child of his age and was interested in critical theories. Here also, he made for himself a theory of his own, based upon various traditional theories and slightly modified, in Fielding's finished theory, by his own practice.

In the *Preface* to *Joseph Andrews,* he starts with the usual Renaissance idea that the characters of comedy are of inferior rank to the characters of serious epic, this difference of rank in the characters constituting one of the essential differences between the serious and the comic.[1]

"Now a comic romance is a comic epic in prose; differing from comedy, as the serious epic from tragedy; its action being more extended and comprehensive; containing a much larger circle of incidents, and introducing a greater variety of characters. It differs from the serious romance in its fable and action, in this; that as in the one these are grave and solemn, so in the other they are light and ridiculous: it differs in its characters by introducing persons of inferior rank, and consequently, of inferior manners, whereas the grave romance sets the highest before us: lastly, in its sentiments and diction; by preserving the ludicrous instead of the sublime."

This distinction between the agents of the serious and of the comic was a commonplace of critical theory of Fielding's time. In his *Poetics, Aristotle* had said: "As for Comedy, this, as we have said, is an artistic imitation of men of an in-

[1]See Spingarn, *Literary Criticism of the Renaissance,* pp. 60-106.

ferior moral bent; faulty, however, not in any or every way, but only in so far as their shortcoming are ludicrous; for the Ludicrous is a species or part, not all, of the Ugly."[2]

Aristotle, it will be noted, does not say anything about rank. His distinction rests on moral grounds. But certain Renaissance critics, among other, Scaliger, made the distinction on the basis of rank.[3] Almost everyone who considered the matter at all either accepted the distinction as one of rank, or else said nothing about it. The distinction seems absurd in many ways, but the theory that the heroes of tragedy, who were assumed to be well-known historical figures, could not be made the subject of comic treatment is not without reason. If one assumes, as most critics did, that the function of comedy is to laugh men's follies to scorn, it will be difficult to get the effect of the ludicrous from depicting the behavior of great heroes and leaders of men, for the assumption in any tradition about a hero is that he is a leader and that he is heroic. This is, obviously, not the whole truth about tragedy and comedy. But it is one distinction between the kind of tragedy known to the critics—that is, the heroic—and the kind of comedy most highly esteemed—that is, the comedies of Plautus and Terence. Bourgeois tragedy, such as *A Woman Killed with Kindness,* has for its dominant emotional tone pathos rather than pity or terror. Even Shakespeare, who was little hampered by critical theorising, makes his tragic heroes of superior rank—that is, leaders in the state—and his merely comic characters, like Dogberry, persons of low rank, or like Falstaff, of negligible social importance.

In spite of what Fielding says about difference of rank in the agents as constituting one of the differences between serious epic and the comic epic, he apparently did not pay very much attention to the distinction, after all, at least so far as tragedy and comedy in the drama are concerned, for

[2]Aristotle, *Poetics,* p. 14.

[3]This actually was the practice of the tragedy of Aeschylus, Sophocles, and Euripidies, and of the comedy of Plautus and Terence. The tragic hero must be free, except for the workings of fate, and high rank helps to give him that freedom.

Fielding was one of George Lillo's most devoted admirers, and Fielding believed *George Barnwell* and *Fatal Curiosity* to be really tragic.[4] The fact that he repeats this traditional view is simply evidence that he *was* accepting a tradition. In his elaborated view of the comic prose epic, the idea about rank is of almost no importance. And, even in this early statement, the phrase "and, consequently, of inferior manners" is of more significance than that about rank, when viewed from the point of view of Fielding's own practice, though his characters are of inferior rank to the heroes of the serious epic.

After thus differentiating the comic from the serious epic, Fielding goes on to define the burlesque and the comic. The distinction about the social consequence of the agents is of importance in differentiating the comic epic from the burlesque epic, such as Scarron's *Virgile Travesti*. True comedy differs from the mock-heroic or the burlesque in that the characters of the latter are persons of great rank made trivial by the way in which they are treated. Fielding will admit burlesque, he says, in diction, but not in the fable or characters. Burlesque, he defines as "the exhibition of what is monstrous and unnatural, and where our delight, if we examine it, arises from the surprising absurdity, as in appropriating the manners of the highest to the lowest, or *è converso*."[5] In the comic, however, "we should ever confine ourselves strictly to nature, from the just imitation of which will flow all the pleasure we can this way convey to a sensible reader."

This distinction between the comic and the burlesque is like Aristotle's between the epic of the commonplace and the mock-heroic. "Thus the agents represented by Homer are better than we; the agents in the epic of the commonplace by Cleophon are on the average level; and those in the mock-heroic travesty of Homer by Hegemon of Thasos—who was

---

[4]See quotation from *The Champion*, Cross, *op. cit.*, Vol. I, p. 200.
"His Fatal Curiosity, which is a Masterpiece in its kind, and inferior only to Shakespeare's best pieces, gives him a Title to be called the best Tragic Poet of his Age."
[5]Fielding was very able in burlesque. His *Tom Thumb* is one of the best burlesques in the language.

the first to engage in the literature of parody—are below the average, as are the personages in the mock-heroic Diliad of Nicochares."[6] Fielding may not have had this distinction in mind, however, for, in the course of a paragraph or so, he quotes with approval the statement of Shaftesbury that there was no such thing as burlesque to be found among the ancients.

Another point about the agents of comedy is that they are given fictitious names. I have already quoted what Le Bossu has to say on the subject of the names of the characters in satire, comedy, and tragedy and epic. I might repeat it here.

"En cette Doctrine, nous trouverons avec Aristote trois sortes d'Actions que les Poëtes emploient. Dans la prémiere, les Choses & les Noms des Personnes sont singuliers & véritables, & non feints ou inventez par le Poëte. Les Satyriques en usent ainsi. Dans la seconde, & les choses & les Noms sont feints & inventez par le Poëte. C'est le stile des Comiques . . . . Dans la troisieme espéce, les Choses sont inventés, mais les Noms ne le sont pas. Ils sont connus par l'Histoire, ou par quelque Tradition . . . . Cette troisieme espéce d'Action est pour la Tragédie, et pour l'Epopée."[7]

Fielding certainly practices this doctrine in his comic prose epic, for all of the events and names are fictitious.[8] Furthermore, he states explicitly in his *Preface* to *Joseph Andrews* that although his characters are taken from life, their persons are obscured in such a way that it would be impossible to recognize them. It is doubtful whether he holds faithfully either to his statement that *Joseph Andrews* is a burlesque only in diction or to his other statement that his persons are so obscured that recognition is impossible. Certainly, neither

---

[6] Aristotle, *op. cit.*, p. 7.

[7] Le Bossu, op. cit., tom. I, pp. 88-89. The idea that the names in comedy are invented is derived from Aristotle's remarks on the "New Comedy", *Poetics*, p. 32. "That Poetry represents the universal has become clear enough in the present stage of Comedy; for the comic poets first combine plots out of probable incidents, and then supply such names for the agents as chance to fit the types—in contrast to the old iambic lampooners, whose method was to begin with particular individuals."

[8] Not quite all of the names are fictitious. He occasionally refers to actual persons. But all of the main characters bear fictitious names.

Richardson nor Colley Cibber would have admitted any such idea. In the main, however, that was Fielding's practice in *Joseph Andrews,* and it surely was in *Tom Jones.*

All of these points which have just been made have to do with a more or less formal definition of comedy as a literary type. They are important as showing how far Fielding accepted the prevailing theories of his day. His own attempt to penetrate the sources of the comic is, however, of more consequence. It is compounded of many things—of Cervantes, Lucian, Swift, his great Triumvirate of Laughter, of course—of Molière, whose plays he knew intimately and some of which he had translated, of Abbé Bellegarde's *Reflections on the Ridiculous,* of the traditional English criticism about "humours". And, finally, he worked out his own ideas, for none of these had precisely Fielding's conception.

Aristotle does not help him here. "Besides, it may seem remarkable," says Fielding, "that Aristotle, who is so fond and free of definitions, hath not thought proper to define the Ridiculous. Indeed, where he tells us it is proper to comedy, he hath remarked that villainy is not its object: but he hath not, as I remember, positively asserted what is. Nor doth the Abbé Bellegarde, who hath written a treatise on this subject, though he shows us many species of it, once trace it to its fountain."[9]

He might have added that neither do Cervantes, Lucian, Swift, although they undoubtedly possessed the comic sense.[10] And, of course, we must admit that no one who has come after or before Fielding has suceeded wholly in tracing the Comic Spirit to its source, although George Meredith, Bergson, and others have written about it suggestively. Ben Jonson, Fielding states, has somewhat the same ideas about the Ridiculous which he himself holds—that is, that the ridiculous arises from affectation.[11]

[9]*Preface* to *Joseph Andrews.*

[10]Addison had some excellent things to say on humor, scattered throughout the *Spectator* Papers, but there is no evidence that Fielding had these things in mind.

[11]Affectation is the object of attack in much of the comedy which Fielding knew, even where the principle is not explicitly stated.

"The only source of the true Ridiculous (as it appears to me)," says Fielding,[12] "is affectation. But though it arises from one spring only, when we consider the infinite streams into which this one branches, we shall presently cease to admire at the copious field its affords to an observer. Now, affectation proceeds from one of these two causes, vanity or hypocrisy: for as vanity puts us on affecting false characters, in order to purchase applause, so hypocrisy sets us on an endeavor to avoid censure, by concealing vices under an appearance of their opposite virtues. And though these two causes are often confounded (for there is some difficulty in distinguishing them), yet, as they proceed from very different motives, so they are as clearly distinct in their operations: for indeed, the affectation which arises from vanity is nearer to truth than the other, as it hath not that violent repugnancy of nature to struggle with, which that of the hypocrite hath. It may be likewise noted, that affectation doth not imply an absolute negation of those qualities which are affected; and, therefore, though, when it proceeds from hypocrisy, it be nearly allied to deceit; yet when it comes from vanity only, it partakes of the nature of ostentation: for instance, the affectation of liberality in a vain man differs visibly from the same affectation in the avaricious; for though the vain man is not what he would appear, or hath not the virtue he affects, to the degree he would be thought to have it; yet it sits less awkwardly on him than on the avaricious man, who is the very reverse of what he would seem to be.

"From the discovery of this affectation arises the Ridiculous, which always strikes the reader with surprise and pleasure; and that in a higher and stronger degree when the affectation arises from hypocrisy, than when from vanity; for to discover anyone to be the exact reverse of what he affects, is more surprising, and consequently more ridiculous, than to find him a little deficient in the quality he desires the reputation of."

[12]*Preface* to *Joseph Andrews.*

Ugliness, misery, and vice can never be the object of laughter, for the last arouses detestation, while the two former arouse pity. And wherever he has introduced these into his novel, they are not as subjects of ridicule, but as subjects of pity or destestation, as the case may be. Thus, Fielding excludes certain subjects as the objects of comic treatment—subjects which *are,* however, the objects of satiric treatment, especially satire of the Juvenalian sort. By implication, he thus excludes satire from the Comic—as does Meredith, of course. No doubt, it was because Fielding felt that Rabelais and Aristophanes had not thus limited the objects of their comedy that he came ultimately to rank them less high than he had earlier in his life. I must say, however, that had I been Fielding, I should not have included Swift, who seems to me more Juvenalian than Horatian.[13]

The incongruity between a person's pretensions and his inner being, or his actual behavior, was, then, the source of the ridiculous for Fielding—as it is, in one way or another, for Bergson, for George Meredith, for Schopenhauer. Fielding was assisted in arriving at this idea, it seems almost certain, by his love for Molière. One of Molière's best known comedies has for its central theme, a theme implied in its title, this very subject. I refer to *Les Précieuses Ridicules,* a comedy about the pretentious women of Madeleine de Scudéry's circle. La Harpe says that, before Molière, the word "précieuse" had a desirable connotation, as defining a woman "d'un merite distingué et de très-bonne compagnie", and that, after Molière, it connoted something ridiculous only.[14] Moliére himself defines his attitude very precisely in *La Critique de l'Ecole der Femmes.*

For instance, Uranie says: "L'honnêteté d'une femme n'est pas dans les grimaces. Il sied mal de vouloir être plus sage que celles qui sont sages. L'affectation en cette matiere

---

[13]Perhaps the works of Swift which Fielding had in mind were such things as *The Tale of the Tub* and *A Battle of the Books* rather than *A Modest Proposal* or even *Gulliver's Travels.*

[14]Moliere, *Oeuvres,* tom. I, p. 416, *n.*

est pire qu'en toute autre; et je ne vois rien de si ridicule que cette delicatesse d'honneur qui prend tout en mauvaise part, donne un sens criminel aux plus innocentes paroles, et s'offense de l'ombre des choses."

The ridiculous here is, by implication, taken to arise from affectation, in this case, the affectation of delicacy. Or take this speech of Elise's on the subject of the word "précieuse".

"Elle se defend du mom, mais non pas de la chose: car enfin elle l'est depuis les pieds jusqu'à la tête, & la plus grande façonniere du monde. Il semble que tout son corps soit demonté, & que les movements de ses hanches, de ses epaules & de sa tête, n'aillent que par ressorts. Elle affecte toujours un ton de voix languissant & niais, fait la moue pour montrer une petite bouche, & roule les yeux pour les faire paroitre grands."

In fact, Fielding had only to meditate upon Molière's great characters in the light of these remarks just quoted to see that in the Frenchman's comedies—as distinct from his farces—affectation of some sort was the source of the ridiculous, as Molière says it was explicitly of *Les Précieuses Ridicules*. There are Tartuffe, the religious hypocrite, his bourgeois gentleman, the Miser (Harpagon), all of them in one way or another exhibiting a kind of affectation, though the affectation is not necessarily the central point of the comedy.

Such characters are characters of humors (I use the word here in the Jonsonian sense). There is the miser, dominated by his one desire for gold. There is the religious hypocrite. There is the prude. One characteristic dominates each person and constitutes his folly. Many of Fielding's characters are of the same sort. Such, for example, are Mrs. Slipslop, Lady Booby, Square and Thwackum. One of Fielding's ideas about the comic has to do with this Jonsonian conception of humors. In one of the *Covent Garden* articles, Fielding is discussing the prevalence of characters of humor in England. In this connection, he makes a statement which is interesting: "Hitherto there is no Mention of the Ridiculous, the Idea of which, though not essential to Humour, is always included in our notions of it. The Ridiculous is annexed to it these two ways, either by the Manner or the Degree in which it is exerted."[15] This idea of the ridiculous supplements the one outlined in the *Preface* to *Joseph Andrews*. Not only affectation, but the dominance of one quality—which may be a kind of affectation, or lead to it—constitutes the ridiculous.

But several of Fielding's greatest characters do not come under this category. Parson Adams is not a character of humor in the Jonsonian sense. He is a character of humor, in the sense in which Meredith defines the word humor. In fact, Meredith uses Parson Adams as an example of the spirit of humor, as opposed to a character embodying the comic spirit.[16] Parson Adams had little affectation. One of the few places in which his pretentions do not match his performance is the scene in which his little boy is reported dead. He has just been lecturing Joseph on the advantages of submitting to one's fate, but when this disaster seems to overtake him,—we are delighted to learn that it has not done so—he finds it as difficult as Joseph had to submit to fate. Parson Adams is, in fact, modeled on Don Quixote, who is not a character of Jonsonian humor. It is somewhat hard to make a *logical* distinction between the two types of ridiculous—that is, between a person like Mrs. Slipslop and Parson Adams—though the difference is immediately obvious. There is irony in Parson Adams, and beauty. In the last analysis, we admire him for the very things which make him absurd, just as we do Don Quixote. And we never admire Mrs. Slipslop, nor Harpagon. We feel a kind of tragedy, or tragic irony, in Harpagon. We never love nor admire him. He evokes the "thoughtful laughter" of Meredith. But our laughter over Parson Adams lies deeper still.

[15]*Covent Garden Journal*, No. 55, July 18, 1752. This article contains a really excellent treatment of the theory of humors.
[16]Meredith, *Essay on Comedy*, edited by Lane Cooper, p. 135. "The Book of Fielding upon Richardson is essentially comic. His method of correcting the sentimental writer is a mixture of the comic and the humorous. Parson Adams is a creation of humor."

In any event, Fielding's practice in the creation of character was wider and more varied than his theory. There is one kind of comedy in Blifil, a Molièresque one, although Molière created a more credible hypocrite in Tartuffe than Fielding did in Blifil. The traditional character of humor like Jonson's Face and Subtle and Brainworm is represented by Mrs. Slipslop, Square, and Thwackum. Don Quixote, who tilts at windmills and believes in the heroic, the rejected buffoon Falstaff calling out "God" three times as he died, live again in Parson Adams, set upon by practical jokers at one moment and the next throwing his hand-copied Aeschylus into the fire when Fanny faints, or rising up in simple, but austere dignity in church to rebuke the egregious Pamela.

Fielding's theory of comedy, then, starts with a traditional conception, but he refines this theory and develops besides a theory of the nature of the ridiculous which is true, though perhaps not the whole truth. His own comedy is richer than his theory of comedy. In his practice, he grasps fully the element of incongruity which lies at the heart of the risible, and, in so doing, evokes our "thoughful laughter". Finally, his comedy is at once thoroughly English and yet universal. Squire Western is unmistakably an eighteenth century squire; yet he is perfectly comprehensible to an American today. Parson Adams is modeled upon a Spanish prototype, but he is as English as Don Quixote is Spanish, even though the source of their absurdity is the same—their common failure to accept the world of fact rather than the ideal world which they have created from their own faith.

The Comic Spirit is, for Fielding, a weapon for making men see their follies. He uses farce, burlesque, satire, irony, humor, wit, anything and everything. He writes a comic version of Homer in several great battle scenes—one of them being the scene between Joseph, the parson, and the hounds in *Joseph Andrews,* and another that between Molly and her rivals in the church-yard in *Tom Jones.* Some of the beatings which Parson Adams receives are pure horse play. The scene

when a great lady refuses to let the naked and miserable
Joseph into the coach has a touch of the satiric, quickly re-
lieved by the simple human kindliness of the coach boy who
succors his fellowman.   This is followed by the ironic touch
of the coach boy's being transported for robbing a hen roost.
We can love Tom Jones or Parson Adams without being at
the same time blind to their ridiculous side.   And, as I have
said, Parson Adams is more than merely a figure for "thoughtful laughter", for we actually admire him, and, with Don
Quixote, he remains the embodiment of all that is absurd and
tragic and admirable in the idealism and simplicity of mankind.   Not once does Fielding fail to make this figure realistic in a simple and homely fashion.   In the scene in Book IV
of *Joseph Andrews* where the parson after various escapades
in the course of the night, creeps, unknowingly, into Fanny's
bed, Fielding makes this remark: "Adams groped out the
bed, and, turning the clothes down softly, a custom Mrs. Adams
had long accustomed him to, crept in, and deposited his car-
case on the bedpost, a place which that good woman had always
assigned him."[17]   In spite of such a detail, Parson Adams
remains a heroic figure, and does not become a figure at which
men can point the finger of scorn for letting himself be ruled
by a woman.

Squire Western is a stock figure in English comedy—the
ignorant country squire, who, when he goes to town, is the
dupe of all.   But, even when we are angry with him for his
stupidity in his management of Sophia, we still are fond of
him.   His stupidity and obstinacy provoke our "thoughtful
laughter", rather than our indignation, and we see deeply into
the folly which parents sometimes display toward their be-
loved children.   He is a better figure in this respect than Sir
Austin Feverel.   One never feels really kindly toward Sir
Austin who is a satiric rather than a comic character. (Meredith
had not, of course, fully developed this theory of comedy when
he wrote *The Ordeal of Richard Feverel*.)

[17]*Joseph Andrews*, Book IV, Ch. XIV.

Nor does Fielding hesitate to make sly fun of his heroines. Sophia's forehead, he says, "might have been higher without prejudice to her". Amelia had a broken nose. To be sure, the broken nose of Amelia militated against her charms as a heroine to such an extent that the novel *Amelia* was less widely sold than Fielding had expected. But, in spite of this, even because of this sly fun, the heroines are the more real.

In his theory of comedy, then, Fielding started with certain Renaissance conceptions. The characters of comedy are of lower rank than those of tragedy, and of inferior manners. He thus opposes to comedy the heroic sort of tragedy rather than the bourgeois tragedy like those of his friend George Lillo. The purpose of comedy is didactic—to teach by example rather than by precept. The source of the Ridiculous is affectation, as affirmed by Ben Jonson, and by Molière. Both the names of his characters and the events of his novels are fictitious, as Le Bossu had said was the practise of the comic writers.

Fielding's comedy is sometimes burlesque, sometimes satiric, sometimes farcical. It is very English—it is the comedy of Shakespeare and Dickens and Thackeray—seldom purely of the mind but touched with some emotion. Beneath all, is the perception of the irony of life, and a belief in the beauty of sanity and essential balance and harmony of spirit. His novels show us that this spirit of sanity and proportion goes with health of mind—and indeed, of body, for his characters are all vigorous, healthy creatures. Sophia has a "sane mind in a sound body" in contrast to Richardson's morbid Clarissa. The sense of the incongruous plays over everything. The favorite sermon of Parson Adams,—the least affected of men— the one about which he is really tremendously vain, is a sermon on vanity. Parson Adams is always the butt of ridicule, but he is bigger than any who ridicule him. Prudential morality, a narrow, unhealthy performing of what is conventional just because it *is* prudent, is made to seem thoroughly absurd and thoroughly bad. One of the best comic things in *Joseph Andrews* is the picture we get there of the prudent Pamela, now Squire Booby's "lady". (The name, Booby, is itself a stroke of the Comic Spirit!) Here Pamela's affectations are stripped from her, and we see her pluming herself on her position and telling Joseph what *he* owes her new position.

Richardson never viewed his characters as the gods might view them—*sub specie aeternitatis*. He was one of them. But the Comic Spirit is Olympian, and Fielding, writing in his "little parlor", breathes that air. I think he probably merely despised Pamela when he write *Shamela*—if he wrote it, as he surely must—but he had learned to laugh Jovian laughter when he wrote *Joseph Andrews,* and there made simple, ridiculous Parson Adams rebuke the virtuous Pamela, lady of Squire Booby, for her behavior in church.

CHAPTER X

CONCLUSION

In Chapter I of Book XIII of *Tom Jones*, Fielding writes his epic Invocation. All good epics have an invocation, and Fielding has followed the rules too carefully to omit one. Instead of invoking the Muse, however, he invokes Genius, Learning, Humanity, and Experience. And these divine ideas —to be a Platonist where Fielding was an Aristotelian—responded bounteously. He had all these gifts, and in abundance. I have attempted to show what his learning was. Any lover of Parson Adams and of the scapegrace Tom Jones will know of the humanity of their creator. He will know as well of Fielding's experience as he follows the shifting scenes in and out of inns, among highwaymen, parsons, London society ladies, West Country squires. Nor can he doubt that the author of *Tom Jones,* very nearly the first English novel and probably still the greatest one, had genius. One aspect of Fielding's genius is apt to be overlooked, however, in the wealth of his other endowments—that, though he was an innovator, consciously writing a new form "not hitherto attempted in our language," he was a traditionalist. Perhaps, we should think of Fielding, not as the first English novelist, but as the last of the Renaissance writers of epic.

In giving to English literature this "new province of writing", Fielding accomplished what so many others had attempted and failed. He had written a modern epic. The old world of personal heroes, of Achilles, Hector, Ajax, Agamemnon, had passed. No Alaric, nor Polexandre, nor Prince Arthur could be made to live—even by a man of genius— with quite the same reality with which Achilles lives. The

ancient epics gave us a picture of their world because they
gave us pictures of the most representative men of those
worlds. In somewhat the same way, Tom Jones is a representative young man of his age. Our modern heroes seldom
hold in their hands the cause of victory or defeat for their
armies; nor do they often sail over unknown seas to found
new nations. Their struggles are with their own natures—
how to do right, or to learn what is the right thing to do—
and with the fairly settled and prosaic society around them.
The modern novel is a thing of great variety, and many novels
are far away from the mood and scope of Fielding's. But
they all have, at the heart of their conception, this in common
—their clinging to the knowledge that, in some way, their
characters and their situations must be representative of at
least a part of the modern world. No Hippogriffs race madly
through the realistic novels we now read. Nor do the heroes
don armor and play the knight errant, as did the heroes of
the heroic romances. And the marvellous is still, as it was for
Fielding, the surprising, not the supernatural.

But that is not all that Fielding achieved. To the realistic
accounts of ordinary men such as we find in *Robinson Crusoe,*
or *Gil Blas,* or *Le Roman Comique,* Fielding added an artistic
pattern. So long as the realistic narrative of the commonplace remained without artistic pattern, its appeal was largely
a kind of *news* appeal. Whatever theory of art one may hold,
the one essential thing in any work of art is that it be a whole.
A history of all the events which occur to one man may be
interesting as biography—true or fictitious though the events
may be. But when these events are arranged into a complex pattern of cause and effect, which may have their focus in
some central theme, then the account becomes a whole, and
communicates to the reader that sense of balance and harmony
which is one of the vital effects of a work of art. In giving
this element of dramatic concentration to his narrative, Fielding thus made his novels works of art and made possible the
great development of modern novel as a literary form. Again,

one may say, that though today our novels vary exceedingly in their form, some of them highly episodic, some of them almost austerely dramatic, all of them, at their best, have a definite pattern—what Fielding and his contemporaries would have called a fable.

It would be interesting to digress here with a discussion of the English novel, past and present. The term "novel" is a very loose one, and is used to name things as diverse as *The Forsyte Saga*—whose title denies its epic impulse and asserts its structural kinship with the Old Norse Sagas—and *Mrs. Dalloway,* a series of episodes of the consciousness. Fielding is not the parent of all these forms. He taught later novelists how to handle large groups of characters and events. He also showed the relation of coincidence and surprise to the marvellous and to life. Perhaps no better justification of the part chance plays in narrative has even been written than what Fielding has to say about the marvellous. To call him the "Father of the English novel" is, however, a little misleading. He is far closer to Homer's *Odyssey* than to James Joyce's *Ulysses.* But he is the father of English prose epic—a form which has been of great significance in the work of many of his great successors, many of whom have freely acknowledged their indebtedness.

Fielding, then, writing in his little parlor, turned to the past and learned how to handle his material, so that the effect should be that given by a whole. He looked at men around him, and remained faithful to the world which he saw. He was traditionalist and innovator, Ancient and Modern. And not the least important of the many things which he gave to English literature are his prefactory chapters, where he tells us what he is doing, showing us show he has utilized the technique of other men, how he has adapted traditional ideas, how he has "invented" his men and their deeds. The history of the English novel begins with Fielding, and no literary historian can write a history of the novel without including him. But the historian of criticism should also study the critical contributions of this literary creator and see how a founder of "a new province of writing "worked out his problems on the basis of critical discussions which had gone on for several centuries and which have their roots ultimately in the remote past.

APPENDIX

The following pages contain a verbatim copy of the pamphlet in the British Museum which gives a list of Fielding's library.

The prices in the right-hand column have been added in ink in the original pamphlet, presumably by the auctioneer. I have not copied an occasional written notation in the left-hand margin, giving the name of the purchaser.

A CATALOGUE of the entire and valuable LIBRARY of BOOKS of the late HENRY FIELDING, Esq.; which (by order of the administrator) will be sold by AUCTION, by SAMUEL BAKER, at his house in *York Street, Covent Garden,* on *Monday, Feb.* the 10th, and the three following evenings, for the benefit of his WIFE and FAMILY. Among many other Valuable books are the following in FOLIO.

Statutes at large down to the 26th year of the Reign of the present King, 34 vol.
Almost all the Reports in Law.
Cay's Abridgment of the Statutes, 2 vol.
Horfman's Conveyancing, 3 vol.
Rymer's Foedera, 20 vol.
State Tryals, 6 vol.
Rushworth's Collections, 8 vol.
Pococke's Travels, 2 vol.
Burnet's Reformation, 3 vol.
Ralph's History of England, 2 vol.
Thurloe's State Papers, 7 vol.
Locke's, Clarke's, Tillotson's, Boyle's, and Bacon's Works.
Thuanus per Buckley, 7 vol.
Dictionaire de Bayle, 5 vol.
Grotii Opera, 4 vol.
Constantini Lexicon, 2 vol.
Dion. Halicarnasseus, ab Hudsono, 2 vol.
Aristophanes Kusteri.
Plato, Gr. Lat. Serrani, 3 vol.

Suidae Lexicon, Kusteri, 3 vol.
Stephani Lexicon Graecum, 4 vol.
Seldeni Opera, 6 vol.
Plutarchi Opera, Gr. Lat. 2 vol. Paris
Demosthenes, Gr. Lat. *Edit. Opr.*
Polybius, Gr. Lat. Casauboni.

There are likewise most of the Greek Commentators on ARISTOTLE, and several Books with Mr. FIELDING'S *MSS.* Notes.

The said collection may be view'd on *Thursday* the 6th and every Day after, till the Time of sale, which will begin at half an hour after five o'clock.

CATALOGUES to be had *gratis* at the place of sale, of Mr. MILLAR in the *Strand;* Mr. DODSLEY'S *Pall Mall;* Mr. MEADOWS in *Cornhill;* and Mr. OWEN'S *Temple Bar.*

CONDITIONS OF SALE

I.   THAT he who bids most is the Buyer, but if any Dispute arises, the Book or Books to be put up to sale again.

II. That no Person advances less than Three pence each bidding under Five shillings; above Five Shillings, Sixpence; and above One Pound, One Shilling.

III. That the Books are supposed to be perfect, but if any appear otherwise before taken away, the Bidder is at his choice to take or leave them.

IV. That each person give in his name, and pay Five shillings in the pound (if demanded) for what he buys.

V.   That no books are to be delivered in the time of selling, unless first paid for.

VI. The books must be taken away at the Buyer's Expence, and the Money paid at the Place of Sale within Three Days after the Sale is ended.

     N.B. Any Gentlemen who cannot attend the sale, may have their Commissions receiv'd and faithfully executed.

> *By their most humble servant,*
> *Samuel Baker.*

First Night's SALE
February 10, 1755.

BOOKS in OCTAVO and INFRA

1. Coke's Reports, 7 vol. *best Edit.* 1738   (2.12.6)
2. Brown's Privilegia Parlimentaria 1704
3. Privilegia Londini, or Laws, Customs, and Privileges
   of London 1716   (0. 1.3)
4. Manwood's Forrest Laws 1741   (0. 1.0)
5. English Pleader, or Collection of Precedents, &c............. 1734   (0. 1.0)
6. Styles's Practical Register 1707
7. Lilley's Continuation of ditto, 2 vol. 1710   (0. 2.0)
8. Shaw's Parish Law...................................... 1748   (0. 2.0)
9. Parson's Answer to the fifth part of Coke's Reports, 4 to. 1606   (0. 1.0)
10. Shaw's Practical Justice, 2 vol. 1733
11. Nelson's Office of a Justice of Peace, 2 vol. 1745   (0. 5.9)
12. Readings upon the Statutes, 5 vol. 1723   (2. 7.0)
13. Cases and Resolutions in the King's Bench, on
    Settlements and Removals 1732
14. Wingate's Britton 1640   (0. 1.9)
15. Compleat Juryman 1752   (0. 1.6)
16. Legal Provisions for the Poor, by S.C. 1725
17. Oeuvres de Boileau, 3 tom. ....*Amst.* 1717   (0. 3.0)
18. L'Iliade and Odyssée d'Homere, per Dacier, 6
    tom. ....*Amst.* 1712   (0. 5.0)
19. Lucien, par Ablancourt, 2 tom. ....*Amst.* 1697
20. Histoire des Revolutions de la Republique Ro-
    maine, par Vertot, 3 tom. ....*Par.* 1720   (0. 2.9)
21. Le Nouveau Testament, par Martin ....*Lond.* 1750   (0. 1.0)
22. Addison's Freeholder   1744   (0. 1.9)
23. Buchanan's Detectioun of the Duinges of Marie
    Quene of Scottes ....   (0. 2.9)
24. Life of Mr. Richard Hooker   1665   (0. 0.6)
25. Les Oeuvres de Sarasin ....*Par.* 1663   (0. 1.0)
26. Bulstrode's Essay on Transmigration in defense of
    Pythagoras   1692   (0. 1.0)
27. Child's Discourse on Trade ....   (0. 2.6)
28. Luciani Opera, Gr. & Lat. a Zuingero, 4 tom ....*Bas.* 1619   (0. 2.0)
29. Les Avantures de Telemaque ....*Lond.* 1745   (0. 1.9)
30. Morus de optimo Reipublicae Statu; & nova
    Insula Utopia ....*Glasg.* 1750   (0. 2.9)
31. Catullus, Tibullus & Propertius, Scaligeri, *Par. H. Stepb.* 1577   (0. 2.3)

32. Revolutions de Portugal, par Vertot. ....*Lond.* 1730 (0. 1.3)
33. Sophoclis Tragoediae, Gr. & Lat. 2 tom. ....*Glasg.* 1745 (0. 3.0)
34. Le Theatre de la Foire, ou l'Opera Comique par
    d'Orneval, 3 tom. ....*Par.* 1721 (0. 4.3)
35. Le Plutus, & les Nuées d'Aristophane, par Mad.
    le Fevre ....*Lyon.* 1696 (0. 1.0)
36. Pensées de Paschal sur la Religion ....*Amst.* 1700 (0. 1.6)
37. Novum Testamentum Graecum, Millii ....*Amst.* 1735 (0. 1.0)
38. Revolutions de Suede, par Vertot ....*Par.* 1695 (0. 1.6)
39. King's British Merchant, 3 vol. 1748 (0. 5.3)
40. Persius's Satires, with notes Lat. and Eng. 1751 (0. 1.6)
41. Le Theatre de P. and T. Corneille, 10 tom. ......*Amst.* 1701 (0.12.0)
42. Cicero's Letters, by Melmoth, 3 vol. 1752 (0.12.0)
43. Toland's Miscellaneous Works, 2 vol. 1747 (0. 5.6)
44. Lucian's Works, by Dryden, 4 vol. 1711 (0. 8.6)
45. Butler's Hudibras, with Notes by Grey, 2 vol. 1744 (0.11.6)
46. South's Sermons, 6 vol. 1722 (0.15.0)
47. Deism Reveal'd, 2 vol. 1749 (0. 7.0)
48. Potter's Antiquities of Greece, 2 vol. ....*Oxf.* 1697 (0. 3.6)
49. Plutarch's Morals, 5 vol. 1694 (0.10.0)
50. Dodwell's Life, by Brokesby, 2 vol. 1715 (0. 1.0)
51. Calamy's Abridgment of Baxter's Life, 2 vol. 1713 (0. 2.0)
52. Polybius's History, by Saville, 2 vol. 1698 (0. 9.6)
53. Plautus's Comedies, Lat. & Eng. by Cook, vol. 1st. 1747 (0. 3.3)
54. Collins's Grounds & Reasons of Religion 1724 (0. 2.6)
55. History of the Devils of London 1703 (0. 1.0)
56. Journey thro' England and Scotland, 3 vol. 1732 (0. 5.6)
57. Petyt's Antient Right of the Commons of England 1680 (0. 2.9)
58. Histoire Critique de l'Etablissement des Bretons
    dans les Gaules, 2 vol. ....*Par.* 1720 (0. 2.9)
59. Grabei Septuaginta, 8 tom. in 4 vol. ....*Oxon.* 1707 (0.13.6)
60. Vita Johannis Barwick ....*Lond.* 1721
61. Smith Miscellanea ....*Lond.* 1686
62. Horatii Opera, in Usum Delphini ....*Lond.* 1694 (0. 2.3)
63. Virgilii Opera, in Usum Delphini ....*Lond.* 1696 (0. 2.9)
64. Herodiani Historia, Gr. & Lat. ....*Oxon.* 1678 (0. 1.6)
65. Theocritus, cum Scholiis Graecis ....*Lond.* 1729 (0. 0.6)
66. Asserii Annales Alfredi Magni, a Wise ....*Oxon.* 1722 (0. 1.6)
67. Juvenalis & Persii Satyrae in Usum Delph. ....*Lond.* 1722 (0. 2.6)
68. Grotius de Jure Belli ac Pacis, cum notis Barbeyrac,
    2 tom. ....*Amst.* 1720 (0. 5.0)
69. Livii Historia, 2 tom. ....*Lond.* 1702 (0. 8.6)

172   UNIVERSITY OF WISCONSIN STUDIES

70. Lucretius de Rerum Natura, a Creech ....*Lond.* 1717
71. Aristotelis Politices, Gr. & Lat. Heinsii ....*L. Bat.* 1621   (0. 1.0)
72. Traité de la Divination du Ciceron, par Desmarais
     ....*Amst.* 1711   (0. 0.6)
73. Rossi Warwicensis Historia Angliae, a Hearne,....*Oxon.* 1745   (0. 2.6)
74. Leland's Itinerary, per Hearne, 9 vol. in 5 ....*Ox.* 1745   (1. 3.0)
75. Fabricii Bibliotheca Latina, 3 tom. ....*Hamb.* 1721   (0. 3.0)
76. Oeuvres de Racine, 2 tom. ....*Par.* 1713   (0. 4.3)
77. Burnet's Travels thro' Switzerland, Italy, &c.....*Rotter.* 1687   (0. 2.0)
78. Causes Celebres & Interessantes, par Pitaval, 22 tom.
     ....*Haye* 1737   (1.19.0)
79. Oeuvres de Gilbert ....*Par.* 1643   (0. 0.6)
80. Le Theatre Italien, de Gherardi, 6 tom. ....*Par.* 1717   (0. 6.0)
81. L'Etat de la France, 6 tom. ....*Par.* 1736   (0. 5.6)
82. Histoire des Revolutions d'Angleterre, par Orleans,
     3 tom. ....*Haye* 1719   (0. 5.0)
83. Essai Philosophique sur l'ame des Betes, 2 tom. *Amst.* 1737   (0. 2.0)
     A Parcel of odd Volumes in Octavo and Duodecimo....   (1. 3.0)
     (Pamphlets) ....   (' 0. 4.6)

QUARTO

84. Fitzherbert's Natura Brevium, with Judge Hale's
     Commentary 1730   (0.15.0)
85. Seldeni Fleta, seu Comment Juris Anglicani 1685   (0. 6.0)
86. Bracton de Legibus 1640   (0.11.0)
87. Gouldsborough's Reports 1653   (0. 0.6)
88. Godbolt's Reperts 1652   (0.14.6)
89. De Paenis Criminalibus 1597   (0. 2.6)
90. Staundford's Pleas of the Crown 1607
91. Justiniani Institutiones ....*Par.* 1659   (0. 1.0)
92. Vinii Comment. Institut. Imperialium ....*L. Bat.* 1726   (0. 9.6)
93. Vossius de Historicis Latinis ....*L. Bat.* 1651   (0. 1.0)
94. .... de veterum Poetarum Temporibus....*Amst.* 1654   (0. 0.6)
95. Aristotle de Rhetorica, Gr. & Lat. Goulstoni ....*Lond.* 1619   (0. 0.6)
96. Spinozae Opera Posthuma 1677   (0. 5.0)
97. Newton's Observations on Daniel, and the Apocalypse 1733   (0. 5.0)
98. Hill's Review of the Works of the Royal Society.... 1751
99. Hooke's Roman History, 2 vol. 1751   (1.15.0)
100. Cruden's Concordance to the Bible 1738   (0.11.0)
101. Cumberland on the Laws of Nature............................ 1727   (0. 6.6)
     A Parcel of Quarto's in various Languages ....   (0. 2.6)

FOLIO

102. Hawkins's Pleas of the Crown, 2 vol. *with a great
     number of MSS Notes by Mr. Fielding* 1726   (1. 2.0)
103. Statutes at large, 5 vol. to the ninth of K. George,
     with the Continuation of all the Acts of Parliament
     from the Ninth of K. George I, to the XXVI of K.
     George the II, 29 vol. the whole making 34 vol........   (10. 0.0)
104. Wilkins Leges Anglo-Saxonicae 1721   (0. 6.6)
105. Year Books, 7 vol. *compleat & best edit.* ....   (3. 3.0)
106. Horsman's Conveyancing, 3 vol. 1744   (3. 0.0)
107. Dalton's Country Justice 1715   (0. 2.6)
108. Skinner's Reports 1728   (0.18.0)
109. Cases in Chancery, 2 parts, with select Cases 1735   (0.15.6)
110. Finch's Reports 1725   (0. 5.0)
111. Levinz's Reports, 3 vol. in 2 1702   (0. 5.0)
112. Oliver's Acts and Ordinances ....   (0. 2.0)
113. Coke's Reports, 3 vol. 1671   (0. 4.0)
114. Jones's (Sir Thomas) Reports 1729   (0.11.0)
115. Hobart's Reports, *best edit.* 1724   (0.12.6)
116. Pusendorf's Law of Nature and Nations, by Barbeyrac 1729   (0.13.0)
117. Rolle's Abridgment 1668   (0.11.0)
118. Barlow's Justice of Peace 1745   (0.13.0)
119. Dyer's Reports, *best edit.* 1688   (0.15.6)
120. Jones' (Sir William) Reports 1675   (1. 1.0)
121. Wood's new Institute of the Civil War 1730   (0. 9.0)
122. Palmer's Reports 1688   (0. 2.6)
123. Keyling's Reports 1708   (0. 5.6)
124. Aleyn's Reports 1688   (0. 4.0)
125. Saunders' Reports, 2 vol. 1686   (0. 2.6)
126. Vernon's Cases in Chancery. 2 vol. 1726   (1.15.0)
127. Sigonius de Antiquo Jure Civium Romanorum,
     Italiæ, &c. ....*Paris* 1576
128. Cowell's Law Dictionary 1708
129. Ventris's Reports. 2 vol. 1701   (0. 7.0)
130. Lord Raymond's Reports. 2 vol. 1743   (2.12.6)
131. Hale's History of the Pleas of the Crown, 2 vol........ 1736   (0.16.0)
132. Hetley's Reports 1657   (0. 3.0)
133. Ley's Reports 1659   (0. 1.0)
134. Booth's Nature and Practice of real Actions 1701   (0. 4.6)
135. Bridgman's Reports 1659   (0. 4.0)
136. Tremaine's Pleas of the Crown 1723   (0. 5.0)
137. Moore's Reports 1688   (0. 4.0)

138. Style's Modern Reports 1658   (0.10.6)
139. Peere William's Reports, 3 vol. 1746   (4. 5.0)
140. Scobell's Acts and Ordinances of Parliament 1658   (0. 3.0)
141. Fitzherbert's Grand Abridgment. 2 vol. 1565   (0. 2.6)
142. Carthew's Reports 1741   (0.15.0)
143. Yelverton's Reports 1674   (0. 2.0)
144. Fitz-Gibbons' Reports 1732   (0.10.6)
145. Savile's Reports 1688
146. Owen's Reports 1656   (0. 3.6)
147. Benloe and Dalison's Reports 1689   (0. 3.0)
148. Carter's Reports 1688   (0. 6.0)
149. Cay's Abridgment of the Statutes, 2 vol. 1739   (3.13.6)
150. Domat's Civil Law and Supplement, 3 vol. 1722   (0.16.0)
151. Shower's Reports, 2 vol. 1708   (1.14.0)
152. Dawson of the Origin of Laws 1694   (0. 2.6)
153. Rolle's Reports 1675   (0.10.6)
154. Davis's Reports 1674   (0. 5.6)
155. Hutton's Reports 1682   (0. 3.0)
156. Comberbach's Reports 1724   (0.11.9)
157. Dalton's Country Justice 1705   (0. 3.0)
158. Modern Reports, 6 vol. 1700   (2. 1.0)
159. Keilwey's Reports 1688   (0. 1.6)
160. Anderson's Reports, 2 vol. 1664   (0. 5.0)
161. Farresley's Cases in King's Bench 1716   (0. 6.0)
162. The same Book 1725   (0. 9.6)
163. Raymond's (Sir Thomas) Reports 1696   (0. 9. 0)
   A Parcel of Folios in various languages ....   (0.12.0)

Second Night's SALE

February 11, 1755.

OCTAVO and *INFRA.*

164. Aeschyli Tragoediae, Gr. & Lat. 2 tom. ....*Glasg.* 1746   (0. 3.0)
165. Causes de la Corruption du Gout, par Dacier. *Amst.* 1715   (0. 0.9)
166. Memoires de Joli, 2 tom. ....*Amst.* 1718   (0. 1.0)
167. Oeuvres de Montfleury, 2 tom ....*Par.* 1705   (0. 2.9)
168. .... de Moliere, 8 tom. ....*Par.* 1718   (0.12.0)
169. Moore's Fables for the Female Sex 1749   (0. 3.6)
170. Orrery's Remarks on the Life and Writings of Swift.... 1752   (0. 2.0)
171. Orr's Sermons 1749   (0. 2.3)
172. Davenant on Grants and Resumptions 1700
173. History of long Livers 1722   (0. 1.6)

174. Phalaris's Epistles, by Francklin 1749   (0. 2.9)
175. Drake's secret Memoirs of Robert Dudley E.
     of Leicester 1706
176. Smith's Compleat Housewife 1730   (0. 2.6)
177. Life of Count Ulfeld 1695   (0. 0.6)
178. Shirley's Plays 1652   (0. 1.0)
179. Kennett's Roman Antiquities 1721   (0. 2.0)
180. Osborn's Works 1682   (0. 1.3)
181. Doctrine &c. of the Mahometans, with the Life
     of Mahomet 1712   (0. 1.9)
182. Maynwaring's Life and Works 1715   (0. 1.6)
183. Life of Sir Thomas Smith 1698   (0. 1.9)
184. Friendly Admonition to the Gentlemen in the Com-
     mission of the Peace 1729
185. Maclaurin's Account of Newton's Discoveries 1750   (0. 3.6)
186. Bohun's Character of Q. Elizabeth 1693
187. Hamilton's Life and Character of Bonnell 1707
188. Kennet's Funeral Sermon on the D. of Devonshire
     with an Account of the Family of Cavendish 1708   (0. 1.0)
189. Life of the Duke of Berwick 1738   (0. 2.0)
190. Lewis's Life of Wickliffe 1720   (0. 1.9)
191. Jeffrey of Monmouth's British History 1718   (0. 2.3)
192. Cary's Discourse on Trade 1745   (0. 1.9)
193. History of Sir John Perrott 1728   (0. 1.0)
194. Smith's Memoirs of secret Services 1699
195. Salmon's Antiquities of Surry 1736   (0. 2.9)
196. Life of Mrs. Manley, with the Key 1717   (0. 1.6)
197. Bullstrode's Memoirs of the Reigns of King Charles
     1st and 2nd 1721   (0. 1.0)
198. Lives of illustrious Persons who died 1713 1716   (0. 1.0)
199. Granville's Troubles of England during 1800 Years,
     2 vols. ....   (0. 3.0)
200. Observations on the Ecclesiastical Jurisdiction of the
     Kings of England 1689
201. Fell's Life of Dr. Hammond 1661
202. Duchal's Sermons 1753   (0. 2.3)
203. Dawson's Memoirs of St. George 1714
204. Cavendish's Memoirs of Woolsey 1708   (0. 0.6)
205. Ashmole's History of the Order of the Garter 1715   (0. 2.3)
206. Memoirs of Arthur E. of Anglesey 1693
207. Bale's Chroncle of Syr Johan Oldecastel.................... 1729   (0. 1.6)
208. Life of Chillingworth 1725   (0. 1.3)

209. Squire's Enquiry into the Foundation of the English
     Constitution 1745 (0. 2.0)
210. Butcher's Antiquities of Stamford and Tottenham
     High-Cross 1717 (0. 1.0)
211. Welwood's Memoirs of Transactions in England.......... 1700 (0. 2.0)
212. Journal Book of the House of Commons, ...1678-1680
213. Memoirs of Capt. Carleton 1743 (0. 1.6)
214. Enquiry into the State of the Union 1717
215. Duck's Life of Chichele 1699 (0. 0.6)
216. Memoirs of Sir John Reresby 1734 (0. 1.6)
217. Inquiry into the Share K. Charles I had in the Trans-
     actions of the E. of Glamorgan 1747 (0. 1.6)
218. Walton's Life of Bp. Saunderson 1678
219. Banier's Mythology and Fables of the Ancients
     explained, 4 vol. 1739 (0.12.6)
220. Pliny's Letters, by Melmoth, 2 vol. 1747 (0. 6.0)
221. Berkely and Prior on Tar Water 1744 (0. 1.0)
222. Collier's Immorality of the Stage and Defences.......... 1699 (0. 1.0)
223. Hoadley on the Terms of Acceptance 1711 (0. 2.0)
224. Chandler's Vindication of Christianity 1728 (1.3)
225. Dodwell's Epistolary Discourse proving that the
     Soul is Mortal 1706 (1.0)
226. Puffendorf's Introduction to the History of Asia,
     Africa, &c. 1705 (1.9)
227. Puffendorf's Introduction to the History of Europe.... 1719 (2.3)
228. Chambaud's French and English Vocabulary 1750 (1.3)
229. Jarvis's Don Quixote, 2 vol. 1749 (8.6)
230. Moyle's Works, 2 vol. 1726 (3.3)
231. Toland's Christianity not Mysterious 1702 (0. 0.6)
232. Life of St. Francis Xavier, by Bohours 1688 (0. 2.6)
233. Creech's Lucretius, 2 vol. 1714 (0. 3.0)
234. Chambaud's French Grammar 1750 (0. 2.6)
235. Treatise partly Theological and partly Political on the
     Liberty of Philosophizing 1689 (0. 1.3)
236. D'Avenant's Essays on Peace and War 1704 (0. 1.0)
237. Hume's sacred Succession, or Priesthood by divine
     Right 1710
238. Birch's Life of Abp. Tillotson 1752 (0. 3.3)
239. Locke on Government 1698 (0. 1.0)
240. Dryden's Juvenal and Persius 1711 (0. 2.3)
241. Osorio's History of the Portuguese, 2 vol. 1752 (0. 5.0)
242. Moreton's History of Apparitions 1738 (0. 2.0)

243. Bolingbroke's Letters on Patriotism 1749 (0. 2.9)
244. Miller's Gardener's Calendar 1745 (0. 2.3)
245. Lives of the Lords Chancellors, 2 vol. 1712 (0. 2.6)

QUARTO

246. Stanley's History of Philosophy 1743 (0.13.0)
247. Grotii Annotationes in Vet. & Nov. Test. in Com-
    pendium Redactae, a Moody ....*Lond.* 1727 (0. 3.3)
248. Hyde Historia Religiones Vet. Persarum ....*Oxon.* 1700 (1.17.0)
249. Les Grandes Custumes de France ....*Par.* 1522 (0. 1.6)
250. Cluverii Geographia, notis Variorum ....*Amst.* 1729 (0. 9.6)
251. Seacome's Memoirs of the Stanley's ....*Liverpool* (0. 8.0)
252. North's Lives of Lord Guilford, &c............................ 1742 (0. 6.0)
253. Dale's Antiquities of Harwich and Dover Courts 1732 (0. 4.6)
254. Lipsii Opera, 6 vol. ....*Aniv. ap. Plant.* 1605 (0. 5.0)
255. Struvii Syntagma Hist. German. 2 tom ....*Jenae* 1716 (0. 3.9)
256. Alex. Aphrodisiensis in sophisticos Aristotelis, Gr.
    ....*Florent. ap. Junt.* 1529
257. Godwin's Catalogue of English Bishops 1615 (0. 1.0)
258. Hederici Lexicon, *cum notis. MSS Henr. Fielding, Lond.* 1732 (1. 1.0)
259. Augustinus de Legibus & Senatus—consultis ....*Lugd.* 1592
260. Oeuvres de Lucian, par Baudoin ....*Par.* (0. 2.0)
261. Histoire du Concile de Trente par Paolo, trad.
    par Amelot. ....*Amst.* 1713 (0. 3.9)
262. Silius Italicus, Drakenborchi ....*Traject* 1717 (0.11.6)
263. Suetonius Pitisci, 2 tom. ....*Leovard* 1714 (0.15.0)

FOLIO

264. Bulstrode's Reports, 3 Parts 1657 (1. 1.0)
265. Latch's Reports 1662 (0. 2.6)
266. Cotton's Abridgment of the Records, by Prynne........ 1657 (0. 4.0)
267. Leonard's Reports, 4 parts 1658 (1. 7.0)
268. Coke on Littleton and Institutes, 3 vol. 1648 (0. 8.0)
269. Popham's Reports 1656 (0. 2.3)
270. Lane's Reports in the Exchequer 1657 (0. 2.6)
271. Croke's Reports, 3 vol. 1669 (0.18.6)
272. Noy's Reports 1656 (0. 3.0)
273. Salkeld's Reports, 2 vol. in one 1717 (0.12.0)
274. Siderfin's Reports, 2 vol. 1683 (0.12.0)
275. Keble's Reports, with the Table, 4 vol. 1685 (0.12.6)
276. Wood's Institute of the Laws of England, *interleaved*
    with MSS. notes of Mr. Fielding. 3 vol. .... (0. 5.0)

345. Eikon Basiliké, with Perencheif's Life of K. Charles.. 1727   (0. 1.6)
346. Essay on Civil Government 1743   (0. 2.6)
347. Farmer's History of Waltham Abbey 1735   (0. 1.9)
348. Life of Milton 1699   (0. 1.3)
349. .... of Sir Walter Raleigh, and Tryal 1677   (0. 1.0)
350. .... of Bp. Ken, by Hawkins 1713   (0. 0.9)
351. Burnet's Essay upon Government 1716   (0. 0.6)
352. Britannia Languens, or a Discourse upon Trade 1680   (0. 0.6)
353. Life of Major Bernardi 1729   (0. 1.0)
354. Knight's Life of Dean Colet 1724   (0. 4.3)
355. Petty's Political Survey of Ireland 1719   (0. 0.9)
356. Paule's Life of Abp. Whitgift 1699   (0. 0.6)
357. Life of Robert E. of Leicester 1727   (0. 2.3)
358. England's Black Tribunal, containing the Tryals of
     K. Charles and his Adherents 1737   (0. 2.3)
359. Memoirs of the Family of Boyle, by Budgell 1732   (0. 2.3)
360. E. of Arlington's Letters to Temple 1701   (0. 1.6)
361. Life of General Monk, by Skinner 1724   (0. 2.0)
362. Auli Gellii Noctes Atticæ, *Variorum*, ...*L. Bat.* 1666   (0. 5.0)
363. Taciti Opera, *Variorum*, 2 tom. ....*Amst.* 1685   (0.15.6)
364. Senecæ Tragœdiæ, *Variorum*, ...*Amst.* 1682   (0. 4.0)
365. Salustius, *Variorum* ....*L. Bat.* 1677   (0. 5.6)
366. Appianus   Alexandrinus   Gr.   &   Lat.   *Variorum*,
     2 tom. ....*Amst.* 1670   (0. 7.0)
367. Q. Curtius, *Variorum* ....*L. Bat.* 1649   (0. 2.0)
368. Luciani Opera, Cr. & Lat. *Variorum*, 2 tom. ......*Amst.* 1687   (0.13.0)
369. Velleius Paterculus, *Variorum*, ...*L. Bat.* 1653   (0. 2.0)
370. Justini Historia, *Variorum*. ....*L. Bat.* 1683   (0. 2.3)
371. Alexander ab Alexandro, *Variorum*, 2 tom. ....*ibid.* 1673   (0. 5.6)
372. Caesaris Commentarii, *Varorium* ....*Amst.* 1697   (0. 1.6)
373. Valerius Maximus, *Variorum*. ....*L. Bat.* 1670   (0. 2.6)
374. M. Felix Octavius, *Variorum*. ....*L. Bat.* 1709   (0. 3.3)
375. Spencer's Works, 6 vol. 1750   (0.12.0)
376. Shakespeare's Works, 9 vol. 1748   (0.14.6)
377. Milton's Poetical Works, 8 vo. 2 vol. 1746   (0. 5.0)
378. English Baronets, 3 vol. 1727   (0. 6.6)
379. British Compendium, 2 vol. 1721   (0. 7.6)
380. Vanbrugh's Plays, 2 vol. 1735   (0. 4.6)
381. Constantia, or a true Picture of Human Life, 2 vol... 1751   (0. 3.9)
382. Wycherley's Plays 1731   (0. 2.6)
383. Pope's Homer, 11 vol. 1750   (1. 7.0)
384. Dodsley's Collection of Old Plays, 12 vol. 1744   (1.10.0)

385. Lettres de Mons. Witt, 5 tom. ....*Amst.* 1725 (0.10.6)
386. Otway's Plays, 2 vol. 1733 (0. 4.0)
387. Prior's Poems 1741 (0. 3.0)
388. Life of Harriot Stuart, 2 vol. 1751 (0. 3.3)
389. Fielding's Enquiry into the Causes of the late Increase of Robbers, &c. 1751 (0. 1.6)
390. Congreve's Works, 3 vol. 1730 (0. 8.0)
391. Dryden's Plays, 6 vol. 1735 (0.13.0)
392.   Miscellanies, 6 vol. 1727 (0.14.0)
393. Lettres, Memoires & Negociations de d'Estrades, 8 tom. ....*Brux.* 1709 (0.10.6)
394. Memoires du Card. De Retz, 4 tom. ....*Amst.* 1719 (0. 6.6)
395. Memoires de Rabutin, 2 tom. ....*Amst.* 1711 (0. 3.3)
396. Shadwell's Works, 4 vol. 1720 (0. 8.6)
397. Farquhar's Works, 2 vol. 1742 (0. 4.6)
398. Southerne's Works, 2 vol. 1721 (0. 5.6)
399. Thompson's Works, 4 vol. 1750 (0.10.0)
400. Rowe's Works, 2 vol. 1747 (0. 4.9)
401. Memoires de Sully, 8 tom. ....*Lond.* 1747 (0.18.6)
402. Addison's Miscellaneous Works, 4 tom. 1746 (0. 7.6)
403. Le Siècle de Louis XIV, 2 tom. ....*Lond.* 1752 (0. 4.0)
404. Traité du Poeme Epique, par Bossu, 2 tom. ....*Haye* 1742 (0. 3.0)
405. La Fausseté des Vertus Humaines, Par Esprit. ..*Amst.* 1710 (0. 1.9)
406. History of Pompey the Little 1752 (0. 1.9)
407. Fielding's Life of Jonathan Wild 1754 (0. 2.0)
408. Dryden's Virgil, 3 vol. 1730 (0. 8.0)
409. Lee's Plays, 3 vol. 1734 (0. 5.0)
410. Steele's 4 Plays 1734 (0. 2.9)

QUARTO

411. Claudianus, *in usum Delphini,* ....*Par.* 1677 (0.18.0)
412. Sophoclis Tragœdiæ cum Scholiis Graecis, Gr. & Lat. Camerarii, ...*ap.P. Steph.* 1603 (0. 6.6)
413. Longinus de Sublimitate, Gr. & Lat. Tolii ....*Traject* 1694 (0. 4.9)
414. Hesiodus, cum Scholiis Græcis, a Heinsio ....*ap. Plant.* 1603 (0. 5.0)
415. Diogenes Laertius, Gr. & Lat. a Meibomio, 2 tom. ....*Amst.* 1692 (0.14.6)
416. Statii Opera, Comment, Lactantii ....*Par.* 1600 (0. 1.0)
417. Luciani Opera, Variorum, a Reitzio, Gr. & Lat., 3 tom. ....*Amst.* 1743 (2.13.6)
418. Hesychii Lexicon, Gr. a Schrevelio ....*L. Bat.* 1668 (0. 9.0)

419. Ainsworth's Dictionary, *with MSS. notes by Mr.*
Fielding 1746   (0.16.0)
420. Homeri Opera, Gr. & Lat. Barnesii, 2 tom. ....*Cant.* 1711   (1.12.0)
421. Homeri Ilias Gr. & Lat. a Clarke, 2 tom. ....*Lond.* 1729
422. Terentius, Phædrus, Bentleii ....*Cant.* 1726   (0. 6.6)
423. Horatius, Bentleii ....*Cant.* 1711   (0. 9.0)
424. Quinctiliani Opera, Burmanni, 4 tom. ....*L. Bat.* 1720   (1. 1.0)
425. Petronius Arbiter, a Burmanno, ...*Traject* 1709   (0.11.0)
426. Valerii Flacci Argonauticon, a Burmanno ....*Leid.* 1724   (0.14.0)
427. Apuleii Opera, in usum Delphini, 2 tom. ....*Par.* 1688   (1. 1.0)
428. Plinii Historia Naturalis, in Usum Delphini, 5 vol. *Par.* 1685   (1.17.0)

FOLIO

429. Walker's Account of the Sufferings of the Clergy
in the Time of the Grand Rebellion 1714   (0. 4.0)
430. Whitlocke's Memorials of English Affairs during the
Reign of Charles 1st 1682   (0. 5.6)
431. Fiddes's Life of Cardinal Woolsey 1724   (0. 8.6)
432. Franckland's Annals of King James and Charles 1st.. 1681   (0. 2.0)
433. State Tracts privatly Printed in K. Charles the IId.
Reign, 2 vol. 1693   (0. 9.0)
434. .... published in K. William's Reign, 3 vol......... 1705   (1.16.0)
435. Abercromby's Martial Atchievements of the Scots
Nation, 2 vol. ....*Edinb.* 1711   (0.17.0)
436. Forbes' full View of the public Transactions in the
Reign of Q. Elizabeth, 2 vol. 1740   (1. 7.0)
437. Bp. Burnet's History of his own Time, 2 vol. 1724   (1. 4.0)
438. .... History of the Reformation of the Church of
England, 3 vol. 1681   (2. 6.0)
439. Thuani Historia sui Temporis, 7 vol. *Lond. ap. Buckley* 1733   (5.15.0)
440. Strypes' Annals of the Reformation and Establish-
ment of Religion in England, 4 vol. 1735   (1. 6.0)
441. Life of Sir Leoline Jenkins, by Wynne, 2 vol. 1724   (0.12.0)
442. Rushworth's Historical Collections, 8 vol. 1682   (4.12.0)
443. Nalson's Collection of Affairs of State, 2 vol. 1682   (0. 5.0)
444. Thurloe's Collection of State Papers, 7 vol...................1742   (3. 6.0)
445. Spelman's English Works 1727   (0.10.6)
446. Harrington's Oceana and other Works 1737   (0.15.0)
447. Machiavel's Works 1720   (0.10.6)
448. Hale's Primitive Origination of Mankind 1677   (0. 3.0)
449. Brown's, (Sir Thomas) Works 1686   (0. 7.0)
450. Reynold's on God's Revenge against Murther 1635   (0. 2.0)

451. Milton's Historical, Political, and Miscellaneous Works, 2 vol. 1738 (1. 5.0)

452. Barrow's Works, 2 vol. 1741 (1. 7.0)

453. A Defence of natural and revealed Religion; being a collection of the Sermons preached at Boyle's Lecture, 3 vol. 1739 (1.12.0)

454. Cave's Lives of the Primitive Fathers, 2 vol................. 1687 (0. 8.6)

455. Chillingworth's Works 1742 (0.10.0)

456. Locke's Works, 3 vol. 1751 (2.10.0)

457. Tillotson's Works, with his life, by Birch, 3 vol. 1752 (2. 3.0)

458. Taylor's Life of Christ and Cave's Lives of the Apostles 1742 (0.13.0)

459. Clarke's Works, 4 vol. 1738 (3.12.0)

460. Boyle's Works, with his Life, 5 vol. 1744 (4. 4.0)

461. Bacon's Works, with his Life by Mallet, 3 vol...............1753 (2.18.0)

462. Holy Bible, by Bill and Newcomb 1706 (0.11.0)

463. Cudworth's True intellectual System of the Universe 1678 (0. 7.6)

464. Strype's Life of Abp. Parker 1711 (0. 3.0)

465. Grafton's Chronicle 1568 (0. 2.0)

466. Dugdale's Origines Juridiciales 1671 (0.10.6)

467. Sprigge's England's Recovery, being the History of the Army under Sir Thomas Fairfax 1647 (0. 1.6)

468. Ware's Antiquities and History of Ireland 1705 (0.10.6)

469. Mariana's History of Spain 1699 (1. 5.0)

470. Gerarde's Herbal, by Johnson 1636 (0.16.0)

471. Le Grande Dictionaire Historique, par Moreri, 6 tom. ....*Amst.* 1717 (1. 7.0)

472. Dictionaire Historique & Critique, par Bayle, 5 tom. ....*Paris* 1734 (3.13.6)

473. Calvini Lexicon Juridicum 1665

474. Grotii Opera omnia, 4 tom. ....*Lond.* 1679 (2. 9.0)

475. Plinii Historia Naturalis Mundi, ...*Francof.* 1599 (0. 5.0)

476. Senecae Opera, a Lipsio ....*Antv.* 1615 (0. 2.6)

477. Josephi Opera, Gr. & Lat. Hudsoni, 2 tom. ....*Oxon.* 1720 (0.15.0)

478. Constantini Lexicon, Graeco-Latinum, 2 tom. 1592 (2. 5.0)

479. Dionysius Halicarn. Gr. & Lat. Hudsoni, 2 vol. *Oxon.* 1704 (2.16.0)

480. Aristophanis Comoediae, Gr. & Lat. Kusteri, *Amst.* 1710 (2. 2.0)

481. Platonis Opera Omnia, Gr. & Lat. Serrani, 2 tom. ....*ap. H. Stephanum* 1578 (5. 0.0)

482. Suidae Lexicon, Gr. & Lat. a Kustero, 3 tom. ....*Cant.* 1705 (1.12.6)

483. Themistii Orationes, Gr. & Lat. Petavii ....*Par.* 1684 (0. 4.6)

Fourth Night's SALE
February 13, 1755.

OCTAVO & INFRA

484. Spectator, 8 vol. 1749 (0.15.6)
485. Tatler, 4 vol. 1749 (0. 8.6)
486. Guardian, 2 vol. 1745 (0. 4.6)
487. Temple's Miscellanies, 2 vol. 1693 (0. 3.3)
488. .... Introduction to the Hist. of England 1695 (0. 1.6)
489. .... Observations on the Netherlands 1673 (0. 1.0)
490. Warburton's Shakespear, 8 vol. 1747 (1.14.0)
491. Le Neve's Monumenta Anglicana, 2 vol. 1717 (0. 2.3)
492. Pope's Works, by Warburton, 9 vol. 8 vo. 1751 (2. 2.0)
493. Orrery's Remarks on Swift's Life and Writings, 8 vo. 1752 (0. 4.9)
494. Swift's Works, 8 vol. ....*Dublin* 1742 (1.15.0)
495. Middleton's Life of Cicero, 3 vol. 1750 (0.10.6)
496. Buckingham's (Sheffield D. of) Works, 2 vol. 1740 (9. 5.6)
497. Ben Johnson's Works, *large Paper,* 6 vol..................... 1716 (0. 7.0)
498. Beaumont & Fletcher's Works, 10 vol. 1750 (1.12.0)
499. Shaftsbury's Characteristicks, 3 vol. 1737 (0.15.6)
500. Salmon's Critical History of England, 2 vol................. 1726 (0. 3.0)
501. Clarendon's History of the Rebellion, *with cuts.* 6 vol. 1732 (1.16.0)
502. Sprotti Chronica a Hearnio, C.M. ....*Oxon.* 1719 (0. 3.6)
503. Bolingbroke's Letters on the Study of History, 2 vol. 1752 (0. 7.0)
504. Fielding's Dramatick Works, 2 vol. .... 1728, &c. (0.13.6)
505. Horatii Opera, *cum figuris, Chart, Max-*
    ....*Lond. ap. Sandby* 1749 (0. 7.6)
506. Virgilii Opera. *cum figuris, Chart, Max.* 2 tom.
    ....*ibid. ap. eund.* 1750 (0.11.6)
507. Tull's Horse Hoeing Husbandry 1751 (0. 3.9)
508. Warburton's Discourse on the Earthquake and fiery
    Irruption which defeated Julian's Attempt to re-
    build the Temple of Jerusalem 1750 (0. 2.3)
509. Abridgment of Hawkins's Pleas of the Crown,
    interleaved with MSS. notes by Mr. Fielding, 4 vol..... 1728 (0.11.0)
510. Montaigne's Essays, 3 vol. 1743 (0. 9.0)
511. Coke's Detection of the Court and State of England,
    3 vol. 1719 (0. 6.0)
512. Salmon's Review of the Hist. of England, 4 vol. 1722 (0. 5.0)
513. Hemingford Historia Edwardi I. II. III. 3 tom. *Oxon.* 1731)   (5.6)
514. Trokelowe Annales Edwardi, II. ....*Oxon.* 1729)   (2.6)

551. Prideaux's Connection, 3 vol. 1716   (6.6)
552. Select Trials at the Old Bailey, 4 vol. 1742   (6.0)
553. Strada de Bello Belgico, 2 tom., ...*Antv.* 1649   (2.0)
    (Young's, 2nd Vol. ....   (0. 1.6)
    (Fielding's Miscell. 1st & 3rd vols. ....   (0. 4.6)
    (Ovid 1st vol. ....   (0. 1.9)
    (Shakespear ? vol. ....   (0. 5.6)
    (Gloss's Cookery ....   (0. 3.9)
    (Pompey & Cookery ....   (0. 1.9)
    (Stevens' Grammar ....   (0. 1.9)
    (Waste ....   (0.15.6)
554. Luciani Opera, Gr. & Lat. Benedicti, 2 tom. ....*Salm.* 1619   (4.6)
555. Mountfort's Plays, 2 vol. 1720   (2.6)
556. Waller's Works 1744   (3.3)
557. Rudimanni Grammatica Lat. 2 tom. ....*Edin.* 1725   (3.0)
558. Francis's Horace, Lat. & Eng. 4 vol. 1747   (8.6)
559. Oeuvres d'Horace par Dacier, 10 tom. ....*Par.* 1691   (11.0)
560. Della Guerra di Fiandra dal Bentivoglio, 3 tom. *Colon* 1635   (9.0)
561. L'Accomplissement des Propheties, par Jurien, 2
    tom., ...*Rotterd.* 1686
562. Female Quixote, 2 tom. 1752   (2.3)
563. The Irish Compendium, *Cuts* 1722   (2.0)
564. Busbequii Epistolæ ....*Oxon.* 1660
565. Sir John Suckling's Works 1719   (2.6)
566. Denham's Works 1719   (2.0)
567. Recherche de la Verité, par Mallebranche, 2 vol. 1688   (3.6)
568. Law's Proposals for a Council of Trade in Scotland.... 1751   (1.3)
569. Legal Provisions for the poor 1725   (0.9)
570. Life of Bishop Bedell 1685   (1.0)
571. Essay for regulating the Law 1727   (1.0)

QUARTO

572. Aurelius Victor in Usum. *Delphini* ....*Par.* 1681   (2.6)
573. Justinus in Usum. *Delphini* ....*Par.* 1677   (6.6)
574. Plauti Comœdiæ, in Usum *Delphini,* 2 tom. ....*Par.* 1680   (0. 8.0)
575. Lucretius de Rerum Natura, in Usum. *Delphini, Par.* 1680   (0. 8.0)
576. Martialis Epigrammata, in Usum. *Delph.* ....*Par.* 1680   (0.10.6)
577. Collection of Scarce Tracts from Lord Somers and
    other MSS. collections, 16 vol. 1748   (4.14.6)
578. Plutarchi Vitæ, Gr. & Lat. Bryani, 5 tom. ....*Lond.* 1729   (2. 1.0)
579. Pemberton's View of Newton's Philosophy 1728   (0. 5.0)
580. Histoire Romaine, par Catro & Rouille, 21 tom. *Par.* 1725   (2. 1.0)

581. Hogarth's Analysis of Beauty 1753 (0. 3.6)
582. North's Examen of Kennet's History 1740 (0. 4.0)
583. Thompson's Historical and Critical Treatise on the
Gout, *sewed* 1745 (0. 1.3)
584. Middleton's Enquiry into the Miraculous Powers of
the Christian Church, *sewed* 1749 (0. 3.0)
585. The Philosophical Transactions abridged from
the beginning to 1733, by Lowthrop, Motte, Eames,
and Martyn, 8 vol. 1716 (2. 2.0)
586. Collection of Petitions and Replies before the Judges
in Scotland ....
587. Histoire Critique du Vieux Testament, par Simon *Par.* 1680
588. Vossius de Historicis Græcis ....*ibid.* 1651 (0. 1.9)
589. Danetii Dictionarium Antiquitatum Romanarum *Amst.* 1701 (0. 1.0)
590. Boyer's French and English Dictionary 1748 (0.13.0)

FOLIO

591. Joan. Gram. Philoponi Commentaria in Analytica
Aristotelis de Anima, Gr. ....*Venet* 1536 (7.0)
592. Alex. Aphrodiseus in Topica Aristotelis Gr.
....*Venet ap. Aldum.* 1513 (10.6)
593. Olympiodorus in Meteora Aristotelis, Gr. ....*ibid.* 1551 (19.0)
594. Procopii Cæsariensis Arcana Historica, Gr. &
Lat. Alemanni ....*Lugd.* 1623 (2.0)
595. Nonius Marcellus, Festus Pompeius & Varro de
Lingua Latina ....*Venet* 1498
596. Alex. Aphrodiseus in Analytica Aristotelis Gr.
.....................................*Venet ap. Aldum* (14.0)
597. Joan, Grammaticus in Posteriora Resolutoria
Aristotelis, Gr. ....*Venet ap. Aldum* 1504
598. Eustratius in Aristotelem de Moribus, Gr.
.....................................*Venet ap. Aldum* 1536
599. Simplicius in Physicas Aristotelis, Gr. ....*ibid.* 1526 (1. 0.0)
600. Joan, Grammaticus in Aristotelem de Generatione &
Interitu,—Alex. Aphrodiseus in Meteorologica & de
Mixione, Gr. ....*Venet ap. Aldum* 1527 (0.12.6)
601. ....; Incertus Author, & Eustratius in posteriora
Resolutoria Aristotelis, Gr. ....*Venet ap. Aldum* 1534
———— Joan, Grammaticus in Aristotelum de Nat-
urali Auscultatione Gr. *Venet* 1535.—Simplicius in
Categorias Aristotelis Gr. ....*Basil.* 1551 (0.16.0)

602. Simplicius in Aristotelem de Caelo, Gr.
....*Venet ap. Aldum* 1526   (0.11.0)
603. Poetæ Græci veteres Tragici, Comici, Lyrici &
Epigrammatarii, Gr. & Lat. ....*Genev.* 1614
604. .... Heroici, Gr. & Lat. ....*Aur. All.* 1606   (0.12.0)
605. Homeri Opera Comment, Eustathii, Gr., 3 tom. ..*Bas.* 1560   (2.12.0)
606. Euripidis Tragœdiæ, Gr. & Lat. a Barnes ....*Cant.* 1694   (1.16.0)
607. Pindari Opera, Gr. & Lat. ....*Oxon.* 1697   (1.11.6)
608. Dion Cassius, Gr. & Lat. Leunclavii ....*Hanov.* 1606   (0.10.6)
609. Polybii Historia Gr. & Lat., Casauboni ....*Par.* 1609   (2. 3.0)
610. Les Histoires de Polybe, par du Ryer ....*Par.* 1655   (0. 2.6)
611. Demosthenis & Aeschenis Opera, Gr. & Lat.
Wolssi ....*Francof.* 1602   (2. 5.0)
612. Platonis Opera, Gr. & Lat. Ficini ....*Francof.* 1602   (1.17.0)
613. Phavorini Lexicon Græcum ....*Romae* 1712   (2. 2.0)
614. Plutarchi Opera, Gr. & Lat. Xylandri, 2 tom. ....*Par.* 1624   (3. 4.0)
615. Aristotelis Opera, Gr. & Lat. Duval, 2 tom. ....*Par.* 1629   (0.16.0)
616. Thucydides de Bello Peloponnesiaco, Gr. & Lat.
a Hudsono ....*Oxon.* 1696   (1. 1.0)
617. Seldeni Opera omnia, a Wilkins, 6 tom. ....*Lond.* 1726   (1.18.0)
618. Eusebii Socratis & Sozomeni Historiae Ecclesiasticæ
Gr. & Lat. 2 tom. ....*Cant.* 1720   (0. 4.0)
619. Stephani Thesaurus, Gr. Ling. 4 tom. ....*Par.* 1572   (3. 1.0)
620. Luciani Opera Lat. ....*Par ap Vascos* 1546   (0. 6.0)
621. Xenophontis Opera, Gr. & Lat. Leunclavii ....*Par.* 1625   (1.13.0)
622. Historiae Romanae Scriptores Latini veteres &
Graeci Minores, Gr. & Lat. 3 tom. ....*Aur. All.* 1609   (0. 5.6)
623. Stephani Dictionarium Historicum, Geogr. & Poet
a Lloydio ....*Lond.* 1686   (0. 1.0)
624. Cato, Varro, Columella & Putilius de Re Rustica *Par.* 1533   (0. 8.6)
625. Stobaei Sententiae Graecae & Latinae ....*Aur. All.* 1609   (0.12.6)
626. Pausaniae Opera, Gr. & Lat. a Kuhnio, ...*Lips.* 1696   (0.17.6)
627. Arriani Opera, Gr. & Lat. Gronovii ....*L. Bat.* 1704   (0. 7.6)
628. Philostrati Opera, Gr. & Lat. ....*Venet. ap. Ald.* 1502
629. Brodaei Epigrammata, Gr. & Lat. ....*France.* 1600   (0. 7.6)
630. Luciani Opera, Gr. & Lat. Bourdelotii ....*Par.* 1615   (1. 8.0)
631. Diodorus Siculus, Gr. & Lat. Rhodomani ....*Han.* 1604   (0.17.0)
632. Clerici Comment in Vet. Testamentum, 4 tom. *Amst.* 1710   (1.18.0)
633. Ammianus Marcellinus a Gronovio ....*Lug. Bat.* 1693   (0.19.0)
634. Strabonis Geographia Notis Causauboni, &c. ....*Amst.* 1707   (1. 9.0)
636. Isocratis Orationes & Epistolae, Gr. & Lat. Wolfii,
....*Par. ap. H. Stepb.* 1593   (0. 5.0)

637. Skinneri Etymologicon Ling. Anglicanae ....*Lond.* 1671 (0. 7.0)
638. Lyndwood Provinciale ....*Oxon.* 1679
639. Aeliani Opera, Gr. & Lat. Gesneri ....*Tigur.* (0. 4.0)
640. Histoire de France par Mezeray, 3 tom, *La Meillieure*
    Edit. ....*Par.* 1643 (6.10.0)
641. Ciceronis Opera Lambini, 4 tom. in 2 vol. ....*Par.* 1566 (0.10.6)
642. Homeri Opera, Gr. & Lat. Spondani. ....*Bas.* 1606 (0. 5.0)
643. Budaei Commentarii Ling. Graecae, *Par. ap. R. Steph.* 1548 (0. 5.6)
644. Lycophronis Opera, Gr. & Lat. Scaligeri ....*Oxon.* (0. 2.0)
645. Herodotus, Gr. & Lat. Galei ....*Lond.* 1679 (0.10.6)
646. Virgilii Opera, a Donato & Honorato ....*Bas.* 1575 (0. 2.0)
647. The Ruins of Palmyra, *with Cuts,* boards 1753 (2.16.0)
648. Wottoni Leges Wallicae, ...*Lond.* 1730 (0. 2.0)
649. Barnes's History of Edward the third and the
    Black Prince 1688 (0. 5.0)
650. Templeman's Survey of the Globe, *On Copper Plates;*
    Moll's Sixty two Maps of the World, *neatly coloured* 1729 (0.10.0)
651. Salmon's modern History of all Nations, *with a great*
    many fine Cuts, 3 vol. 1744 (1.18.0)
652. Pineda's Spanish Dictionary 1740 (0.13.0)
653. *Law Manuscripts, by Mr. Fielding,* 5 vol................ (0.13.0)

FINIS.

I—ORIGINAL SOURCES, INCLUDING ANTHOLOGIES

Addison, Joseph. (Papers in) *The Spectator.* 8 vols. London, 1898.

Apuleius, Lucius. *The Golden Ass.* (Reprint of 1566 translation by William Adlington in the Abbey Classics.) Boston, 1922.

Ariosto, Ludovico. *Orlando Furioso.* Milan, n. d.

Bayle, P. *Dictionnaire historique et critique.* Paris, 1697.

Blackmore, Sir Richard. *Alfred,* an Epick Poem in Twelve Books. London, 1723.

Blackmore, Sir Richard. *Eliza,* an Epick Poem in Ten Books. London, 1705.

Blackmore, Sir Richard. *Essays upon Several Subjects.* 2 vols. London, 1717.

Blackmore, Richard. *King Arthur,* an Heroick Poem in Twelve Books. London, 1697.

Blackmore, Richard. *Prince Arthur,* an Heroick Poem in Ten Books. London, 1695.

Blackwell, Thomas. *An Enquiry into the Life and Writings of Homer.* London, 1735.

Boileau, Nicolas. *Oeuvres.* 3 vol. Amsterdam, 1717.

Boyle, Roger, Earl of Orrery. *Parthenissa.* London, 1655-1656.

Butcher, S. H. *Aristotle's Theory of Poetry and Fine Art,* with a Critical Text and a Translation of the Poetics. London, 1895.

Butler, Samuel. *Hudibras.* 2 vol. (with notes by Zachary Grey). London, 1744.

Bysshe, Edward. *The Art of English Poetry.* London, 1708.

Camoens, Luiz. *The Lusiads,* translated by Richard Burton. 2 vol. London, 1880.

Catulli, Tibulli, Propertii. *Opera de Nova editio.* Josephus Scaliger, Jul. Caesaris F. recensuit. Paris, 1577.

Cervantes Saavedra, Miguel de. *The Ingenious Gentleman Don Quixote of la Mancha,* translated by Peter Anthony Motteux (Bohn's Library). 2 vols. London, 1919.

Cervantes Saavedra, Miguel de. *The Travels of Persiles and Sigismunda.* London, 1619.

Chapelain, Jean. *De La Lecture des Vieux Romans*, avec des notes par Alphonse Feillet. Paris, 1870.

Chapelain, Jean. *La Pucelle*, ou La France Delivrée. Poëme Heroique. Paris, 1656.

Chapelain, Jean. *Opinion sur le poëme d'Adonis*. Paris, 1623.

Congreve, William. *Incognita*, or Love and Duty Reconcil'd. Edited by H.F.B. Brett-Smith. (In the Percy Reprints). Oxford, 1922.

Cooper, Lane. *Aristotle on the Art of Poetry*. New York, 1913.

Coras, J. de. *Jonas.* Paris, 1663.
    Samson. Paris, 1665.
    Josué Paris, 1665.
    David Paris, 1665.

Cooke, A.S. *The Art of Poetry*: The Poetical Treatises of Horace, Vida, and Boileau, with the translations by Howes, Pitt, and Soame. Boston, 1892.

Dacier, A. *La Poëtique traduite en François*, avec des Rémarques. Paris, 1692.

Dacier, Andre. *Remarques critiques sur les Oeuvres d'Horace*. Paris, 1683.

Dacier, André. *Nouveaux Eclaircissemens sur les Oeuvres d'Horace*. Paris, 1708.

Dacier, Mme. *Des Causes de la corruption du goût*, Paris, 1714.

Dacier, Anne. *L'Iliade et Odyssée d'Homere*. 6 vol. Amsterdam, 1712.

Dacier, Mme. Anne. *L'Iliade d'Homère, traduite en François avec des Rémarques.* Avec quelques Reflexions sur la Preface Angloise de M. Pope. Paris, 1719.

Desmarets, de Saint-Sorlin. *Clovis, ou la France chrestienne* Paris, 1657.

Dennis, John. *Remarks on a Book entitled Prince Arthur, an Heroick Poem.* With some General Critical observations and Several New Remarks upon Virgil. London, 1696.

Dennis, John. *Select Works*. 2 vols. London, 1718.

de Scudéry, Georges. *Alaric,* on Rome Vaincue Poëme Heroique. Paris, 1685.

de Scudéry, George (and Madeleine). *Artamenes; or the Grand Cyrus.* Englished by F.G., Esq. 10 vols. London, 1691.

de Scudéry, Madeleine. *Ibrahim,* ou l'Illustre Bassa. Paris, 1641.

Dryden, John. *Essays, Selected and Edited by W. P. Ker.* 2 vols. Oxford, 1926.

Dryden, John. *Translation of Virgil's Aeneid.* 3 vol. London, 1730.

Du Bellay, D. *Oeuvres Choisies,* publiées par L. Becq. de Fouquières. Paris, 1876.

Durham, W. H. (Editor). *Critical Essays of the Eighteenth Century.* 1700-1725. New Haven, 1915.

Fénélon, Francois de Salignac. de la Mothe. *Les Avantures de Télémaque.* Avec Preface—Discours de la Poesie Epique, Par M. Ramsay. London, 1745.

Fielding, Henry. *Covent-Garden Journal.* Edited by Gerard Edward Jensen. 2 vols. New Haven, 1915.

Fielding, Henry. *The Tragedy of Tragedies,* or the Life and Death of Tom Thumb the Great. Edited by James T. Hillhouse. New Haven, 1918.

Fielding, Henry. *Works,* edited with a biographical essay by Leslie Stephen. 10 vols. London, 1882.

Haslewood, J. *Ancient Critical Essays upon English Poets and Poesy.* 2 vols. London, 1811-1815.

Heliodorus. *An Aethiopian Romance.* Translated by Thomas Underdowne (1587). (Revised and partly rewritten by F. A. Wright, for the Broadway Translations). London and New York, n.d.

Huet, Abbé. *Un Traité sur l'Origine des Romans—*Preface to *Zayde, Histoire Espagnole,* par M. de Segrais. Paris, 1670.

Jonson, Ben. *Timber,* or Discoveries made upon Men and Matter, edited by F. E. Schelling. Boston, 1892.

Le Bossu, R. P. *Traité du Poeme Epique.* Paris, 1675.

Le Moyne, Père. *Saint-Louis* ou le Heros chrestien. Poëme heroique, avec Traite du poeme heroique. Paris, 1658.

Le Sage, Alain René. *Gil Blas.* Paris, 1715-1735.

Longinus. *On the Sublime,* translated by A. O. Prickard. With appendix containing passages from Dionysius of Halicarnassus, Plutarch, Dion Chrysostum, Lucian, Cassius Longinus. Oxford, 1926.

Lucian. *The Works of Lucian of Samosata,* translated by H. W. Fowler, and F. G. Fowler. 4 vols. Oxford, 1905.

Lucian, Oeuvres, de la Traduction de M. Perret, Sr. d'Ablancourt. Amsterdam, 1709.

Mambrunus, Petrus. *Constantinus sive Idolatria Debellata.* Paris, 1658.

Meredith, George. *An Essay on Comedy,* edited by Lane Cooper. New York, 1918.

Mesnardieres, J. de La. *La Poëtique.* Paris, 1640.

Minturno, Antonio. *L'Arte Poetica.* Venice, 1564.

Moliere, Jean B. P. *Oeuvres Complètes,* nouvelle Edition avec des remarques nouvelles par M. Félix Lemaistre. 3 vol. Paris, 1862.

Montesquieu. *Essai sur le goût.* Paris, 1721.

Ogilby, John. *Translation of Virgil.* London, 1684.

Padelford, F. M. *Select Translations from Scaliger's Poetics.* (Yale Studies in English). New York, 1905.

Petronius. *The Satyricon,* translated by J. M. Mitchell. (In the Broadway Translations). London & New York, 1923.

Pope, Alexander. *Works,* edited by Rev. Whitwell Elwin and W. J. Courthope. 10 vols. London, 1882.

Puttenham, G. *The Arte of English Poesie,* edited by E. Arber. London, 1869.

Rapin. *Discours academique sur la comparison entre Virgile et Homère.* Paris, 1668.

Rapin, R. *Reflections on Aristotle's Treatise of Poesie.* Made English by Mr. Rymer, by whom is added some reflections on English Poesie. London, 1694.

Saint-Amant, Marc-Antoine Gérard, Sieur de. *Moise Sauvé.* Paris, 1653.

Sarasin, J. Fr. *Oeuvres, rassemblées par Paul Festuigière.* 2 vols. Paris 1926.

Scarron, Paul. *Le Roman Comique.* Paris, 1651-1657.

Scarron, Paul. *Le Virgile Travesti.* Paris, 1648.

Schinz, Albert. *Eighteenth Century French Readings.* New York, 1923.

Schinz, Albert, and King, Helen M. *Seventeenth Century French Readings.* New York, 1915.

Shaftesbury, Anthony, Earl of. *Characteristics of Men, Manners, Opinions, Times, etc.* Edited by John M. Robertson. London 1900.

Sidney, Sir Philip. *The Defense of Poesy,* otherwise known as An Apology for Poetry, edited by A. S. Cook. Boston, 1890.

Spingarn, J. E. *Critical Essays of the Seventeenth Century.* Oxford, 1908.

Swift, Jonathan. *A Tale of a Tub,* to which is added *The Battle of the Books* and *The Mechanical Operation of the Spirit.* Edited by A. C. Guthkelch and D. Nichol Smith. Oxford, 1920.

Swift, Jonathan. *Works.* 8 vols. Dublin, 1742.

Tasso, Torquato. *I Discorsi dell'Arte Poetica.* Milan, 1901.

Tasso, Torquato. *La Gerusalemme liberata.* Milan, 1895.

Vossius, G. J. *Poeticarum Institutionum.* Amsterdam, 1547.

Webbe, W. A. *Discourse of English Poetrie,* edited by E. Arber. London, 1871.

Wilson, Thomas. *The Arte of Rhetorique.* London, 1553.

Wilson, Thomas. *The Rule of Reason,* conteinyng the Arte of Logique. London, 1551.

II—SECONDARY SOURCES

Blanchard, Frederic T. *Fielding the Novelist: A Study in Historical Criticism.* New Haven, 1926.

Bosdorf, E. *Enstehungsgeschichte von Fieldings Joseph Andrews.* Weimar, 1908.

Bourgoin, A. *Les Maîtres de la Critique au xviième Siècle.* Paris, 1889.

Campbell, Lily B. *Scenes and Machines on the English Stage during the Renaissance: A Classical Revival.* Cambridge (University Press), 1923.

Castro, Américo. *El pensamiento de Cervantes.* Madrid, 1925.

Clark, John. *A History of Epic Poetry.* Edinburgh, 1900.

Comparetti, D. *Vergil in the Middle Ages,* translated by E. F. M. Benecke. London, 1895.

Cross, Wilbur L. *The History of Henry Fielding.* 3 vols. New Haven, 1918.

Delaporte, P. V. *Du merveilleux dans la littérature française sous le regne de Louis XIV.* Paris, 1891.

Denniston, J. D. *Greek Literary Criticism.* London & Toronto, 1924.

Digeon, Aurélion. *Le Texte des Romans de Fielding.* Paris, 1923.

Digeon, Aurélion. *The Novels of Fielding.* London, 1925.

Dobson, Austin, *Fielding.* London, 1909.

Dobson, Austin. *Eighteenth Century Vignettes,* 3 vols. Oxford, 1892-1896.

Dolder, Ernst. *Henry Fielding's Don Quixote in England.* Zurich, 1907.

Düber, R. *Beiträge zu Henry Fieldings Romantechnik,* Halle, 1910.

Duchesne, Julien. *Histoire des Poëmes Epiques Français du XVII e Siècle.* 1870.

Egger, E. *Essai sur l'Histoire de la Critique chez les Grecs.* Paris, 1887.

Faguet, Emile. *En Lisant Molière.* Paris, 1914.

Godden, G. M. *Henry Fielding: A Memoir,* including newly discovered letters and records with illustrations from contemporary prints. London, 1910.

Hamelius, P. *Die Kritik in der Englischen Literatur des 17. und 18. Jahrhunderts.* Leipzig, 1897.

Hugon, Cécile. *Social France in the XVIIth Century.* London, 1911.

Ker, W. P. *Epic and Romance.* London, 1926.

Menéndez y Pelayo, M. *Historia de las Ideas Esteticas en España.* 9 vols. Madrid, 1890-1896.

Morgan, C. E. *The Rise of the Novel of Manners*: 1600-1740. New York, 1911.

Murray, Gilbert. *The Rise of Greek Epic*. Oxford, 1907.

Rigault, Hippolyte. *Histoire de la Querelle des Anciens et des Modernes*. Paris, 1856.

Saintsbury, George. *A History of English Criticism*. Edinburgh & London, 1911.

Whitney, Lois. *Primitivistic Theories of Epic Origins*, in *Modern Philology*, vol. XXI, No. 4, May, 1924.

Williams, Ralph C. *Two Studies in Epic Theory*, in *Modern Philology*, vol. XXII, No. 2, Nov. 1924.

Williams, Ralph Coplestone. *The Merveilleux in the Epic*. Paris, 1925.

Wolff, Max Ludwig. *Geschichte der Romantheorie*. Nuremberg, 1915.

Wood, Paul S. *Opposition to Neo-Classicism in England between 1660-1700*. Modern Lang. Assn. Vol. XLIII. No. 1. March, 1928.

INDEX

196

DATE DUE

GAYLORD			PRINTED IN U.S.A.